# Sanctions and the
# Search for Security

 *A project of the International Peace Academy*

# Sanctions and the Search for Security

## CHALLENGES TO UN ACTION

David Cortright
George A. Lopez

with Linda Gerber

LYNNE
RIENNER
PUBLISHERS

BOULDER
LONDON

Published in the United States of America in 2002 by
Lynne Rienner Publishers, Inc.
1800 30th Street, Boulder, Colorado 80301
www.rienner.com

and in the United Kingdom by
Lynne Rienner Publishers, Inc.
3 Henrietta Street, Covent Garden, London WC2E 8LU

**Library of Congress Cataloging-in-Publication Data**
Cortright, David, 1946–
    Sanctions and the search for security : challenges to UN action  / David Cortright and
    George A. Lopez, with Linda Gerber.
    "Project of the International Peace Academy."
    Includes bibliographical references and index.
    ISBN 1-58826-053-4 (alk. paper)
    ISBN 1-58826-078-X (pbk. : alk. paper)
    1. United Nations—Sanctions.   2. Economic sanctions.   3. Security, International.   I.
    Lopez, George A.   II. International Peace Academy.   III. Title.
    JZ6373.C67   2002
    341.5'82—dc21
                                                                                  2002017819

**British Cataloguing in Publication Data**
A Cataloguing in Publication record for this book
is available from the British Library.


Printed and bound in the United States of America

      The paper used in this publication meets the requirements
⊗    of the American National Standard for Permanence of
      Paper for Printed Library Materials Z39.48-1984.

    5 4 3 2 1

# Contents

*Foreword,* William Graham                                         vii
*Foreword,* David M. Malone                                         ix
*Acknowledgments*                                                   xi

1   Themes and Trends of the Sanctions Era                           1

2   The Iraq Quagmire                                               21

3   Smart Sanctions, Limited Impacts: UN Policy
    in Afghanistan                                                  47

4   Success in the Making? The Evolution of
    UN Sanctions in Angola                                          61

5   Sanctions and Regional Security: The Crisis in West Africa      77

6   Following the Money Trail: Targeted Financial Sanctions         93

7   Carrots and Sticks for Controlling Terrorism                   115

8   Beyond Symbolism: Travel and Aviation Sanctions                133

9   Sanctions Sans Commitment: Arms Embargoes                      153

10  The Viability of Commodity Sanctions:
    The Case of Diamonds                                           181

11  Reform or Retreat? The Future of UN Sanctions Policy           201

*List of Acronyms*                                                 225
*Bibliography*                                                     227
*Index*                                                            239
*About the Book*                                                   249

# Foreword

*William Graham*

It gives me great pleasure to introduce this volume on UN Security Council–mandated sanctions.

When the Canadian government gave thought, in the mid-1990s, to how it might best focus its efforts during its next term on the UN Security Council, it concluded that working to improve the effectiveness of UN sanctions regimes would be a fitting and useful priority. Of the very few instruments available to the Council to encourage implementation of its decisions, sanctions are the most frequently used.

It was clear that several of the sanctions regimes mandated by the Council earlier in the 1990s were not working well. Some, indeed, seemed counterproductive. Canada's House of Commons Standing Committee on Foreign Affairs and International Trade, which I then chaired, recognized this important factor in its report of April 2000 on sanctions against Iraq and urged the establishment of sanctions regimes that are more targeted at those responsible for the conditions that the UN seeks to change.

On taking its seat in the Council in January 1999, Canada agreed to chair the Council committee on sanctions against the National Union for the Total Independence of Angola. In carrying out this responsibility, Ambassador Robert Fowler and his colleagues revolutionized the Council's approach to sanctions issues. They showed that greater effectiveness was possible, if a willingness existed to recognize the importance of economic factors in contemporary conflicts and if the Council was prepared to "name and shame" those governments, nonstate actors, and individuals actively undermining sanctions regimes.

Canada provided financial support to the International Peace Academy for the completion in 2000 of the forerunner of the present volume, *The Sanctions Decade: Assessing UN Strategies in the 1990s*, also by David Cortright and George A. Lopez. In it, the authors carefully analyzed the twelve existing sanctions regimes, documenting their successes and failures. The volume immediately became a valuable working tool for policymakers at the UN and in capitals around the world. It also proved of considerable interest to the broader public.

The present volume surveys the Council's experience with these cases and several new ones, seeking to distill more generally applicable lessons on sanctions that Canada hopes the Council will take into account in its future decisionmaking. I am also pleased that the efforts of Canada's Security Council delegation feature prominently in this account of how sanctions have changed during the last few years.

I am delighted that Canada was also able to provide financial support for the preparation of this volume. I congratulate the International Peace Academy on the quality of the work and recommend it highly to all those interested in sanctions and the many issues they raise.

*—William Graham*
*Minister of Foreign Affairs of Canada*

# Foreword

## David M. Malone

It is with great pride that the International Peace Academy (IPA) sponsors this volume. Two years ago, its two authors, David Cortright and George A. Lopez, published *The Sanctions Decade: Assessing UN Strategies in the 1990s* to considerable acclaim. This book instantly became an essential reference tool for policymakers and for many in the scholarly world. It examined all the sanctions regimes mandated by the UN Security Council during the 1990s, drawing often incisive and always useful conclusions on each. It argued that sanctions can only work as incentives to compliance and further negotiation and that they need to be integrated within broader political strategies in order to be effective.

The present volume, both companion piece and sequel, adopts a complementary approach. While updating the reader on the various sanctions regimes detailed in the earlier book, it adopts a crosscutting strategy. It seeks to distill overall conclusions for policymakers on the types of sanctions that appear to work (or do not) and the sorts of strategies required to enhance effectiveness of UN action through this instrument.

The authors have monitored closely the Security Council's decisions involving enforcement of its mandates over many years now. Their experience and the depth of their knowledge are clearly on view in this volume. Their aims are simple: to improve Security Council decisionmaking and UN implementation of these decisions by providing a framework through which lessons from the past can be analyzed.

The failure in 2001 of a Security Council working group to agree on guidelines governing the application of sanctions was discouraging, if perhaps unsurprising, given the leeway its members wish to retain over individual decisions. It is our hope that this volume and its recommendations may prove useful to Security Council delegations, representatives of other member states, capitals, the UN Secretariat, and to the broader scholarly and policy communities as they ponder resorting to sanctions in the future.

We and the authors are deeply grateful to the government of Canada for its financial support of our work on this topic.

*—David M. Malone*
*President, International Peace Academy*

# Acknowledgments

This book is a collaborative effort of dozens of colleagues. We owe the greatest debt to Linda Gerber, who managed every phase of this project; arranged numerous interviews; and maintained liaison with researchers, the publisher, and the International Peace Academy (IPA). She wrote the first draft of Chapter 10 and provided important corrections and editing comments on nearly every section of the manuscript. She edited every word and note in the book and has been an indispensable partner in all phases of this work.

We benefited greatly from the research, writing, and editing support of other staff members at the Fourth Freedom Forum, particularly Alistair Millar, who wrote part of Chapter 2, and Jennifer Glick, who produced the charts and other graphic materials and edited the manuscript. Barnabas Martin provided important research assistance, and Ann Pedler, Ruth Miller, Brian Alexander, and Miriam Redsecker offered valuable administrative support. Additional research support came from Erica Cosgrove, who wrote a number of very useful research memoranda, and from Kristi Nelson and Colin Rowat.

Our most important partner in this project was the IPA. Without the creative initiative and financial support of the IPA, this book would not have been possible. This volume is the second in a series of studies for the IPA and was inspired by IPA president David Malone. Malone provided support and encouragement throughout the process, and he offered IPA facilities for meetings and research interviews. We also benefited from the support of IPA vice president and former U.S. ambassador to Sierra Leone John Hirsch, and from other IPA staff, including Karin Wermester, Simon Chesterman, and Marlye Gélin-Adams.

With the UN Security Council as the principal subject of our inquiry, we depended greatly on obtaining information and documentation from UN officials. We are especially grateful to Joseph Stephanides, director of Security Council Affairs in the Department of

Political Affairs, for assisting us in obtaining information and arranging interviews with relevant UN staff members. Among the officials we interviewed were Steve Avedon, Tatiana Cosio, Aleksandar Martinovic, Loraine Rickard-Martin, Manuel Bessler, Andrew Cox, Randy Rydell, David Biggs, and Anna Frangipani-Campino. We thank these officials for their willingness to be interviewed and for their responses to numerous inquiries.

We conducted many interviews outside the UN with former officials, nongovernmental experts, and academic scholars. Among those who provided important assistance were Peter Andersen, Loretta Bondi, Tamar Gabelnick, Joost Hiltermann, Jeffrey Laurenti, Ed Luck, Andrew Mack, Meghan O'Sullivan, Jack Patterson, Jim Paul, John Rempel, William Reno, Barnett Rubin, Rachel Stohl, Joe Stork, and Joanna Weschler.

Colleagues at the Joan B. Kroc Institute for International Peace Studies at the University of Notre Dame supported our project and provided substantive input. We gained much from the insights of Peter Wallensteen, professor of peace and conflict studies at Uppsala University in Sweden, who was a visiting fellow at the Kroc Institute in 2001. We are also grateful to Scott Appleby, director of the Kroc Institute, who provided constant encouragement and support, and to Linda Brady for administrative assistance.

The financial support of the Ministry of Foreign Affairs of the government of Canada has been crucial to this project. We wish to thank the Canadian foreign minister, William Graham, and his colleagues in the Department of Foreign Affairs and International Trade in Ottawa. Canada's exemplary leadership within the United Nations has contributed significantly to international security and global governance.

We gratefully acknowledge the encouragement and support of the Board of Directors of the Fourth Freedom Forum. The Forum's financial support and extensive research files were indispensable to the success of this project. We express a special thank you to the Forum's founder and chairman, Howard S. Brembeck, whose vision of a more lawful and secure world animates our work. For the support of all those who contributed so importantly to this work, we are deeply grateful.

—*David Cortright*
—*George A. Lopez*

# 1

# Themes and Trends of the Sanctions Era

In our earlier book, *The Sanctions Decade,* we explored in detail the twelve cases of United Nations (UN) Security Council sanctions imposed during the 1990s.[1] Although we employed a case-specific and historical approach, we also examined the tension between achieving political compliance and minimizing adverse humanitarian impacts. We noted the tendency to view political effectiveness solely in terms of coercive means, derived most often from a punishment model of sanctions, and contrasted this with a bargaining model in which more refined types of sanctions were integrated with inducements. Finally, we provided a variety of practical recommendations for sanctions reform among member states and within the various organs of the UN, most specifically the Security Council and the Secretariat.

*Sanctions and the Search for Security* has been undertaken to explore important trends and themes in light of two realities that have emerged in recent years. The first is the breadth of UN innovations in sanctions design and implementation that have developed "on the ground" since 1999. The second reality involves the need to assess critically the Security Council's own efforts to undertake a serious sanctions reform process. Our purpose in writing this book is not only to chronicle the complex UN sanctions of recent years but also to stimulate the ongoing policy-scholarly debate and the process of UN sanctions reform.

We believe that in a relatively brief time and in diverse and numerous ways, sanctions have become integral, if not indispensable, instruments of multilateral action, designed to preserve regional security or enhance the prospects for effective regional peacekeeping. This reality has not yet become part of the critical consciousness of the UN bureaucracy or its member states. Although some particular sanctions mechanisms are remarkably innovative and well adapted to local circumstances, in most cases sanctions still lack the supportive institutional

1

structures needed to enhance their effectiveness and ability to contribute to greater peace and security.

## Themes Explored in This Book

Our recent research and interactive work with the diplomatic and expert communities have revealed several notable themes that now characterize the sanctions enterprise of the Security Council.[2] They are evident in ongoing sanctions episodes, newly undertaken cases, and the more refined, "smarter" sanctions—financial, arms, travel, and commodity sanctions—that have become commonplace. We examine these themes along multiple dimensions of the search for security in a chaotic and changing set of regional environments.

The themes that reappear throughout this volume and warrant initial discussion include:

- the development of effective innovations and nuanced formulations of more targeted and selective sanctions;
- the dramatic increase in the monitoring of sanctions compliance through the use of independent investigative commissions and panels of experts;
- the ambiguities and discrepancies that emerge between sanctions theory and effective sanctions formulation and implementation;
- the assertion of power politics and large-state national concerns, often in a narrow sense, in the workings of Security Council policy and sanctions reform discussions;
- the changing nature of sanctions targets and environments, which increasingly involve factions within failed states, regional security crises, or the general breakdown of human security;
- the difficulties associated with imposing sanctions on a target economy already plagued by disintegration, a shadow economy, and criminalization;
- the pattern of targeted regimes responding to the threat of sanctions with bargaining offers;
- the rise in prominence of nongovernmental organizations (NGOs) as external critics, sanctions monitors, and participants in the process of sanctions policy reform.

Some of these themes, such as the changing role of NGOs, are integral to understanding every sanctions case. Other themes, such as the reassertion of big power politics, are more pronounced in particular cases, such as Iraq or Afghanistan, or in the sanctions reform process. We devote full chapters to some of the themes and discuss others in several different chapters.

In addition to examining these themes, we review the attempt of the Security Council to institutionalize the process of sanctions reform through a formal working group. We recount the formation of the working group in April 2000 and explain the differences, largely rooted in the Iraq experience, that prevented the Council from reaching agreement.

We argue in this volume that, despite the failure of sanctions to produce political compliance in many cases and notwithstanding the difficulties experienced by the sanctions reform working group at the Security Council, UN practice is undergoing a sea change that has significantly advanced the sophistication of the sanctions instrument. The UN use of Chapter VII has evolved considerably since August 1990, when Security Council Resolution (SCR) 661 imposed sanctions on the government of Iraq for its invasion of Kuwait. That enforcement action emerged from the prevailing punitive concept of sanctions, which assumed that fully enforced and comprehensive trade sanctions, aimed at completely choking off the target economy, were the best strategy for translating economic pain into political change.[3] The general trade sanctions against Iraq were followed quickly by similarly broad measures imposed on the former Yugoslavia and Haiti. By mid-decade, it was widely acknowledged within the UN community that these sanctions involved terrible and often unacceptable trade-offs in the pain-gain equation.[4] The negative humanitarian impacts of sanctions began to weigh heavily on member states, with many nations openly questioning whether the gains achieved by extracting such large-scale humanitarian costs were consistent with the UN Charter.[5]

Beyond these significant humanitarian concerns, it was also apparent that the full-scale strangulation of a national economy did not necessarily produce equivalent economic pain for the government leaders who were responsible for the reprehensible policies that the world had condemned via sanctions. The prospect for political compliance by these elite rulers with the demands of the world community was low. Faced with these realities, in the late 1990s the Security Council made dramatic improvements in the design and implementation of economic sanctions. As we detail in several chapters, the change was evident in the new sanctions imposed against the Taliban in Afghanistan and the Taylor government in Liberia, as well as in the extension and adaptation

of earlier sanctions against the National Union for the Total Independence of Angola (UNITA) and the Revolutionary United Front (RUF) in
Sierra Leone.

## Toward More Targeted Sanctions

The considerable refinement in sanctions policymaking may surprise
observers who have not closely followed the myriad innovations in
recent years. The sharpening of economic sanctions is neither an acci-
dent nor a product of trial and error. The specialized and more precisely
targeted sanctions we explore in Chapters 6 through 10 were direct
results of a series of expert meetings, commissioned investigations, and
policy exercises intended to improve the use of the sanctions instrument.

The two most important and dynamic policy initiatives for smarter,
more targeted sanctions were the Interlaken process, sponsored by the
Swiss government, and the Bonn-Berlin process, sponsored by the
German government. In the former, the Swiss government took the lead
in 1998 and 1999 in convening groups of academic experts, international civil servants, lawyers, NGO staff, and diplomatic and banking
experts in two major seminars at Interlaken, Switzerland. The purpose
of these meetings was to ascertain the scope of targeted financial sanctions as potentially effective means of focusing selective pressure on
decisionmaking elites, as we explore in Chapter 6. The Interlaken
process sought to build on advances in the fight against international
money laundering. Participants were guided through a series of working
groups to determine the extent to which financial sanctions could
achieve goals similar to or better than those of large-scale, comprehensive sanctions regimes by effectively putting pressure on designated
lists of government leaders and elites.

Building on the Interlaken process, the German Foreign Ministry
asked the Bonn International Center for Conversion (BICC) to spear-
head a parallel initiative on the refinement of travel bans and arms
embargoes, two different forms of complementary sanctions, which we
examine in Chapters 8 and 9. Seminars were convened in Bonn in 1999
and Berlin in 2000. The Bonn-Berlin process was noteworthy for several reasons. The designers considered travel bans and arms embargoes
within one conference framework, sketching the logical linkages
between the two and also examining the unique features of each. The
conference organizers grouped the arms issues into three distinct areas

of concern, with a special focus on monitoring. The seminars also developed model language for Security Council resolutions and national legislation to enhance the enforcement of arms embargoes.[6]

## Blending Theory with Policy

In various chapters, we examine some of the recent scholarly debate about sanctions and explore how differing theoretical frameworks may offer guidance to policymakers as they consider particular kinds of sanctions mechanisms. From this ongoing debate, we attempt to compare the utility of sanctions as a means of coercion with the utility of sanctions as a means of persuasion, thus combining sticks and carrots. We examine the combination of sanctions and incentives in several of the cases, including Angola and Afghanistan. This theme also guides our discussion in Chapter 7 on the role of economic statecraft as a potentially powerful tool in the new global campaign to counter terrorism.

Sanctions and incentives have also been used to encourage UN member states to comply with Security Council measures. Because the UN lacks its own enforcement machinery, it must rely on the voluntary cooperation of member states to achieve compliance with its mandates. This cooperation can be obtained either through positive forms of assistance and encouragement or through the application of pressure. States naturally prefer the former. Although the Security Council itself cannot offer much assistance, it can and often does work with individual member states, regional organizations, and international financial institutions to ensure the provision of technical and financial support. When countries surrounding Yugoslavia requested assistance to implement comprehensive sanctions imposed by SCR 757 (1992), European agencies cooperated with the UN to provide the expertise and financing for sanctions assistance missions. When the United States sought to gain the cooperation of Pakistan in the campaign against terrorist networks in Afghanistan, it lifted sanctions that had been imposed in response to the testing of nuclear weapons and provided substantial economic assistance and debt relief.

If positive inducements are not successful or are unavailable, it may be necessary to apply pressure to gain compliance. If assistance is offered but either is rejected or proves insufficient to gain cooperation, secondary measures may be appropriate. A number of the expert panels created to examine sanctions implementation recommended that the

Security Council impose sanctions against those who violate sanctions. The panel reports provided voluminous documentation of states, entities, or individuals blatantly disregarding sanctions. If such violations carry no penalty, there is no incentive to comply. To remedy this problem, it is necessary at times to apply secondary pressures on those who violate sanctions. The Security Council applied this principle in 2001 when it imposed sanctions against Liberia (SCR 1343) because of its violation of sanctions against the RUF in neighboring Sierra Leone. This decision may presage a new determination by the Council to apply pressure on those who violate its sanctions mandates.

## Power Politics Among the Permanent Five

One aspect of the recent assertion of power politics has been the shift away from what seemed to be a generalized commitment to sanctions cooperation among the Permanent Five members of the Security Council to a greater tendency by individual nations to use sanctions to serve more narrow national interests. In the first part of the 1990s, the Security Council became sharply proactive in addressing peacekeeping, security, and human rights concerns.[7] A more cooperative working relationship among the Permanent Five prompted UN watchers to wonder if the organization had finally reached a level of maturity in the post–cold war world akin to that envisioned by its founders fifty years earlier. Even when the Permanent Five disagreed about certain sanctions issues—as was the case with the distinct French, Chinese, and Russian concerns about various extensions of the Iraq sanctions—their disagreement tended to take the form of abstaining on critical votes rather than threatening to exercise the veto.

Although certain dimensions of that earlier cooperative trend have continued, recent years have witnessed more pronounced differences among the Permanent Five, especially the United States, the United Kingdom, and Russia, and attempts to dominate particular sanctions episodes. In the attempts to develop smarter sanctions in Iraq, as we discuss in detail in Chapter 2, the United States and the United Kingdom took the lead but ran into strong counterpressure from Russia. In the sanctions against the Taliban, as analyzed in Chapter 3, Russia and the United States dominated the proceedings and strong-armed the Council into adopting a package of measures that had little support from other Council members.

In the early 1990s, Lisa Martin noted that international organizations are often subject to a certain kind of "hijacking" of the sanctions process.[8] The longer a sanctions episode continues, Martin maintained, the greater the vested interests of the powerful states in that episode. Following this logic, it is no surprise that British and American assertiveness in maintaining sanctions against Iraq has been a prevailing theme of the internal politics of the Council. Similarly, the dominant interest of various European powers in sanctions against a variety of sub-Saharan actors has been based in part on former colonial arrangements and concerns. Efforts by the United States and Russia to dominate the formulation of sanctions against the Taliban were based largely on those countries' special interests. Thus, although once there was what seemed to be a generalized commitment to sanctions as a mode of the Permanent Five dealing with "threats to peace," individual nations are now more likely to use sanctions to serve narrow national interests.[9]

Another manifestation of power politics has emerged as an irony in the Council's attempts to impose more targeted and focused sanctions. The more sanctions target a specific faction within an internal conflict or control the trade and movement of specific commodities, the more likely it is that some among the Permanent Five will object to them. France, despite its desire to bring peace and security to West Africa and its support for UN arms and diamond embargoes, was unwilling to support a commodity embargo against timber exports from Liberia. By identifying this particular export as the focus of control, the Council placed France, which imports a high percentage of Liberia's timber exports, in the perceived position of carrying a higher cost burden than other Permanent Five states. This example illustrates that, unlike general trade sanctions, which may lead to relatively diffuse costs among participating nations, targeted and selective sanctions lead to more focused costs for some sender states. This differential cost may make states feel more burdened than they would by general trade sanctions and affects the commitment of those states to sustain support for sanctions. In some Permanent Five states, these effects can lead to domestic debate about the utility of participating in the proposed smart sanctions.

## Differences over Sanctions Reform

Political differences among the Permanent Five impeded the attempt of the Security Council to produce a formal report on sanctions reform. In the late 1990s, a number of member states on the Council began to argue for a new structure and road map on sanctions reform. Although the Council had displayed considerable creativity and flexibility in sharpening sanctions policies in individual cases, the ad hoc nature of these changes left many observers and practitioners uneasy. There was no commonly accepted set of rules and procedures. Sanctions policy still seemed to be a rudderless ship, guided only by exigencies of the moment, unable to chart a course toward a clear destination. There was fear that the mistakes made on Iraq could be repeated. There was hope that a more formalized political and legal framework would enhance the effectiveness of sanctions in the future.

These concerns led to the proposal for a formal Security Council working group on sanctions reform. The government of Canada assumed leadership of the reform process in early 2000. Under the guidance of Foreign Minister Lloyd Axworthy, Canada used its position as president of the Council in April of that year to gain approval for the creation of a formal working group. The group was constituted as a committee of the whole and was charged with developing recommendations on the structure and substance of sanctions by November 2000.

Although there was broad agreement in the Council on the need for the working group, it was not long before differences appeared regarding its expectations and goals. A pervasive Iraq sanctions fatigue weighed heavily on the group's deliberations, as continuing differences over sanctions against Iraq cast a shadow over the process. The creative policies and initiatives for reform that had developed in other cases in recent years were largely obscured. Every proposal was put to the test of whether it "would have worked" in Iraq. Council members thus viewed reform recommendations through the lens of the worst-case scenario. The process became bogged down as long-simmering differences over Iraq boiled to the surface.

The difficulties within the working group were reflected in the first decision that had to be made, the selection of the group's chair. As various candidates were considered, objections were raised largely on the basis of previous positions on sanctions against Iraq. Some member states opposed candidates who were seen as being too close to the U.S./UK position, whereas other countries objected to candidates who were considered overly sympathetic to the French view. As the members searched for an ambassador without a vocal, preestablished position on Iraq or sanctions in general, the name of Anwarul Chowdhury, permanent representative to the United Nations of Bangladesh, emerged as a compromise candidate. Even as member states finally agreed on the selection of chair, however, differences on substantive issues continued to impede the process.

Chowdhury defined the agenda of the working group according to a set of principles and recommendations that had previously surfaced in the Security Council. These ideas were stated most clearly in an October 1998 paper by the chairs of the sanctions committees and a January 1999 note by the president of the Security Council.[10] Chowdhury organized the work into three clusters, dealing with the administration of sanctions, the design of Security Council resolutions, and monitoring and assessment. These three areas of reform corresponded to the suggestions and actual policy developments that emanated from within the Security Council itself and from a variety of governmental and nongovernmental sources. There was broad agreement within the UN community and beyond that improvements were needed in the administration, design, and monitoring of sanctions policies.

Because of the delay in selecting a chair, the working group's proceedings did not commence until the summer of 2000. The group held nearly two dozen hearings with various sanctions experts and practitioners. As the work proceeded, it became clear that the November reporting deadline would not be reached. Chowdhury worked in a methodical, deliberate, and consensus-building manner in the hope of overcoming the various differences within the group. Through a mixture of private sessions and public hearings, Chowdhury managed to forge a consensus on most matters, but he could not overcome continuing differences on two major issues.

The most divisive matter for the working group was the question of time limits or, stated differently, when to terminate sanctions. France argued vigorously for adopting a formal recommendation that time limits be included in all Security Council sanctions. Anxious to avoid the experience in Iraq, where sanctions continued indefinitely because a permanent member could block their easing or suspension, France wanted to require an affirmative vote for the continuation of sanctions. Russia and other members of the working group supported the French position. The United States and the United Kingdom, on the other hand, opposed time limits. They maintained that time limits would permit a targeted regime to adopt a "hunkering down" strategy. The focus of the target's energies would be holding out until the sanctions were lifted rather than meeting the necessary conditions for compliance with UN mandates. As members of the Council debated their differences, Chowdhury attempted in vain to find a compromise.

It is ironic that the working group split over this principle because in practice the question of time limits was readily accepted in specific cases. As we note in our examination of various cases, time limits were approved in the case of the arms embargo against Ethiopia and Eritrea (SCR 1298, 2000) and were also adopted in the cases of the arms embargo and further sanctions against Afghanistan (SCR 1333, 2000) and the diamond embargo and other sanctions against Liberia (SCR 1343, 2001). In all three cases, the United States and the United Kingdom joined with France, Russia, and other Council members to approve provisions establishing sanctions for a period of one year, which, of course, could be renewed. For the United States and the United Kingdom, a concept agreeable in specific cases was not acceptable as a general principle. Their generic opposition reflected a desire to avoid its application in the case of Iraq.

The second major difference involved how sanctions committees should make their decisions. The United States and the United Kingdom wanted to retain the existing consensus rule, whereas France, Russia, and other countries argued that decisions should be made on the basis of a majority vote. At stake was the issue of whether a single state, by listing an objection in a sanctions committee, could impose its will on other members and deny progress in cases where states might want to see more flexibility in the way sanctions are applied. Once again, the Iraq case loomed in the background. The U.S. practice of placing a large number of holds on the import of dual-use goods into Iraq had generated increasing opposition and concern among members of the Council.[11] A rule requiring a majority vote for such matters would directly affect this practice. France and its supporters on the Council wanted to see such a change as a way of reducing the inordinate number of holds, but the United States insisted on retaining the right of individual member states to block approval of specific dual-use imports. Again, no agreement was reached.

As the working group timeline stretched past November, Chowdhury attempted to complete the process and issue an official report by the end of 2000. He scheduled a press conference for the second week of December in the hope that a deadline would force the Council to reach agreement. Despite intensive discussions, however, the differences remained. Chowdhury was forced to cancel the press conference. He subsequently stepped back from the process and some months later left New York on reassignment.

Although the formal reform process of the Chowdhury working group was a failure, the Security Council continued to make progress in refining the practice of economic statecraft. The disappointment arising from the failure of the working group was tempered by the reality of ongoing reform and innovation in the actual formulation and implementation of sanctions policy. In practice, the Council generated an unprecedented series of policy refinements as it shifted toward a smarter sanctions strategy. These innovations and the cases in which they apply comprise the subject of this book.

## Failed States and Shattered Economies

The complex environments of brutal, factional intrastate violence in which most sanctions have been imposed recently vary from the "traditional" conditions of earlier sanctions episodes. In the early 1990s, UN actions were focused on fully viable nations such as Iraq and Libya and nominally viable states like Haiti. As we examine in Chapter 9, recent sanctions have targeted leaders of armed factions fighting internal wars or newly emerging leaders of failing states beset by war.

Through the work of Robert Jackson, William Reno, and others, we have come to understand that a significant segment of the international community is composed of quasi- or failed states. These entities are characterized by the absence of traditional government. Ruling elites in these states lack the capacity to provide law and order or to ensure a functioning and transparent economy.[12] Although external factors—such as natural disaster, dramatic changes in the world economy, or the withdrawal of a patron nation's support—can lead to conditions of state failure, more frequently they have resulted from the scourge of internal war. Within these violent conflicts operate factional, ethnic, or regional leaders whose brutality makes them the target of UN sanctions.

The political and military conditions of such environments pose substantial challenges to UN policymakers. Initially, the issue of denying resources to violent actors who brutalize innocents or bringing these actors and other warring parties to the bargaining table is quickly followed by concerns with minimizing the negative consequences of sanctions in situations that are already disastrous for most civilians. Another problem involves ensuring adequate monitoring and enforcement of the embargoes by neighboring states that themselves lack political and economic capacity and may be experiencing internal tensions.

The failed state environment usually exists within a regional crisis of insecurity and conflict. In all the sanctions episodes of recent years, UN measures have targeted actors within broader regional conflicts. The source of instability has been not just the internal disintegration of a failed state but a wider web of regional turmoil.[13] Under these circumstances, it becomes difficult to imagine peace and stability coming to

Afghanistan, Sierra Leone, or Angola solely through changes within those particular nation-states. Changes must also occur in the region. In the case of Afghanistan, where the focus of sanctions was exclusively the Taliban regime, the role of Pakistan as a major source of arms and financial support for the Taliban was a crucial element of the equation. In Sierra Leone and Liberia, the UN faced the challenge of developing a comprehensive system of security for the entire region. The war that has ravaged Angola for decades is connected to a broader crisis of insecurity and conflict throughout central and southern Africa.

It might be overly optimistic to assume that the Security Council can or should structure an entire well-integrated peacekeeping and security system for a given region. Yet recent episodes illustrate that in the absence of some grander security design and coordinated peacemaking strategy among regional and international actors, sanctions alone have little chance of success.[14] We address these issues and their implications in several of the cases examined.

The economies of failed states are characterized by decentralization and criminalization. Black marketers and armed entrepreneurs inside and outside these countries take advantage of the inability of central institutions to provide security and regulate economic activity. In an atmosphere of generalized chaos, these actors mobilize labor and resources, by gunpoint if necessary, to produce and market contraband goods in violation of international standards or UN sanctions. Warlords and ruling elites often exercise centralized control of these networks, either directly or indirectly. Thus, failed states are characterized by different layers of a shadow economy whose benefits accrue to ruling elites and armed factions. The wider population, already suffering from war and physical displacement, is further victimized by this economic dislocation.[15]

The shadow economy of a failed state constitutes a very different target from the traditional national economy that is usually envisioned as the target of sanctions. The ability of external actors to control exports and imports through sanctions presumes a flow of goods through functional institutions of trade. Controlling the flow of selected goods assumes cross-national transactions that are regulated by the market rather than political forces and that function according to transparent, predictable procedures. In failed states, economic relations vary over time and operate outside any legitimate system of taxation, documentation, or accountability. Under these conditions, when external actors like the UN Security Council impose sanctions, traditional mechanisms for monitoring or controlling commerce may be irrelevant to the actual flow of goods on the ground. Enforcement options, such as border monitoring, presume conditions of peace and stability and levels of functional state authority that may not exist.[16]

In an octopuslike failed national economy, with market forces radiating like tentacles in many different directions, neither regional institutions nor economic and political incentives can ensure the proper enforcement of sanctions. Further, in countries faced with complex humanitarian emergencies brought on by war and displacement, economic sanctions may be destructive of local relief activities. At the same time, as international aid workers in various locales will acknowledge, sanctions busting intermingles all too easily with international efforts to remedy the plight of victimized civilians. In a typical scenario, small arms may enter a given conflict zone through the private relief flights that operate in these risky, unregulated environments. Pilots who deliver vaccines and medical supplies to humanitarian agencies may use the last bit of empty space on the same plane to deliver unmarked crates of AK-47s or SA–7 rocket launchers.

Scholars and policymakers have not sufficiently understood or appreciated the role of sanctions in the context of regional security or within a failed state environment and shadow economy. The reality of life on the ground in failed states means that sanctions, as tools for constraining and controlling the political behavior of perpetrators of violence, face serious limitations. Warlords generate sufficiently high profits from these economic networks that they can usually absorb the extra costs sanctions may impose. Under such a system of huge personal rewards, targeted leaders have very little incentive to end violence or build viable institutions and nations based on the rule of law. They have no incentive to participate in the creation of an open, growing, and inclusive economy free of criminal and black market behavior.

## The Power of a Threat

Although our review of current and past sanctions cases confirmed many of our preconceived hypotheses, we were surprised by some unexpected findings. One such finding was that the threat of sanctions is often more powerful than the sanctions themselves. In several cases, we found a common pattern of targeted regimes responding to the mere threat of sanctions with bargaining gestures or offers of partial compliance. This pattern occurred in at least seven cases.

- In Somalia, the imposition of sanctions in January 1992 led to a cease-fire agreement among warring factions in Mogadishu, although the accord did not last.
- In Libya, the Qaddafi regime made several offers in the early part of 1992, before and immediately after sanctions were imposed, to turn over suspected terrorists for trial in international or Arab tribunals. None of the proposals was acceptable to the Security Council, however.
- In June 1993, just as sanctions were being imposed but had not yet been implemented, the military junta in Haiti agreed to enter negotiations that led to the Governors Island agreement.
- The government of Sudan responded to diplomatic sanctions in April 1996 and the threat of stronger measures to come by sending a letter to the Security Council indicating that Osama bin Laden had been asked to leave the country. In fact, bin Laden departed Sudan within weeks of the imposition of sanctions.
- In Sierra Leone, the military junta responded to the imposition of sanctions in February 1997 by signing an agreement in Conakry to restore the elected government.
- In Afghanistan, the Taliban responded to the threat of sanctions in 1999 by offering to present the bin Laden case to an Islamic tribunal, a proposal that was deemed unacceptable.
- In Liberia, the Taylor government announced a series of sweeping measures in early 2001, before sanctions went into force, purporting to comply with the UN demand to cut off support for the RUF, although the Secretary-General could not verify these claims.

The initial offers made by targeted regimes in these cases were partial and limited, usually falling far short of Security Council demands. The conciliatory offers were partly a delaying tactic, but they were also a negotiating gambit, a bargaining gesture designed to test the prospects for dialogue. In circumstances such as these, in which a regime is facing the first shock of coercive pressure, the target's initial position is usually not meant to be taken as a final offer. It is a way of testing the other side, of laying out a marker. Such offers may provide a basis for beginning the process of negotiation and dialogue. In some cases, such as Haiti, the bargaining leads to agreement, although the accord may not be enforced. In the other cases, including most of those under review, the initial offers are rejected, and the Security Council proceeds to impose sanctions.

A corollary development in many of these cases has been a hardening of positions and a period of diplomatic stalemate following the actual implementation of sanctions. When the initial offers are rejected, the targeted regime retreats and refuses to make any further gesture toward compliance. In some cases, such as Afghanistan, the regime becomes even more insular. In others, such as Libya, a long diplomatic stalemate ensues. The reason for this retrenchment may be the very effectiveness of sanctions in sparking an initial reaction. The initial offers and compromise gestures are indications that sanctions can influence internal debates within the targeted regime, even in very rigid and authoritarian systems such as Libya or Liberia. The reversal after sanctions are imposed may occur because the moderate factions that had argued for concessions are discredited. When the conciliatory gestures are rejected, hard-liners win and positions become more inflexible.[17]

These realities do not mean that the Security Council should embrace every offer that comes from a targeted regime. In some cases, they are merely part of a strategy by the target to weaken the resolve of its adversaries and undermine the coalition of states arrayed against it. In other instances, though, the initial gesture may reflect a genuine effort by the targeted regime, or at least a faction within it, to find a diplomatic solution. In these instances, it may be appropriate to attempt to test the sincerity of the target, perhaps through a special negotiating effort, as in Haiti, or by postponing the implementation of sanctions in exchange for a further quid pro quo. If a process of reciprocity can be established, it may lead to further cooperation and a possible settlement of the dispute. At the very least, an initial bargaining offer or conciliatory gesture from a targeted regime should occasion an attempt at dialogue, perhaps through a quick diplomatic mission, to determine the prospects for additional movement toward compliance.

The pattern of initial response to sanctions deserves special consideration in sanctions policy making. It may hold possibilities for the development of a bargaining process that can lead to at least partial compliance. It is an indication of the way in which sanctions can influence the decisionmaking calculus of a targeted regime. It should be seen as a sign of sanctions impact and a possible opening to dispute resolution. In future cases, international bodies may wish to develop strategies for responding to this initial receptivity to compromise.

## The Nongovernmental Sector

As we document in various chapters, the role of NGOs in sanctions formulation, implementation, monitoring, and evaluation cannot be overstated. Issue-focused and operational NGOs preassess conditions in probable sanctioned environments and engage in the monitoring and verification of humanitarian, economic, and political conditions on the ground during sanctions episodes. Independent research groups have been influential in examining the utility of sanctions reform proposals as well as doing various impact assessments and analyses of the kinds of conditions under which sanctions are likely to succeed. Beginning with the well-known study of the Institute for International Economics in Washington, D.C., in 1990, and through much of the work by ourselves and other sanctions analysts since 1990, a transnational network of researchers has provided the UN system and its member states with expertise that was previously unavailable.

Scholarly centers have been complemented by NGOs that have a broad range of human rights and other policy interests. The significance of these groups has been well documented by various analysts. The transnational networks have been critical to the work of UN specialized agencies as well as to the general policy community's understanding of international issues.[18] It is no surprise, then, that as these organizations have become increasingly interested in the dynamics of internal war, they have also engaged in intense scrutiny of sanctions and their relation to humanitarian conditions. The NGO sector contributed substantial reform recommendations to the Chowdhury working group. National group affiliates of NGOs have lobbied hard with their governments on behalf of specific sanctions implementation and reform measures. The ability of the UN to respond to concerns about sanctions monitors and the particular impacts of sanctions has been greatly facilitated by the work of these agencies. Our case studies illustrate that NGO networks have served as a kind of shadow extension of the Security Council and have helped to meet the Secretariat's need for up-to-date information about the relative impacts of sanctions, particularly on the most vulnerable populations.

## Conclusion

The maturation of the sanctions mechanism within the Security Council framework is evident. Expert working groups, scholarly researchers, NGOs serving as advocates, and the judgment of diplomats schooled in prior sanctions cases have combined to transform sanctions policy making. Recent targeted and selective sanctions episodes bear little resemblance to the broad-based, blunt measures imposed just a decade ago.

As UN officials have engaged in learning, adaptation, and reform, they have developed and implemented increasingly sharpened and specialized sanctions mechanisms. Analysis of these trends provides the impetus for this book.

Ironically, however, the most recent reforms have been applied in extreme circumstances, in which brutal factional violence and general economic and political disarray have made them less effective than they might have been in the early 1990s against nations with fully functioning governments. The contemporary targets of UN sanctions are increasingly nonstate actors who are driven by a desire for personal enrichment and power rather than a larger political agenda. These actors derive benefits from the very economic anarchy they have created, which reinforces their elusiveness and shields them from the effects of country-specific sanctions. They have no interest in cooperating with the UN system but rather seek to circumvent international authority by a variety of ingenious and illegal means. This characteristic lowers the potential for sanctions success and raises questions about the relationship between sanctions and the necessary wider framework of peacemaking and security embedded in regional conflicts.

In this book, we examine these colliding ironies, present up-to-date assessments of the ongoing cases of Security Council sanctions, and dissect the particular forms of smart sanctions that have developed in theory and practice over the past few years. We conclude in Chapter 11 with specific recommendations for how praxis, politics, and scholarly inquiry can help the UN Security Council coalesce around an agenda for more refined and effective sanctions policies.

## Notes

1. David Cortright and George A. Lopez, with Richard W. Conroy, Jaleh Dashti-Gibson, and Julia Wagler, *The Sanctions Decade: Assessing UN Strategies in the 1990s* (Boulder, Colo.: Lynne Rienner Publishers, 2000).

2. For this volume, we were able to interview dozens of individuals involved in the formulation, implementation, or monitoring of sanctions within the UN community. In addition, we worked with a few key experts (mentioned in the acknowledgments by name) on narrower aspects of sanctions and particular countries' cases.

3. The dominance of the coercion model of comprehensive trade sanctions may very well have been a result of the preeminence of the 1990 study of the Institute for International Economics, which at the time was the only longitudinal analysis of data available to policymakers seeking systematic knowledge of the success of past sanctions. That study was unambiguous about the predominant effectiveness of general trade sanctions, arguing that "if sanctions can be imposed in a comprehensive manner, the chances of success improve." See Gary C. Hufbauer,

Jeffrey S. Schott, and Kimberly Ann Elliott, *Economic Sanctions Reconsidered: History and Current Policy*, 2d ed. (Washington, D.C.: Institute for International Economics, 1990), 101–102.

4. The precise contours of this trade-off between the humanitarian impact of sanctions and the political gains associated with sanctions success are examined in Thomas G. Weiss et al., eds., *Political Gain and Civilian Pain: Humanitarian Impacts of Economic Sanctions* (Lanham, Md.: Rowman and Littlefield, 1997), and in Cortright and Lopez, *The Sanctions Decade,* 13–36.

5. In fact, the litany of concern about the humanitarian impact of sanctions stretched all the way to the Secretary-General, who noted early in his tenure, "Humanitarian and human rights policy goals cannot easily be reconciled with those of a sanctions regime." See Kofi Annan, quoted in United Nations General Assembly, *Annual Report of the Secretary-General on the Work of the Organization,* A/53/1, New York, 27 August 1998, 64.

6. Most of the working papers of the expert meetings and the final working group documents are available on the Internet. For the Interlaken process, see <www.smartsanctions.ch> (20 September 2001). For the Bonn-Berlin process, see <www.bicc.de> (20 September 2001). More detailed strategic reports focused on implementation of these approaches are available from the Swiss Confederation, United Nations Secretariat, and Watson Institute for International Studies at Brown University, *Targeted Financial Sanctions: A Manual for Design and Implementation* (Providence, R.I.: Thomas J. Watson Jr. Institute for International Studies at Brown University, 2001).

7. For a very credible and succinct treatment of these themes, see Karen A. Mingst and Margaret P. Karns, *The United Nations in the Post–Cold War Era* (Boulder, Colo.: Westview Press, 2000), 74–116, 158–198; and Keith Krause and W. Andy Knight, eds., *State, Society, and the UN System: Changing Perspectives on Multilateralism* (Tokyo: United Nations University Press, 1995).

8. Lisa Martin, *Coercive Cooperation: Explaining Multilateral Economic Sanctions* (Princeton, N.J.: Princeton University Press, 1992).

9. The role of national interests in sanctions and economic policy making has been best discussed in two recent edited collections, one by Richard N. Haass and Meghan L. O'Sullivan, *Honey and Vinegar: Incentives, Sanctions, and Foreign Policy* (Washington, D.C.: Brookings Institution, 2000); and another by Jean-Marc F. Blanchard, Edward D. Mansfield, and Norrin M. Ripsman, eds., *Power and the Purse: Economic Statecraft, Interdependence, and National Security* (London: Frank Cass, 2000).

10. United Nations Security Council, *Chairs of the Sanctions Committee, Issue Paper Concerning the Sanctions Imposed by the Security Council*, New York, 30 October 1998; and United Nations Security Council, *Note by the President of the Security Council,* S/1999/92, New York, 29 January 1999.

11. As of September 2001, the net value of oil for food import applications on hold stood at more than $4 billion, representing nearly 17 percent of all applications reviewed by the Iraq sanctions committee. See United Nations Security Council, *Report of the Secretary-General Pursuant to Paragraph 5 of Resolution 1360* (2001), S/2001/919, New York, 28 September 2001, par. 15.

12. Robert Jackson, *Quasi-States: Sovereignty, International Relations and the Third World* (Cambridge: Cambridge University Press, 1990); and William Reno, *Warlord Politics and African States* (Boulder, Colo.: Lynne Rienner Publishers, 1998).

13. This pattern is most evident in sub-Saharan Africa. See I. William

Zartman, ed., *Collapsed States: The Disintegration and Restoration of Legitimate Authority* (Boulder, Colo.: Lynne Rienner Publishers, 1995); Jean-Francois Bayart, Stephen Ellis, and Béatrice Hibou, *The Criminalization of the State in Africa* (Bloomington: Indiana University Press, 1999); and Kempe Ronald Hope Sr. and Bornwell C. Chikulo, eds., *Corruption and Development in Africa* (New York: St. Martin's Press, 2000).

14. For a general argument in this direction, see John Gerard Ruggie, *Constructing the World Policy: Essays on International Institutionalization* (New York: Routledge, 1998); for an argument on the specific role of international organizations in creating such an integrated system, see Robert C. Johansen, "Building World Security: The Need for Strengthened International Institutions," in Michael T. Klare and Yogesh Chandrani, eds., *World Security: Challenges for a New Century* (New York: St. Martin's Press, 1998), 386–407. The most comprehensive set of essays developing a coordinated approach is available in Luc Reychler and Thania Paffenholz, eds., *Peace-building: A Field Guide* (Boulder, Colo.: Lynne Rienner Publishers, 2001); the most carefully integrated argument about these issues is provided in Elizabeth M. Cousens and Chetan Kumar, eds., *Peacebuilding as Politics: Cultivating Peace in Fragile Societies* (Boulder, Colo.: Lynne Rienner Publishers, 2001), esp. 183–220.

15. With the exception of William Reno, cited above, anthropologists have been ahead of economists and political scientists in documenting and interpreting the meaning of these shadow economies and the pattern of brutal violence that surrounds them. See Carolyn Nordstrom, *A Different Kind of War Story (Ethnography of Political Violence)* (Philadelphia: University of Pennsylvania Press, 1997).

16. An exceptional set of portraits of these interrelated trends is provided in Mats Berdal and David M. Malone, eds., *Greed and Grievance: Economic Agendas in Civil Wars* (Boulder, Colo.: Lynne Rienner Publishers, 2001).

17. We are indebted for this insight to Meghan O'Sullivan, personal communication, 7 October 2001.

18. Insights about these generalizations emerge in the work of an important cohort of scholars, from Thomas Risse-Kappen, ed., *Bringing Transnational Relations Back In* (Cambridge: Cambridge University Press, 1995) through, most recently, Susan Burgerman, *Moral Victories: How Activists Provoke Multilateral Action* (Ithaca, N.Y.: Cornell University Press, 2001).

# 2

## The Iraq Quagmire

After more than eleven years of continuing sanctions, the United Nations has been unable to achieve its objectives in Iraq. The sanctions have constrained Iraq's military capabilities, but they have not succeeded in convincing Saddam Hussein's government to comply fully with the UN mandate on disarming weapons of mass destruction. On the contrary, Iraqi defiance of UN policy has deepened and become more strident over the years. As sanctions fatigue has spread, particularly among frontline states, Iraq has aggressively pursued policies to undermine the sanctions, and international compliance has steadily eroded. Unauthorized trade has increased, and commercial and transportation links with Baghdad have multiplied.

In the face of this crisis, in late 2000 the United States and the United Kingdom led an effort within the UN Security Council to ease prohibitions on civilian trade while bolstering restrictions on the import of weapons and military-related goods. Spurred on by nongovernmental groups and independent researchers, the two governments developed a so-called smart sanctions plan for Iraq in the spring of 2001. The proposal attempted to address concerns about humanitarian hardships in Iraq while maintaining financial and military controls on the Baghdad regime. Most governments supported the smart sanctions plan, but Russia rejected it. The result was further stalemate, although discussions continued within the Security Council on ways of modifying the sanctions and resolving the crisis over Iraq.

In this chapter, we examine the Iraq sanctions impasse. After reviewing the debate over the UN disarmament mandate in Iraq, we address concerns about humanitarian conditions, describe the significant changes that have occurred in the oil for food program, recount the

This chapter was coauthored by Alistair Millar.

attempts of the Security Council to restructure the sanctions, and offer our own prescriptions for how to reform sanctions and achieve UN objectives in Iraq. For a listing of selected Security Council resolutions on Iraq, see the box on page 24.

## The Dispute over Disarmament

The concern over fulfilling the UN arms inspection and verification mandate has dominated the discourse on sanctions in Iraq. The Gulf War cease-fire resolution, Security Council Resolution (SCR) 687 (1991), required the "destruction, removal, or rendering harmless of Iraq's weapons of mass destruction" as a condition for lifting sanctions. As we have recounted elsewhere, much progress was achieved in fulfilling these requirements during the 1990s.[1] According to reports by the United Nations Special Commission (UNSCOM) and the International Atomic Energy Agency (IAEA), efforts to eliminate nuclear weapons and long-range ballistic missile capabilities were largely completed by 1998. Substantial progress was also achieved in dismantling chemical weapons facilities and stockpiles.[2] Inspectors were less successful in eliminating biological weapons capabilities and in learning of the history of the biochemical program. This lack of success resulted primarily from Baghdad's unwillingness to cooperate fully with UN inspections. It also emanated from the dual-use nature of many of the ingredients and precursor elements involved in such weapons, as well as the inherent difficulty of attempting to prevent the use of biological elements for weapons purposes. The Hussein government's resistance to the inspections fueled a UN fear that there was much to hide.

On balance, many experts agree that by 1998, Iraq's most dangerous weapons capabilities were largely eliminated. This was the opinion of the independent panel of experts established by the Security Council in 1999 to assess disarmament and weapons monitoring issues. The panel concluded that "in spite of well-known difficult circumstances, UNSCOM and the IAEA have been effective in uncovering and destroying many elements of Iraq's proscribed weapons programs . . . the bulk of Iraq's proscribed weapons programmes has been eliminated."[3] Even Richard Butler, the embattled former chairman of UNSCOM, acknowledged that Iraqi disarmament declarations were nearly complete by 1998. In his book *The Greatest Threat*, Butler

## IRAQ, Security Council Resolutions

| Resolution Number | Action |
|---|---|
| 661[a] | **6 August 1990**<br>Imposed comprehensive, mandatory sanctions<br>Created the sanctions committee<br>Banned all trade<br>Imposed an oil embargo and an arms embargo<br>Suspended international flights<br>Froze Iraqi government financial assets and prohibited financial transactions |
| 670 | **25 September 1990**<br>Imposed aviation and maritime sanctions |
| 687 | **3 April 1991**<br>Established terms of the cease-fire<br>Established a set of eight specific conditions for the lifting of sanctions |
| 706 | **15 August 1991**<br>Authorized the oil for food program<br>Permitted the sale of up to $1.6 billion in Iraqi oil over a six-month period<br>Directed that proceeds be deposited in a UN escrow account to finance humanitarian imports, war reparations |
| 986[b] | **14 April 1995**<br>Established a new formula for oil for food<br>Permitted the sale of up to $1 billion in Iraqi oil every three months<br>Gave Baghdad the primary responsibility for distribution of humanitarian goods |
| 1153 | **20 February 1998**<br>Extended the 986 program<br>Raised the level of permitted oil sales to $5.25 billion every six months<br>Permitted revenues to finance urgent development needs |
| 1284 | **17 December 1999**<br>Established a new UN Monitoring, Verification and Inspection Commission (UNMOVIC)<br>Lifted the ceiling on the level of permitted oil sales<br>Outlined procedures for the completion of the weapons verification process<br>Declared the Council's intention to suspend sanctions for renewable 120-day periods if Iraq cooperated with UNMOVIC and IAEA |

| 1302 | **8 June 2000** |
|------|------|
|      | Established a panel of experts to report on the humanitarian situation |
| 1352 | **1 June 2001** |
|      | Extended the 986 program |
|      | Expressed the intention to consider new arrangements to facilitate civilian trade |
| 1360 | **3 July 2001** |
|      | Extended the 986 program |

*Notes:* a. Dates indicate time of Security Council decision. In some cases, actual imposition time may be later. Lists for this and all subsequent case studies include sanctions-related resolutions only.
b. Resolution 986 did not come into force until December 1996.

wrote, "In the chemical and missile areas . . . the declarations had improved and were *almost* [emphasis in original] full, final, and complete." Butler told Russian officials in December 1998 that the final accounting of Iraq's weapons of mass destruction could be completed within six to eight weeks if Baghdad cooperated.[4] Scott Ritter, one of UNSCOM's most aggressive inspectors, wrote in a June 2000 article:

> It was possible as early as 1997 to determine that, from a qualitative standpoint, Iraq had been disarmed. Iraq no longer possessed any meaningful quantities of chemical or biological agent . . . and the industrial means to produce these agents had either been eliminated or were subject to stringent monitoring. The same was true of Iraq's nuclear and ballistic missile capabilities.[5]

Despite Iraq's frequent obstruction of UNSCOM's efforts, substantial, hard-won progress was achieved in eliminating its weapons programs.

In response to this progress, Russia, France, and other countries urged the Security Council to certify the partial completion of the UN disarmament mandate. Moscow called for a partial lifting of sanctions as a means of acknowledging the progress achieved and encouraging further cooperation from Baghdad. Such a step would have been in keeping with cooperation theory, which emphasizes the importance of reciprocating concessions. When the target of coercive pressure complies with the sender's demands, however grudgingly, a reciprocal gesture to ease coercive pressure can help to encourage further cooperation. The United States rejected proposals for easing sanctions pressure, however, showing little interest in applying this principle in Iraq. Nor did Iraq provide any indication that it was interested in cooperation on inspections. The policy options on Iraq were reduced to Iraqi obstinacy and U.S. bombing.

Together with the United Kingdom, the United States refused to consider any incentives to encourage Iraqi compliance. Washington and London used their positions as permanent members of the Security Council to block attempts to scale back the sanctions on Iraq or to use that leverage to achieve other concessions. The United States in particular maintained a policy of hostility toward Iraq, placing a large number of holds on goods examined by the sanctions committee. It continued an ongoing punitive foreign policy toward Iraq that included regular bombing.

This combination of continued Iraqi truculence and U.S. inflexibility led to a number of crises between UNSCOM and Iraq. The most serious came in the fall of 1998 and led to the complete collapse of the weapons inspection process in December 1998. UNSCOM left Iraq just ahead of an intensive U.S./UK bombing raid intended to punish Baghdad and presumably compel new compliance. Iraq cut off all cooperation with UNSCOM and refused to accept any further disarmament inspections. The UN disarmament mission, which had been so successful in identifying and eliminating much of Iraq's weapons of mass destruction, came to a halt.

In an attempt to resurrect the inspections process, the United Kingdom led a Security Council effort to replace UNSCOM with a new weapons monitoring commission, the UN Monitoring, Verification, and Inspection Commission (UNMOVIC), authorized in SCR 1284 (December 1999). Under the leadership of Swedish diplomat Hans Blix, UNMOVIC assembled a new team of weapons inspectors with a mandate to complete the disarmament inspections in Iraq promptly. SCR 1284 spelled out a plan for UNMOVIC's return to Iraq, for the completion of weapons inspections, and for the suspension of sanctions within a year of Iraqi compliance. Iraq steadfastly refused to accept the UNMOVIC mission, however, demanding an immediate end to sanctions. The stalemate continued. Meanwhile, no UN weapons inspections occurred in Iraq. All monitoring cameras and tags left by UNSCOM were rendered inoperable. The Security Council was unable to verify the absence of weapons of mass destruction or to complete the final disarmament of Iraq.

## Responding to the Humanitarian Crisis

Concerns about the humanitarian consequences of sanctions have played a major role in the debate over UN policy in Iraq and have eroded support for sanctions. Children and other vulnerable populations have suffered severely since 1990. Increased infant and child mortality rates indicate that hundreds of thousands of children have died prematurely.[6] These preventable deaths resulted from severe malnutrition and disease—conditions set in place by the combination of the bombing of Iraq's infrastructure during the Gulf War and the maintenance of comprehensive trade sanctions.[7] The Hussein regime exacerbated these conditions for political purposes by repeatedly rejecting options for alleviating the crisis. This humanitarian catastrophe prompted a worldwide outpouring of sympathy for the Iraqi people and led to mounting public opposition to continued sanctions.[8]

The Security Council addressed the humanitarian crisis by creating the oil for food program, authorized in SCRs 706 (1991) and 986 (1995). Humanitarian relief could have come much earlier than it did if the Baghdad government had accepted the program when it was first proposed by the Security Council in 1991, or if Iraq had agreed to implement the 1995 proposal more quickly, which it impeded until 1997. Despite Baghdad's reluctance and obstruction of the program, the oil for food effort delivered significant quantities of food, medicine, and other humanitarian supplies. From 1997 through September 2001, the program generated approved oil sales valued at $28.6 billion. Nearly $16 billion worth of humanitarian and civilian infrastructure goods was imported, with another $12.8 billion worth of supplies in the pipeline.[9]

The Security Council steadily expanded the scale of the program over the years. With the passage of SCR 1153 in February 1998, the Council raised the level of authorized oil sales to $5.25 billion every six months and for the first time agreed to allow the use of these revenues for rehabilitation of Iraq's shattered economic infrastructure. With the adoption of SCR 1284 in December 1999, the ceiling on permitted oil sales was lifted entirely, allowing Iraq to export as much oil as it could produce. The lifting of limits on oil exports coincided with a significant rise in world oil prices, resulting in a sharp increase in Iraqi oil revenues. For a depiction of the level of oil sales from each six-month period through the oil for food program, refer to Figure 2.1. In addition to lifting all limits on oil exports, the United Nations steadily expanded the categories of imports that can be purchased with Iraqi oil revenues.

**Figure 2.1   Iraqi Oil Revenues Through the Oil for Food Program**

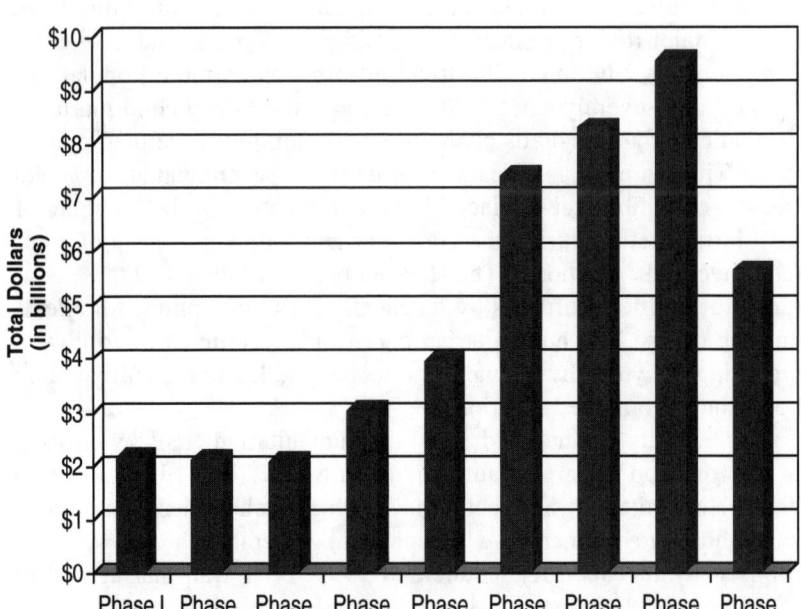

These categories, designed to promote civilian economic activity and infrastructure development, include oil production, electricity, agriculture, water and sanitation, education, housing, transportation, and telecommunications. The program was no longer simply an oil for food relief effort. The emphasis shifted from humanitarian relief to broader economic development and projects that contribute to the rebuilding of essential civilian infrastructure.

By early 2000, it was no longer accurate to describe UN policy as an oil embargo. Iraqi oil exports were not prohibited but merely regulated. Unlimited exports were allowed, although revenues continued to be deposited in the UN escrow account and were subject to controls designed to prevent the purchase of any weapons or military-related goods. By the fall of 2000, daily oil production was between 2.6 and 2.8 million barrels, levels approaching the rates before the Gulf War.[10] Oil export revenues during the second half of 2000 were nearly $10 billion—hardly what one would call an oil embargo.

## Denying Help

As Iraqi oil revenues increased sharply, the funds available in the UN escrow account for humanitarian and civilian economic needs expanded accordingly. Despite the Security Council's efforts to increase the funds available for humanitarian relief, however, the government of Iraq did not take full advantage of the 986 program. Iraq periodically halted oil exports, and it was slow to utilize the available revenues. During the 180-day period ending 30 April 2001, estimated oil revenues were only $5.7 billion, approximately $4 billion less than in the previous 180-day period. According to the May 2001 report of Secretary-General Kofi Annan, the decline in revenues was due "predominantly to the reduced rate of oil exports."[11] The September 2001 report of the Secretary-General confirmed that program implementation has "suffered considerably because . . . the volume of oil exports . . . has been reduced or totally suspended by the Government of Iraq."[12] In late 2000, Iraq refused to pump oil because of the Security Council's rejection of its proposal for a per barrel surcharge. Iraq again withheld oil exports in June and July 2001 in response to the Security Council's declared intention to restructure sanctions while retaining financial and military controls. By playing politics with oil exports, Baghdad lost substantial revenues that were intended to meet the humanitarian needs of its people.

The Iraqi government not only withheld oil exports but did not use the funds available to order needed imports. According to the Secretary-General's May 2001 report, as of mid-May of that year, the government of Iraq had not submitted a single application for the purchase of goods in the health, education, and water and sanitation sectors or for spare parts for the oil industry.[13] The failure to order supplies for the health sector was particularly striking in light of Baghdad's continued declaration of health crises caused by a shortage of supplies, medicines, and replacement parts for medical equipment. The lack of orders was labeled "regrettable" by the Secretary-General. In a society in which the privations of war and sanctions had caused severe health problems, the government refused to avail itself of the hundreds of millions of dollars available to order health supplies for its people.

Equally surprising was Baghdad's lack of purchases of spare parts and equipment for the oil industry. As previous UN studies noted and as confirmed in a recent report by a panel of oil experts, the Iraqi oil industry has suffered from serious problems of disrepair and inadequate production capacity. It was in recognition of these needs that the Security Council agreed to add the category of oil spare parts and equipment to the 986 program as one of the first nonhumanitarian sectors to be funded. Iraq initially did not take advantage of this program, however. During the first 180-day period of 2001, it submitted no applications for the purchase of oil spare parts and equipment. In the previous 180 days of the program, the total value of applications for oil spare parts and equipment was only one-third of the authorized allocation.

Secretary-General Annan's frustration was evident in his May 2001 report: "With all the efforts made for the provision of funding for oil spare parts and equipment, I can only reiterate my regret expressed in previous reports that there has been no major improvement in the submission of oil spare parts applications."[14] As a result, according to the oil experts, Iraq "continues to face significant technical and infrastructural problems, which unless addressed will result in a reduction of crude oil from the current levels."[15] The oil production situation comprised another of the ongoing, bitter ironies of the quagmire of Iraqi sanctions. The Baghdad regime found new, self-destructive (to Iraqi society at least) ways to worsen the effects of sanctions.

Another way Iraq undermined the 986 program was by delaying or refusing to issue visas to UN staff. According to the Secretary-General, nearly one-third of the UN applications for visas during the first 180-day period of 2001 were still pending. These delays and refusals were "adversely affecting the implementation of the programme as a whole."[16] The obstruction of visa applications was specifically targeted at UN operations in the three northern governorates in the Kurdish region. The Secretary-General's report expressed his "deep concern over the current visa situation and the negative impact that the interruption in essential activities is having on the humanitarian situation in the three northern governorates."[17] Baghdad's actions particularly hampered UN efforts to rehabilitate the electricity sector in the northern governorates.

*Real Relief?*

In an attempt to survey health and nutritional conditions within Iraq and to evaluate the impact of the 986 program, the Security Council adopted SCR 1302 (2000), authorizing an independent scientific study of humanitarian conditions. Baghdad refused to permit the UN scientific team to enter the country, however. The government of Iraq apparently did not want to know or have other governments and the UN learn whether the 986 program was improving humanitarian conditions or if there were continuing needs that could be addressed through additional relief efforts. The external perception of continued humanitarian disaster was useful to the Baghdad regime in a perverse way, as a means of generating sympathy and support for an end to sanctions.[18]

Despite the many difficulties associated with its implementation and notwithstanding the lack of precise scientific data, the 986 program helped to ameliorate humanitarian conditions in Iraq. The reports of the Secretary-General indicate that the program has made a positive contribution to improving social conditions. The Secretary-General reported in April 1999 that the program "has met its priority objective in making available basic food items and health supplies."[19] According to the March 1999 report by the panel of independent experts, the 986 program "played an important role in averting major food shortages and to a considerable extent has helped to alleviate the health situation, especially in the North."[20] In the northern governorates, where the United Nations rather than the government of Iraq has managed the relief program (and where private relief organizations operate), nutritional levels and health conditions have improved considerably. A May 2000 study published in the *Lancet* found that although infant mortality and nutritional levels worsened in the southern and central regions of Iraq, infant and child survival rates in the north actually improved during the latter part of the 1990s.[21]

The May 2001 report of the Secretary-General concluded: "Over the past four years, the humanitarian programme has contributed not only to arresting the decline in but also to improving the living conditions of the average Iraqi."[22] The Secretary-General reported "a marked improvement in water quality," thanks in part to the delivery of water and sanitation equipment as part of the 986 program.[23] Deliveries of water treatment equipment and supplies halted further deterioration of existing water and sanitation systems, according to the report.[24] A 2001 report of the World Food Programme stated that the 986 program produced "a significant increase in the food available compared to the pre–SCR 986 period."[25] Although economic and social conditions within Iraq remain difficult, the 986 program has made an important contribution to averting greater hardships and improving the lives of the Iraqi people. It could have made an even greater contribution had it benefited from the cooperation of the Iraqi government. The September 2001 report of the Secretary-General concluded that "with the improved funding level for the programme, the Government of Iraq is indeed in a position to address the nutritional and health concerns of the Iraqi people."[26]

*The Decline in Support for Sanctions*

Concerns over humanitarian suffering in Iraq prompted substantial campaigns for the lifting of sanctions in various Arab states, France, the United Kingdom, the United States, and many other countries. Religious and humanitarian groups mounted significant efforts to deliver humanitarian aid and demand that policymakers ease sanctions pressures. Some of the opposition groups distinguished between military and civilian sanctions, but many did not. The message was simply "lift sanctions," with no reference to maintaining the arms embargo. These campaigns were aided by the resignations of successive UN humanitarian coordinators in Iraq: Denis Halliday, UN coordinator for Iraq, resigned in September 1998, and Hans von Sponeck, director of the oil for food program, departed in March 2000. Halliday and von Sponeck condemned the continuing sanctions and asserted that the 986 program was incapable of relieving the pervasive suffering of the Iraqi people.

By summer 2000, UN sanctions in Iraq were unraveling, which was partly the result of the inevitable erosion that occurs with sanctions that have been maintained for such an inordinately long period. It was also due to factors specifically associated with this case: continuing divisions among the permanent members of the Security Council, widespread public concern for humanitarian suffering in Iraq, and the Baghdad regime's elaborate and multipronged efforts to subvert sanctions compliance. The divisions within the Security Council were evident during the debate over SCR 1284, when Russia, France, and China abstained on final passage of the resolution. Policy differences narrowed somewhat in 2001, when the United States and the United Kingdom offered a plan for restructuring sanctions, but Russian objections continued to block consensus.

By the fall of 2000, citizen groups that opposed sanctions and nations with differing political motives began to openly defy the sanctions by chartering flights to Baghdad. A number of advocacy groups, such as Voices in the Wilderness in the United States, had openly violated the sanctions previously by entering Iraq from Jordan and delivering humanitarian aid. But these efforts did not attract as much attention as the flights to newly reopened Saddam Hussein International Airport. Some of the organizations sponsoring flights sought approval from the Security Council sanctions committee in New York, but many of the trips were unauthorized. Dozens of flights arrived in Baghdad in the latter half of 2000. The flights carried relief supplies and human rights campaigners and, in some cases, businesspeople seeking contracts.

Welcomed by Iraqi officials with celebration and fanfare and widely reported by the media internationally, the flights to Baghdad were a dramatic sign of sanctions defiance.

Far more serious, if less visible, evidence of the unraveling of sanctions came with the rise of unauthorized trade between Iraq and its neighbors. Jordan and Syria began to reopen diplomatic and commercial ties with Iraq. As Iraqi oil revenues sharply increased, new opportunities arose for both authorized and unofficial trade. Jordanian prime minister Ali Abu Ragheb traveled to Baghdad in November 2000, as did Syrian prime minister Mohammad Mustapha Miro in August 2001. Syria signed a free trade agreement with Iraq in January 2001, and the two countries discussed reopening and rebuilding a long-dormant pipeline to carry Iraqi oil.[27] Turkish trade with Iraq increased as well. Oil smuggling along the Iranian coastline also rose, earning the Baghdad regime as much as $500 million annually outside the controls of the UN escrow account. Total Iraqi earnings from these and other oil-smuggling operations were estimated at $600 million in 2000.[28]

Sensing that the tide was shifting in its favor, the government of Iraq intensified its efforts to break free of sanctions. In fall 2000, Baghdad demanded that companies purchasing oil under the 986 program pay a surcharge on each barrel of oil into a separate fund not controlled by the United Nations. When the UN Security Council turned down the proposal, Iraq turned off the oil spigots. As a result, exports dropped from approximately 2.3 million barrels a day in fall 2000 to less than 1 million barrels a day in December 2000. The pipelines were reopened after a few days, but Baghdad continued to apply pressure on oil purchasers to pay the surcharge. Major oil companies and reputable buyers refused Baghdad's demands, but some purchasers, often small, obscure firms or such entities as the Ukrainian Communist Party, continued to buy Iraqi oil.[29] According to a confidential report by oil overseers attached to the Office of the Iraq Programme at the United Nations, some of these buyers were paying a surcharge of twenty to fifty cents per barrel.[30]

Iraq found other ways to manipulate oil contracts to obtain uncontrolled revenues. The normally routine task of selecting oil purchasers became a matter of the highest political importance. Decisions were made not by the State Oil Marketing Organization but by a special committee in the presidential office chaired by the deputy president. Purchasers were chosen on the basis of their willingness to pay kickbacks to Iraq and manipulate contracts to provide hard currency to the regime. In some cases, the official selling price included costs for delivery to one destination, when the oil actually went to another destination where transportation costs were lower. The purchaser agreed to share the difference in transportation costs with the Baghdad regime. Officials at the British Mission to the United Nations estimated that these machinations generated up to $1 billion a year in extra revenues, shared between the purchasers and the regime.

Further evidence of the erosion of sanctions came in October 2000, when the government of Jordan ordered a halt to the inspection of Iraqi-bound cargo arriving at the port of Aqaba. The inspections at Aqaba dated from 1994, when the UN hired Lloyd's Register to monitor goods destined for Iraq. These dockside inspections were a substitute for maritime interception, which had caused delays and increased costs for shippers. Jordan gave no explanation for its decision to halt the inspections by Lloyd's Register, although it indicated at the time that new arrangements would be provided. A year later, the monitoring of Iraqi-bound cargo had not resumed. The end of cargo monitoring at Aqaba, combined with the departure of UNSCOM inspectors from Iraq, left the United Nations with no means of determining whether Iraq was importing military equipment and rebuilding its weapons capability.

## The Call for Change

By the fall of 2000, U.S. and British policymakers recognized that the sanctions policy in Iraq had reached a crisis point and that major change would be necessary. Officially, the outgoing Clinton administration refused to consider any modifications in the comprehensive trade sanctions, but behind the scenes, pressure built for a strategy of easing restrictions on civilian imports while preserving and tightening controls on weapons and military-related goods. As recognition of the need for change spread and after the 2000 elections in the United States resulted in a new administration, the opportunity emerged for a significant restructuring of sanctions policy.

Because of continuing policy differences within the Security Council, however, and pervasive sanctions fatigue among policymakers in the United States and other countries, member states were unable to agree on strategies for redefining the sanctions mix and securing on-site weapons inspections. Instead, much of the impetus for change came from outside the diplomatic community. Human rights groups, independent research centers, and nongovernmental organizations exerted pressure for change and developed specific policy options. Some of these groups, as in the case of our own initiative, were able to build on long-standing research that was mixed with the latest thinking within the diplomatic community.

Human Rights Watch began the process of reappraisal in a letter and corresponding memorandum to then–U.S. permanent representative to the United Nations Richard Holbrooke. The documents addressed both eroding compliance with sanctions and continuing concerns about humanitarian hardships experienced by Iraqi citizens. Human Rights Watch urged the Council to "revise the embargo so as to enable the rehabilitation of the country's civilian economy while retaining comprehensive import restrictions of all military goods and rigorous monitoring of dual-use materials."[31] The Human Rights Watch letter and memorandum were, up to that time, the most thorough attempt to reframe UN policy in Iraq. As we found in our subsequent interviews with officials from the United States and other countries, the documents had a significant impact. A number of policymakers credited Human Rights Watch with stimulating new thinking on Iraq.

One of the first public discussions of restructuring sanctions occurred in September 2000 at a State Department conference called "States Challenging International Norms." Speakers included Human Rights Watch director Kenneth Roth and one of the authors of this book. Roth used the occasion to repeat the Human Rights Watch call for easing civilian sanctions and tightening restrictions on military goods. We seconded Roth's recommendations and emphasized the logic of the suggested approach. Civilian trade sanctions had caused widespread harm and were undermining international support for UN policy. Military sanctions, however, were rather successful in containing Iraq's weapons capabilities. Why not drop the former and retain the latter?

Following the State Department conference, the Fourth Freedom Forum and the Joan B. Kroc Institute for International Peace Studies at the University of Notre Dame launched a special research project to examine options for restructuring the sanctions. We conducted a technical study to determine exactly how the Council could remove sanctions on civilian imports while maintaining effective controls on the purchase or smuggling of military-related goods. The study focused on administrative options for maintaining control over Iraqi oil revenues while permitting unrestricted civilian trade. It also examined technical means of establishing external monitoring of Iraqi-bound cargo.[32] The study was released at an International Peace Academy forum attended by more than 100 UN officials, reporters, and policy experts. At approximately the same time, Meghan O'Sullivan of the Brookings Institution in

Washington, D.C., produced a study proposing a similar loosening of civilian sanctions and tightening of military controls.[33] The Brookings report was widely circulated to decisionmakers and policy experts in the United States. The Brookings Institution also hosted an important policy seminar on this topic in December 2000, chaired by Richard Haass, who went on to become the director of the Policy Planning Staff of the U.S. Department of State. In May 2001, the Watson Institute for International Studies at Brown University teamed up with the Decision Support Center of the Center for Naval Warfare Studies in Newport, Rhode Island, for a sanctions simulation exercise aimed at the same purpose—redesigning UN policy to ease restrictions on civilians while tightening the monitoring and control of weapons-related goods.

These independent nongovernmental initiatives played an important role in stimulating new thinking and identifying policy options. The various meetings and interview sessions gave policymakers an opportunity to discuss and consider new proposals. They provided a forum for the exchange of information and the cross-fertilization of ideas. These unofficial discussions bypassed the formal and politicized deliberations of the Security Council and allowed policymakers to explore new possibilities. During the Fourth Freedom Forum/Kroc Institute study, we met with more than 100 officials from approximately twenty governments. During these sessions, we found ourselves sometimes answering questions from one Security Council member state about the positions of other Council members on our draft recommendations. It was clear from these sessions and from direct comments by individual ambassadors and UN officials that our study and other independent research efforts contributed significantly both to the necessary creative thinking that helped produce an openness to change and to the search for specific mechanisms of implementation and monitoring.

## The Turn Toward Smart Sanctions

The first indication of a possible breakthrough in generating a new structure for sanctions came in February 2001, when U.S. secretary of state Colin Powell visited the Middle East and met with leaders from Syria, Jordan, and other countries.[34] During his trip, Powell used the term *smart sanctions* and spoke of the new administration's interest in "reenergizing" sanctions. Powell outlined the general contours of a new sanctions policy that would ease restrictions on civilian imports while strengthening the embargo on weapons and military-related goods. The goal of U.S. policy, Powell explained, would be to "ensure that UN sanctions are targeted at the Iraqi regime's attempts to develop weapons of mass destruction, while sparing the people of Iraq from any suffering."[35] Powell urged the leaders of Syria, Jordan, Turkey, and other neighboring states to support the proposed new strategy. He reportedly received assurances from Syrian president Bashar al-Assad that the oil pumped through a reopened pipeline with Iraq would be subject to the same kind of revenue controls as other elements of the sanctions regime.[36]

Powell's initiative seemed to suggest a major change in U.S. policy. But it was a shift in which the secretary of state was conceptually and practically far ahead of his agency and the U.S. Congress. The details of the new approach had not been worked out. Many in Washington were uncertain about, if not skeptical of, the new approach, fearing it was "going soft on Saddam." We discovered during interviews with dozens of State Department officials soon after Powell's meetings in the Middle East that the officers who would be responsible for implementing a new U.S. policy were not adequately briefed and had virtually no idea what the new strategy might entail.

One glaring problem was the collection of policies that would be needed if a new engagement with countries in the region was to occur. It was not yet determined how the United States would handle the incentives and agreements the secretary of state might want to provide Syria, for example, when that country was still on the U.S. terrorism list, a designation that prohibited the trade and aid relationships that would be needed to seal any new sanctions deal. To rescind the terrorist designation, the administration would need substantial evidence of changed Syrian behavior. The U.S. government would also need to assess the implications of such policy changes on Israeli-Palestinian relations and the Middle East peace process. Neither the domestic nor the foreign policy groundwork needed to accomplish such changes had been done, even as Powell was heading to Congress to sell the new approach on Iraq.

The lack of knowledge about smart sanctions was widespread. Soon after Powell's announcement, one of the authors received a call from a national reporter who had accompanied Powell to the Middle East. "Several of us in the press pool were asking ourselves, 'What are smart sanctions?'" the reporter said. "No one in the secretary of state's party could tell us, so we were hoping you could help." In the days following

Powell's trip, there seemed to be no one in the new administration who could explain with any precision what a smart sanctions policy would entail.

The United Kingdom took on the task of developing the details of the new policy. The British had a special interest in championing a new sanctions resolution, as they were the key architects of SCR 1284 and had been leading the search for new mechanisms to gain Iraqi acceptance of UNMOVIC. The British Mission to the United Nations took the lead in drafting a new resolution and building Security Council support for the plan. The initial goal was to adopt a new plan by early June 2001, to coincide with the 180-day rollover of the 986 program. The United Kingdom worked closely with the United States in drafting the plan, and the two governments worked to gain the support of France, China, and Russia. Differences among the Permanent Five remained, however. France wanted more freedom for oil companies to invest in Iraq. It saw the control of finances through the escrow account as the equivalent of maintaining trade sanctions. China expressed its well-known reservations about the sanctions policy in general. Russia demanded a timetable for the complete lifting of sanctions.

As part of the diplomatic horse trading to win support for the plan, U.S. representatives on the sanctions committee released many of the holds they had placed on oil for food contracts. On 1 June 2001, for example, the United States announced that it was lifting holds on some $800 million in business deals, including substantial contracts for companies in Russia, China, and France. Similar releases were announced a month later, when the Council addressed the restructuring plan again.[37] For nonpermanent members of the Council, these actions only solidified their skepticism, if not cynicism, regarding the entire sanctions enterprise.

Although British and U.S. officials made significant headway in gaining support for restructured sanctions, they were unable to meet their early June deadline. One of the major stumbling blocks was the list of dual-use goods authorized under SCR 1051 that would be subject to continued sanctions committee review. The United States and the United Kingdom wanted a long list, whereas France and Russia wanted a shorter, more focused list. The Council instead adopted SCR 1352 (2001), which expressed its intention to consider new arrangements for facilitating civilian trade and improving the flow of nonweapons imports.[38] The resolution also extended the 986 program for another month, to give time for diplomats to hammer out the details of the new sanctions plan.

The UK/U.S. plan, as detailed in an early June draft resolution, proposed significant changes in the Iraq sanctions regime. Its principal provisions were as follows:

- Restrictions on civilian imports would be lifted; all commodities and products other than specifically prohibited weapons and military-related goods would be sold freely.
- Weapons and military-related imports would continue to be banned; dual-use items on a newly created Goods Review List would be subject to review and approval by the sanctions committee.
- States sharing land borders with Iraq would be permitted to import up to 150,000 barrels of oil per day, provided that payment to Iraq was either in the form of nonmilitary goods or deposits to the UN escrow account.
- The Secretary-General would be asked to draw up a preapproved list of companies and trading organizations authorized to handle the sale or supply of Iraqi oil so that oil exports would be channeled only through authorized entities.
- All non-Iraqi civilian aircraft would be permitted to land in or take off from Iraq, provided that the aircraft submitted to inspection at designated airfields outside Iraq.
- The Secretary-General would be asked to devise procedures for the land-based monitoring of commodities and products exported to Iraq and would also be authorized to provide assistance to Iraq's neighbors for the proposed monitoring efforts.

The UK/U.S. draft resolution incorporated many of the suggestions of nongovernmental organizations and private research groups for restructuring sanctions in Iraq.[39] It did not, however, incorporate a number of additional suggestions that could have made it more appealing to other governments and increased its likelihood of success. Among the additional steps suggested were the following:

- permitting controlled foreign investment in Iraq's oil industry;
- lifting restrictions on non-oil exports from Iraq;
- streamlining the review of dual-use items, perhaps through contracting with commercial firms;
- minimizing the large number of import applications placed on hold by the sanctions committee;
- creating a cash component in the 986 program for the purchase of locally produced agricultural and other goods;

- developing a new compensation mechanism to assist neighboring states in sanctions implementation and to begin paying Iraq's foreign debt;
- utilizing electronic tagging technologies to assist in the monitoring of dual-use imports;
- establishing sanctions assistance missions in neighboring states to support border monitoring efforts;
- establishing an independent investigative commission to report on violations of the continuing arms embargo; and
- suspending U.S. and UK overflights and bombing missions.

## An Opportunity Lost?

Notwithstanding the limitations in the UK/U.S. draft resolution, it represented a significant change in approach and offered hope that the Security Council might at last reach agreement on easing civilian sanctions while maintaining tight controls on weapons imports. British and U.S. diplomats managed to win support for their plan from fourteen of the fifteen countries on the Security Council, including France and China. The support of the latter two was particularly significant because they had abstained on the previous major Iraq resolution, SCR 1284. But the proposal foundered on determined Russian opposition. Russia threatened to use its veto power to prevent adoption of the UK/U.S. draft resolution. Faced with such adamant rejection, UK and U.S. officials had no choice but to withdraw their plan. The Council instead passed another continuing resolution extending the 986 program.

In November 2001 the Security Council again postponed a decision on restructuring sanctions, but it moved slightly closer to a resolution of the dispute. In adopting SCR 1382, the Council extended the 986 program for another six months, but it also agreed to adopt a Goods Review List as proposed in the UK/U.S. plan. SCR 1382 took note of the proposed Goods Review List, which was attached as an annex, and said that the Council "decides that it will adopt the List . . . subject to any refinements . . . beginning 30 May 2002."[40] Russia joined the consensus in approving SCR 1382, but sharp differences remained over the content of the proposed Goods Review List and the overall direction of UN policy in Iraq.

On the face of it, the Russian objections to the UK/U.S. plan were based on Moscow's long-held view that sanctions should be lifted if Iraq resumed cooperation with UN weapons inspectors. According to a statement by Alexander Yakovenko, official spokesman of Russia's Ministry of Foreign Affairs, "The essence of our proposals is . . . suspending and then completely lifting economic sanctions, tied with the restoration of cooperation by Iraq with the United Nations in the disarmament field."[41] The Russian alternative to the UK/U.S. proposal reflected this emphasis on lifting sanctions. It proposed that, once Baghdad permitted UNMOVIC to reestablish a weapons monitoring system inside Iraq, sanctions on all nonmilitary goods should be suspended and funds in the escrow account should be returned to Iraqi authority. Under the Russian proposal, the embargo on weapons exports to Iraq would continue, but the only provision for enforcement would be the requirement that states notify the sanctions committee of all exports to Iraq. No mechanism for financial control or monitoring imports was proposed, other than the review of contracts by the sanctions committee. The Russian proposal also called for the Council to "consider" the termination of all sanctions 180 days after UNMOVIC and the IAEA certified the completion of the remaining disarmament tasks.[42]

The Russian proposal reflected fundamental differences about how to enforce an arms embargo. The UK/U.S. plan called for maintaining the UN escrow account as a means of ensuring that Iraqi oil revenues were not used to purchase weapons and military-related goods. The Russian proposal relied on member states to notify the sanctions committee of exports to Iraq. One proposal utilized mandatory financial controls, whereas the other depended on the willing compliance of member states. The record of UN embargoes that have relied on voluntary compliance is not very encouraging, however. As documented in Chapter 9, few member states have demonstrated the capacity or the political will to prevent the export of weapons to embargoed countries. UN arms embargoes have not been very effective in stemming the flow of arms to Angola, Sierra Leone, Ethiopia, Eritrea, and other conflict zones. There seems little reason to expect that an embargo against Iraq, with its lure of vast oil revenues and large appetite for arms purchases, would enjoy greater compliance. By contrast, the UK/U.S. proposal had the advantage of maintaining financial controls and thus provided an enforcement mechanism for screening and preventing the import of weapons and military-related goods.

Some observers have suggested that the Russian desire to lift sanctions had as much to do with economic self-interest as with concerns about arms policy. The Russian newspaper *Nezavisimaya Gazeta* quoted Iraqi deputy prime minister Tariq Aziz telling Russian officials that "a correct policy will bring economic benefits" for Russian companies.[43] On 3 July 2001, the very day the Council gave up its attempt to reform the sanctions policy, Iraqi trade minister Mehdi Saleh announced that Moscow would be rewarded with "priority in contracts and trade dealings."[44] *The Economist* also pointed to the favored position of Russian oil companies in winning contracts in Iraq and the influence of these interests on Russian policy.[45] Such an explanation would be consistent with the previously noted theme of great power politics dominating UN sanctions policy.

## Inducing Iraqi Compliance

The search for an endgame in Iraq has been frustrated not only by the differing agendas of the Permanent Five and the resulting disunity within the Security Council but also by Iraq's continued defiance of UN demands. Baghdad has been unwilling to cooperate because it perceives an opportunity, given the recent erosion of international compliance, to break free of UN sanctions. It also fears that even if the disarmament mandate is fulfilled, the United States will prevent the Council from lifting sanctions. Iraq's fears about U.S. intentions appear to be well founded, given the frequent statements of U.S. officials that sanctions will continue as long as Saddam Hussein remains in power.[46] SCR 1284 included a timetable for lifting sanctions in conjunction with the completion of UN weapons inspections, but that resolution called merely for suspension rather than termination and required an affirmative decision to renew the suspension every 120 days. That would allow the United States or any other member state to end the suspension and reimpose sanctions. In light of the intransigence of U.S. policy toward Iraq, Baghdad could reasonably expect that Washington would find reason to do exactly that. Under these circumstances, Iraq has little or no incentive to comply with UN demands.

Iraq's fears of permanent hostility and unending sanctions must be addressed if a solution to the crisis is to be found. Quieting these fears will require a policy of inducements as well as sanctions. An alternative strategy would maintain targeted pressure for compliance, as proposed in the UK/U.S. plan, but would also provide assurances that sanctions will be fully lifted if Iraq cooperates, as specified in the Russian proposal. The Security Council could pledge that sanctions against Iraq would not only be suspended but fully terminated upon completion of the disarmament mandate. This policy would be in keeping with paragraph 22 of the original Gulf War cease-fire resolution, SCR 687. That resolution specified that the oil embargo against Iraq would be lifted when the disarmament mandate was completed. A clarification and restatement of the Council's obligation to lift the oil embargo, as provided in paragraph 22 of SCR 687 (1991), could be a powerful incentive for gaining Iraqi compliance.

The proposed lifting of sanctions would be conditioned on the resumption of unfettered inspections and the certification by UNMOVIC and the IAEA that Iraq's capabilities for developing weapons of mass destruction have been fully eliminated. There can be no backing away from the requirement for a final round of weapons inspections and the dismantling of Iraq's weapons of mass destruction. To weaken or soften this requirement would undermine global nonproliferation efforts and damage the authority of the United Nations.

Policy options the Security Council should consider to implement the proposed inducement strategy include the following:

- suspending some sanctions provisions if Iraq permits weapons inspectors from UNMOVIC and the IAEA to reenter Iraq; such a gesture of reciprocation in response to initial Iraqi cooperation might create momentum for other concessions;
- suspending all sanctions within sixty days of the establishment of an ongoing monitoring and verification system within Iraq, rather than after 120 days as provided by SCR 1284;
- dropping the requirement in SCR 1284 for periodic affirmative votes to renew the sanctions suspension, provided that Iraq continues to cooperate with the ongoing monitoring and verification system;
- specifying clearly and unequivocally that upon completion of the weapons inspection mission and certification of Iraq's complete disarmament, the sanctions against Iraq will be terminated as required by paragraph 22 of SCR 687.

The proposed assurances and gestures of flexibility would demonstrate a good-faith effort to find a diplomatic solution. If combined with a shift toward more targeted and effective smart sanctions, the proposed inducements could help to change Baghdad's political calculations and encourage a new policy of cooperation with UN resolutions. The combination of more focused and effective sanctions and a more flexible, incentives-based diplomacy offers the best hope for encouraging Iraqi compliance and ending the sanctions impasse. In such an effort, the cooperation of the Permanent Five would be essential for success. Whether the renewed cooperation among the Permanent Five generated by the events of 11 September 2001 will provide the catalyst for such new consensus and action remains to be seen.

# Notes

1. See our discussion in David Cortright and George A. Lopez, with Richard W. Conroy, Jaleh Dashti-Gibson, and Julia Wagler, *The Sanctions Decade: Assessing UN Strategies in the 1990s* (Boulder, Colo.: Lynne Rienner Publishers, 2000), 37–61; and David Cortright and George A. Lopez, "Are Sanctions Just? The Problematic Case of Iraq," *Journal of International Affairs* 52, no. 2 (Spring 1999): 735–755.

2. United Nations Security Council, *Letter Dated 22 November 1997 from the Executive Chairman of the Special Commission Established by the Secretary-General Pursuant to Paragraph 9(b)(i) of Security Council Resolution 687 (1991) Addressed to the President of the Security Council*, S/1997/922, New York, 24 November 1997; United Nations Security Council, *Report of the Executive Chairman on the Activities of the Special Commission Established by the Secretary-General Pursuant to Paragraph 9(b)(i) of Resolution 687 (1991)*, S/1998/332, New York, 16 April 1998; and United Nations Security Council, *Letter Dated 9 April 1998 from the Secretary-General Addressed to the President of the Security Council, Appendix: Fifth Consolidated Report of the Director General of the International Atomic Energy Agency Under Paragraph 16 of Security Council Resolution 1051 (1996)*, S/1998/312, New York, 9 April 1998.

3. United Nations Security Council, *Letters Dated 27 and 30 March 1999, Respectively, from the Chairman of the Panels Established Pursuant to the Note by the President of the Security Council of 30 January 1999 (S/1999/100) Addressed to the President of the Security Council*, S/1999/356, New York, 30 March 1999, par. 25.

4. Richard Butler, *The Greatest Threat: Iraq, Weapons of Mass Destruction, and the Crisis of Global Security* (New York: Public Affairs, 2000), 51, 203.

5. Scott Ritter, "The Case for Iraq's Qualitative Disarmament," *Arms Control Today* 30, no. 5 (June 2000): 8.

6. Two of the most rigorous and comprehensive scientific studies of the humanitarian costs of sanctions are Richard Garfield, *Morbidity and Mortality Among Iraqi Children from 1990 to 1998: Assessing the Impact of Economic Sanctions*, Occasional Paper Series 16:OP:3 (paper commissioned by the Joan B. Kroc Institute for International Peace Studies of the University of Notre Dame and by the Fourth Freedom Forum, March 1999 <www.fourthfreedom.org/php/t-si-index.php?hinc=garf.hinc> [4 September 2001]); and Mohamed M. Ali and Iqbal H. Shah, "Sanctions and Childhood Mortality in Iraq," *Lancet* 355 (May 2000): 1837–1857.

7. For a detailed review of the combined impact of war and sanctions, see Eric Hoskins, "The Humanitarian Impacts of Economic Sanctions and War in Iraq," in Thomas G. Weiss et al., eds., *Political Gain and Civilian Pain: Humanitarian Impacts of Economic Sanctions* (Lanham, Md.: Rowman and Littlefield, 1997), 91–148.

8. Cortright and Lopez, "Are Sanctions Just? The Problematic Case of Iraq."

9. United Nations Office of the Iraq Programme, *Weekly Update, 20 October 2001,* <www.un.org/depts/OIP/latest/wu2Oct01.html> (4 October 2001).

10. Robin Allen, "Iraqi Smugglers Net Oil Bonanza," *Financial Times,* 27 March 2001.

11. United Nations Security Council, *Report of the Secretary-General Pursuant to Paragraph 5 of Resolution 1330 (2000),* S/2001/505, New York, 18 May 2001, par. 4.

12. United Nations Security Council, *Report of the Secretary-General Pursuant to Paragraph 5 of Resolution 1360 (2001),* S/2001/919, New York, 28 September 2001, par. 5.

13. United Nations Security Council, *Report of the Secretary-General Pursuant to Paragraph 5 of Resolution 1330 (2000),* S/2001/505, par. 15.

14. Ibid., par. 25.

15. United Nations Security Council, *Letter Dated 6 June 2001 from the Secretary-General Addressed to the President of the Security Council, Annex, Report of the Team of Experts Established Pursuant to Paragraph 15 of Security Council Resolution 1330 (2000),* S/2001/566, New York, 6 June 2001, par. 16.

16. United Nations Security Council, *Report of the Secretary-General Pursuant to Paragraph 5 of Resolution 1330 (2000),* S/2001/505, par. 121.

17. Ibid., par. 134.

18. The subject of accurate accounting of the impact of sanctions on the humanitarian and health sectors continues to be a matter of considerable controversy. Antisanctions groups in the United States and Europe continually cite figures of as many as 1 million deaths since 1991. We believe that these numbers are exaggerated. See Garfield, *Morbidity and Mortality Among Iraqi Children from 1990 to 1998;* see also David Cortright, "A Hard Look at Iraqi Sanctions," *The Nation* 273, no. 18 (3 December 2001): 20–24, and the responding colloquy in *The Nation* 274, no. 2 (21 January 2002): 2, 26.

19. United Nations Security Council, *Review and Assessment of the Implementation of the Humanitarian Programme Established Pursuant to Security Council Resolution 986 (1995), December 1996–November 1998,* S/1999/481, New York, 28 April 1999, par. 53.

20. United Nations Security Council, *Letters Dated 27 and 30 March 1999, Respectively, from the Chairman of the Panels Established Pursuant to the Note by the President of the Security Council of 30 January 1999 (S/1999/100) Addressed to the President of the Security Council,* S/1999/356, 39.

21. Ali and Shah, "Sanctions and Childhood Mortality in Iraq."

22. United Nations Security Council, *Report of the Secretary-General Pursuant to Paragraph 5 of Resolution 1330 (2000),* S/2001/505, par. 123.

23. Ibid., par. 76.

24. Ibid., par. 77.

25. World Food Programme, *Assessment of the Adequacy of SCR 986 Food Basket,* North Coordination Office, Erbil, Iraq, 2001, §1.4.

26. United Nations Security Council, *Report of the Secretary-General Pursuant to Paragraph 5 of Resolution 1360 (2001),* S/2001/919, par. 105.

27. Farouk Choukri, "Syrian PM to Seal End to 20-year Rift with Landmark Baghdad Visit," Agence France Presse, 20 May 2001.

28. "Iraq Smuggled $600 Million Worth of Oil in 2000," Reuters, 6 February 2001, <www.GulfNews.com> (20 February 2001).

29. Carl Mortished, "Oil Boycott over Iraqi 'Breach of UN Scheme,'" *Times* (London), 8 January 2001.

30. Carola Hoyes, "U.S. Toughens Line on Iraq Oil Sanctions Violations," *Financial Times,* 27 February 2001, 5.

31. Letter to United Nations Security Council from Hanny Megally, Director, Human Rights Watch, 4 January 2000, <www.hrw.org/press/2000/01/iraq-ltr.htm> (9 October 2001).

32. See David Cortright, Alistair Millar, and George Lopez, *Smart Sanctions: Restructuring UN Policy in Iraq,* policy brief (Goshen and Notre Dame, Ind.: Fourth Freedom Forum and Joan B. Kroc Institute for International Peace Studies), April 2001.

33. Meghan O'Sullivan, "Iraq: Time for a Modified Approach," policy brief 71 (Washington, D.C.: Brookings Institution, February 2001).

34. Jane Perlez, "Powell Proposes Easing Sanctions on Iraqi Civilians," *New York Times,* 27 February 2001, A1.

35. Barry Schweid, "UN May Monitor Iraqi Smuggling," Associated Press, 26 March 2001.

36. Jonathan Wright, "Syria Agrees to UN Supervision of Pipeline," Reuters, 26 February 2001.

37. Colum Lynch, "Trade Deal Won Chinese Support of U.S. Policy on Iraq," *Russian Impost,* 6 July 2001, A17.

38. United Nations Security Council, *Security Council Resolution 1352 (2001),* S/RES/1352, New York, 1 June 2001.

39. The draft resolution also embodied ideas from the February 2001 study by The Brookings Institution in Washington, D.C. See O'Sullivan, "Iraq: Time for a Modified Approach."

40. United Nations Security Council, *Security Council Resolution 1382 (2001),* S/RES/1382, New York, 29 November 2001, par. 2.

41. "Statement by Alexander Yakovenko, the Official Spokesman of Russia's Ministry of Foreign Affairs, in Connection with the Discussion in the UN Security Council of the Iraqi Question," 1231-27-06-2001, Moscow, 27 June 2001, <www.In.mid.ru/base_e.htm> (9 October 2001).

42. Russian Federation, "Draft Resolution on Iraq," 01.42846, New York, 26 June 2001.

43. Reported in Jeffery Bartholet and Christian Caryl, "Bolting from Baghdad," *Newsweek,* 7 July 2001.

44. Quoted in Edith M. Lederer, "Iraq's Oil Money Undermines Sanctions," Associated Press, 5 August 2001.

45. "Smart Exit," *The Economist,* 7 July 2001, 45.

46. In November 1997, then–U.S. president Bill Clinton stated that "sanctions will be there until the end of time, or as long as [Hussein] lasts." Quoted in Barbara Crossette, "For Iraq: A Dog House with Many Rooms," *New York Times,* 23 November 1997, A4.

# 3

## Smart Sanctions, Limited Impacts:
## UN Policy in Afghanistan

The Security Council measures imposed against the Taliban in Afghanistan embodied in one episode all the varied frustrations, limited effects, and ironies of the contemporary sanctions era. At one level, as we detail below, the specific provisions incorporated into the sanctions resolutions were carefully crafted, sharply focused, and "smart" in every dimension that the UN system had developed since the late 1990s. At another level, however, Security Council policy toward Afghanistan was driven by the great power concerns of Russia and the United States, with only limited support from other states. The UN sanctions were poorly enforced and had little direct effect in convincing the Taliban regime to comply with UN demands and cease its harboring of Osama bin Laden and other terrorists. When the investigation into the terrorist attacks of 11 September 2001 pointed to the al-Qaida network and bin Laden, the Taliban still refused to extradite him. The subsequent U.S.-led military campaign largely bypassed the Security Council and made no reference to the ongoing sanctions. The United States went to the Council to gain support for the far-reaching counterterrorism measures of Security Council Resolution (SCR) 1373, as we note in Chapter 7, but the United Nations remained tangential to the ultimate fate of the Taliban. After initially playing a major role in the struggle against terrorism, the sanctions in Afghanistan were relegated to the sidelines.

In this chapter, we examine the dual reality of sanctions in Afghanistan: innovative design but inadequate implementation. We review the changing objectives of UN policy and the details of Security Council sanctions and then assess the social impacts of the sanctions and the controversy that emerged over the prospect of exacerbating already severe humanitarian hardships. After discussing proposed efforts to improve monitoring, we conclude with an assessment of the political impacts of the sanctions, arguing that although the sanctions

had little direct impact, they nonetheless contributed to the isolation of the Taliban.

## Pressuring the Taliban

Well before the terrorist attacks of 11 September and the subsequent military campaign, the UN Security Council imposed sanctions against the Taliban regime because of its support for terrorism. Aviation and financial sanctions were imposed against the Taliban in SCR 1267 (1999), and an arms embargo and other measures were added in SCR 1333 (2000). The sanctions were designed to end Taliban support for international terrorism. SCR 1267 demanded that the Taliban cease using its territory to harbor international terrorists and that it turn over Osama bin Laden to "proper authorities" for his role in the bombing of U.S. embassies in Africa in August 1998.[1] Security Council resolutions also expressed concern about the continuing war in Afghanistan, the opium trade, and discrimination against women.

After the overthrow of the Taliban regime and the installation of a UN-brokered interim authority in Kabul, the Security Council restructured the sanctions. In January 2002 it adopted SCR 1390, lifting the aviation sanctions but continuing the financial sanctions on targeted Taliban and al-Qaida leaders and entities. Among the measures imposed in SCR 1390 were a freeze on financial assets, a ban on travel or transit, and a prohibition on the supply of arms and related military goods and services. The measures imposed in SCR 1390 were similar to and adopted some of the language of the sweeping counterterrorism provisions contained in SCR 1373 (2001).

The coercive measures imposed against the Taliban regime were among the most innovative ever adopted by the Security Council. Member states consciously attempted to apply lessons from the Swiss and German reform initiatives. The sanctions were targeted precisely against the Taliban leadership. They were carefully designed to avoid adverse humanitarian consequences. The UN Office for the Coordination of Humanitarian Affairs (OCHA) was asked to submit an early assessment of humanitarian impacts. The arms embargo included precise language banning not only weapons and military goods but all forms of military assistance and training. Acetic anhydride, the chemical used for processing opium into heroin, was also banned. SCR 1333 established a committee of experts to recommend ways of improving sanctions monitoring and also continued the trend toward time limits,

---

### AFGHANISTAN, Security Council Resolutions

| Resolution Number | Action |
|---|---|
| 1267 | **15 October 1999**<br>Created the sanctions committee<br>Imposed aviation and financial sanctions against the Taliban regime |
| 1333 | **19 December 2000**<br>Demanded cessation of support for terrorism<br>Demanded extradition of Usama bin Laden for trial<br>Imposed an arms embargo, travel sanctions, and an assets freeze on the Taliban<br>Imposed diplomatic restrictions<br>Broadened aviation sanctions<br>Requested a committee of experts |
| 1363 | **30 July 2001**<br>Established a monitoring mechanism<br>Established the Sanctions Enforcement Support Team to assist neighboring states with enforcement measures |

---

establishing a one-year time line for the new sanctions measures. All these provisions were refinements in the art of economic statecraft.

## Changing Goals

The imposition of Security Council sanctions represented a change in UN policy. Earlier in the decade, the UN had attempted to broker a negotiated peace settlement between the Taliban and the Northern Alliance forces clinging to a small pocket of territory in the north of the country. When the Council imposed a one-sided arms embargo on the Taliban with SCR 1333 (2000), it effectively preempted a General Assembly call for an arms embargo on both parties.[2] Human Rights Watch and other nongovernmental organizations supported the call for an arms embargo on both sides, arguing that the Taliban and the Northern Alliance were each implicated in serious violations of human rights and humanitarian law.[3] Russia and the United States opposed such a policy, however. Russia in particular served as a major weapons supplier to the embattled forces in the north. The United States grew increasingly concerned about the extremist practices of the Taliban leadership, especially with regard to the harboring of terrorists and the mistreatment of women. The 1998 bombings of U.S. embassies in Africa sharply focused U.S. policy on the former. Washington moved ahead with its own actions against the Taliban, freezing financial assets and pressing for similar action at the Security Council. For a list of Security Council measures taken against the Taliban, see the box on page 50. After the 11 September attacks, the Northern Alliance became a strategic ally in the military campaign against the Taliban and benefited from large-scale arms deliveries, supplied primarily by Russia.

The long-term goal of UN policy had been to end the armed conflict in Afghanistan by creating a more representative government in Kabul that respected human rights. The emphasis on preventing terrorism was added with the imposition of Security Council sanctions. In Afghanistan, as in other cases under review, the UN position shifted over the years from that of a neutral arbiter to a partisan seeking to isolate and coerce an abusive regime. Even before the 11 September attacks, the Security Council came to recognize that a fundamental change in or removal of the Taliban leadership was necessary to end support for terrorism, bring the armed conflict to a halt, and prevent further human rights abuse. Within the Security Council, the United States and Russia took the lead in urging a more coercive strategy toward the Taliban. Each country had its particular reasons for pressuring the Taliban. Russia sought to contain the spread of Islamic extremism in central Asia, and the United States wanted to bring Usama bin Laden to justice for his role in previous terrorist attacks. Together they pushed a sometimes reluctant Security Council to adopt more forceful measures against the Taliban.

## The Social Impacts of Sanctions

When sanctions were initially imposed, concerns about their possible humanitarian impacts in Afghanistan stirred controversy. In light of the grave social conditions and the severe food and refugee crises in the country, a number of countries expressed doubts about the wisdom of imposing sanctions. Even Secretary-General Kofi Annan expressed reservations when the sanctions were strengthened in December 2000:

"it is not going to facilitate our peace efforts, nor . . . our humanitarian efforts," he told a press briefing.[4] Because the sanctions against Afghanistan were highly targeted, however, and were designed to avoid generalized harm to the civilian population, their social impacts were limited.

At the time the sanctions were imposed, the Office of the UN Coordinator for Afghanistan released a study which assessed vulnerability and humanitarian impacts. The preliminary findings of the study, released in August 2000, stated: "UN Security Council sanctions have had a tangible negative effect on the Afghan economy and the ability of humanitarian agencies to render assistance."[5] Some member states and officials in the UN Secretariat expressed doubts about the report's conclusions. A subsequent official version of the report, released in December 2000, provided a more measured and balanced assessment of humanitarian impacts. According to the final report, the effects of the aviation sanctions and other measures were relatively small: the "direct impacts of sanctions on the humanitarian situation are limited."[6] A December 2000 paper from the U.S. State Department came to similar conclusions: there was no evidence of measurable humanitarian impacts. As the State Department report noted, the sanctions did not prevent civilian trade, and humanitarian exemptions from the flight ban were provided for medical needs and religious pilgrimages. According to the report, the sanctions committee "never denied a request for a humanitarian flight waiver."[7]

The most direct sanctions effects resulted from the ban on international flights of Ariana Afghan Airlines, the only airline in Afghanistan. Flights outside the country were banned, except for humanitarian purposes. Overseas maintenance arrangements were severed. According to the December 2000 OCHA assessment, the results were "a sharp fall in revenues" for the airline company and a "long-term decline in the airline's capacity."[8] The Taliban authorities who controlled the airline lost income. Afghans who depended on the airline also suffered some loss of income and employment.

When sanctions were initially imposed in November 1999, Afghanistan experienced sharp fluctuations in exchange rates and prices. The cost of wheat in Kabul jumped 55 percent from October to November 1999 and rose a further 10 percent in the following month. This increase appeared to be a market reaction to the threat of sanctions, according to newspapers in Pakistan.[9] A subsequent analysis by UN researchers revealed, however, that other factors caused the increase in food prices and that markets ultimately stabilized and absorbed the initial shock of sanctions. The principal factor pushing up food prices in October 1999 was a decision by the newly installed military government in Pakistan to suspend the export of wheat to Afghanistan.[10] The restrictions imposed by the Musharaff regime in Islamabad had a greater impact on the Afghan economy than UN sanctions.

The UN assessment reported that humanitarian agencies were unable to address the overwhelming nutritional, medical, and refugee assistance needs of the Afghan population. This problem was not due to sanctions, however, but to a lack of financial support from the international community and difficulties in gaining the cooperation of Taliban officials. The April 2001 report of the Secretary-General noted that donor countries provided only $85 million out of the $250 million requested to address the humanitarian crisis.[11] Taliban restrictions on the employment of women also hindered humanitarian operations. The Taliban banned most UN agencies from employing Afghan women. Only when the World Food Programme threatened to cut off the supply of wheat to subsidized public bakeries in June 2001 did Taliban officials agree to permit the hiring of local women to survey household nutritional needs.[12]

Afghanistan has indeed experienced a humanitarian catastrophe, with health conditions among the worst in the world and a huge percentage of the population forced from their homes.[13] But these conditions resulted from decades of war, the collapse of government and economy, and the lack of attention to humanitarian needs by Taliban authorities. Internal restrictions imposed by the warring factions also contributed to humanitarian hardships.[14] UN sanctions did not cause these conditions. According to the April 2001 report of the Secretary-General, "Sanctions are not responsible for the current humanitarian situation."[15]

## Improved Monitoring

When the Security Council imposed the arms embargo and strengthened sanctions in December 2000, it created a committee of experts to examine how these measures could be monitored more effectively. This move was further evidence of the institutional learning that has taken place within the UN on the need for more vigorous monitoring and enforcement efforts. The committee of experts was patterned after other investigative panels, including the UN Commission of Inquiry for Rwanda, and the Angola and Sierra Leone expert panels. It was asked to recommend specific mechanisms for strengthening sanctions and ensuring that they were properly monitored. The committee report, issued in May 2001, included a groundbreaking proposal to create a special UN monitoring and coordination office for sanctions in Afghanistan.

Although the six countries neighboring Afghanistan claimed to be implementing the sanctions, the committee noted that their border control capabilities varied widely. This statement was a polite way of acknowledging that customs services and security efforts in the surrounding states were inadequate. The committee concluded that implementation would be enhanced if monitoring capabilities could be strengthened and supported. It recommended the creation of an Office for Sanctions Monitoring and Coordination–Afghanistan. As proposed, the mechanism would have been the most ambitious sanctions monitoring effort ever attempted by the Security Council. It was modeled after the sanctions assistance missions that operated in the countries surrounding the former Yugoslavia in 1993 through 1995. However, those missions were created and supported primarily by European institutions. The proposed monitoring mechanism for Afghanistan was to be a completely UN-funded and UN-administered effort.

The mechanism was to consist of two parts. The first was an Office for Sanctions Monitoring and Coordination based in New York. The office was to have a director and specialists in such fields as illegal arms trafficking, drug and money laundering, and counterterrorism.[16] The second element of the monitoring mechanism would be teams of experts in the field, working alongside border control and security services in the countries bordering Afghanistan. These sanctions enforcement support teams would assess capability gaps and assist the host countries in modernizing all aspects of customs monitoring and border control. They would also make recommendations for improvements in equipment and training to these countries to better enforce the sanctions.[17]

The Security Council responded favorably to the committee's proposal. In July 2001, the Council approved SCR 1363, formally establishing a five-person monitoring group at UN headquarters in New York, to be followed by a sanctions enforcement support team of up to fifteen members to be deployed in the countries surrounding Afghanistan.[18] The UN Secretariat was in the midst of planning for the creation of the headquarters unit when the terrorist attacks occurred on 11 September. Preparations for the sanctions monitoring program were suspended during the military campaign against the Taliban but were resumed following the regime's overthrow. Paragraph 9 of SCR 1390

(2002) assigned the group to assist with monitoring the continued financial, travel, and arms sanctions on Taliban and al-Qaida individuals and entities.

## The Challenge of Enforcement

The committee of experts report acknowledged the difficulty of attempting to embargo arms in a country already overflowing with weapons. Afghanistan suffered from a "surfeit of weaponry, particularly small arms and light support weapons," according to the report. They had been acquired over decades of war from many sources. The committee noted, however, that the Taliban depended on special fuels and lubricants to operate its major weapons systems. The committee recommended that the arms embargo be broadened to include a special focus on aircraft turbine fuel and possibly the special fluids and lubricants needed for armored vehicles.[19] Cutting off the supply of these critical fuels and lubricants could improve the effectiveness of the arms embargo. The committee also recommended stricter international control and regulation of arms brokers. Similar recommendations were made by the investigative panels for Angola and Sierra Leone. According to the committee report:

> Countries must be encouraged to adopt legislation to strictly control this nefarious trade. Consideration should be given to registering all known arms brokers and dealing severely with those acting in contravention of national legislation or embargoes established by the United Nations.[20]

The committee drew attention to the supply of military recruits from religious schools *(madrasas)* in Pakistan. Other researchers also noted the dependence of the Taliban on support from Pakistan.[21] According to the report from the Swiss Center for Peacebuilding:

> Since 1994 the government and military of Pakistan have provided comprehensive assistance to the Taliban, including military supplies, training, [and] assistance with recruitment of Pakistani and Afghan *madrasa* students.[22]

The committee urged that efforts be made to regulate the *madrasas* and the movement of people into and out of Afghanistan. How this could be done without blocking the flow of war victims and refugees out of Afghanistan, however, was not explained.

## Political Impacts

The political effects of Security Council sanctions were ambiguous. The initial Taliban response to the imposition of sanctions suggested a willingness to find a way of meeting Security Council demands. Taliban leaders offered a number of proposals for isolating bin Laden and bringing him to trial. Among the suggestions was a plan for Islamic scholars to examine the evidence against bin Laden and bring the case before an Islamic court. The Taliban also offered to permit a trial by videotape in U.S. courts conducted under Islamic law. These proposals were inadmissible legally and unacceptable politically in the United States. They nonetheless indicated that sanctions motivated the Taliban to find a way of distancing itself from bin Laden and his terrorist network. In the fall of 1999, after sanctions were approved but before they were enacted, bin Laden wrote a letter to Supreme Taliban Leader Mullah Muhammad Omar offering to leave Afghanistan. This letter was evidence that sanctions, or at least the threat of sanctions, could affect the political calculations of bin Laden and his Taliban hosts.[23] Some observers believe that the Taliban would have been willing to see bin Laden and his terrorist network depart if a graceful exit could have been arranged.[24] No compromise was reached, however, and after sanctions were imposed, positions hardened.

One of the concerns motivating UN policy was the production and marketing of opium and heroin. During the 1990s, Afghanistan became by far the largest producer of opium in the world, supplying as much as 79 percent of world demand in 1999.[25] Trafficking in Afghan-generated narcotics became a major source of criminality and instability in the region and worldwide. In July 2000, Mullah Omar issued an edict banning opium poppy cultivation. It was interpreted by some as a gesture of conciliation by the Taliban and a possible sign of compliance with Security Council demands. But other factors may have been involved. The committee of experts created by SCR 1333 reported that the Taliban had accumulated such a sizable stock of opium and heroin before the ban that they wanted to stop production to prevent prices from declining. The report of the committee noted that the price of opium and heroin increased tenfold in the months after the ban on poppy.[26] According to an Iranian official, the stockpile of drugs in

Afghanistan was sufficient to supply market demand for years to come.[27] The report of the committee of experts noted that heroin seizures in Europe remained at high levels during the first quarter of 2001, with the majority of heroin shipments originating in Afghanistan.[28] Despite the prohibition on poppy cultivation, the Taliban continued to reap substantial revenues from narcotics trafficking.

After the imposition and strengthening of Security Council sanctions, the Taliban leadership became more inflexible in its bargaining position and more dismissive of international public opinion. Sanctions prompted the Taliban to renege on an earlier written agreement to participate in UN-brokered efforts to achieve a negotiated end to the fighting.[29] Secretary-General Kofi Annan stated in his April 2001 report that "the capacity of the UN to act as an honest broker has not been compromised by the imposition of sanctions."[30] In fact, however, the Security Council was not a neutral party, and the Taliban no longer considered the UN an impartial mediator. The Taliban showed its contempt for international opinion and its disdain of non-Islamic culture when it ordered the destruction of the statues of Buddha at Bamiyan in March 2001. Within the Taliban, decisionmaking became increasingly secretive and centralized around Mullah Omar.[31] The Taliban used the imposition of external sanctions to tighten its controls on Afghan society. The role of al-Qaida and the "Arab-Afghan" fighters increased.

When sanctions were initially imposed, skeptics questioned whether economic sanctions, no matter how effectively implemented, could help to resolve the crisis in Afghanistan. What was the point of sanctioning a country whose economy was already, in the words of the Center for Peacebuilding report, "almost entirely illegal"?[32] By the late 1990s, Afghanistan had become an example of what William Reno has called a "shadow state," a country with little or no formal governmental structure. The usual components of political authority—the rule of law, formal decisionmaking mechanisms, public accountability, and political power-sharing procedures—were largely lacking.

Even in the absence of political pluralism, however, UN sanctions proved to be an effective means of exerting economic and political pressure on the Taliban. The sanctions did not bring about compliance with UN demands, but they imposed economic and political costs that made it more difficult for the Taliban to consolidate power and gain legitimacy. They had the important function of preventing the Taliban regime from gaining acceptance as the legitimate state authority in Afghanistan. The strong Security Council support for sanctions sent a message to third parties that the Taliban was a pariah regime to be isolated rather than engaged. The message worked, for even before the 11 September attacks, only three countries offered diplomatic recognition to the Taliban. The sanctions consolidated and intensified the isolation of the Taliban regime and frustrated its ambitions for economic development and political legitimacy. To that extent, they were partly successful and laid the groundwork for the military campaign against the regime that followed in the wake of the terrorist attacks.

In light of the U.S.-led military operations against the Taliban and the political and humanitarian repercussions of these events for the people of Afghanistan, it is tempting to dismiss the imposition of sanctions by the Security Council as a meaningless exercise. Doing so would be a mistake. At the very least, the attempts to sanction a regime for violations of international norms regarding terrorism, women's rights, and the drug trade were novel in intention and in form. The selective and adaptive nature of the sanctions was particularly striking and was specifically constructed to avoid exacerbating the preexisting humanitarian crisis. To the extent that the highly targeted sanctions managed to avoid adverse social impacts while nonetheless exerting pressure on the Taliban leadership, they were remarkably successful.

Although the sanctions did not succeed in ending Taliban support for terrorism, they helped to isolate and weaken the regime in a manner that made the U.S. and international response to the attacks of 11 September 2001 more effective. The isolation of the regime served notice on bystander states that attempts to circumvent the sanctions and engage with the regime would be costly in political terms, if not economically. Even before 11 September, the Taliban regime was considered an international pariah, certified as such by the imposition of UN sanctions. The subsequent military overthrow of the Taliban built upon the economic hardships generated by sanctions to increase the prospects that the harboring of terrorists in Afghanistan would come to an end.

## Notes

1. United Nations Security Council, *Security Council Resolution 1267 (1999)*, S/RES/1267, New York, 15 October 1999, par. 2.

2. United Nations General Assembly, *A/RES/50/88 A-B: 95th Plenary Meeting 19 December 1995*, A/RES/50/88, New York, 19 December 1995.

3. Human Rights Watch, *Afghanistan: Crisis of Impunity: The Role of Pakistan, Russia, and Iran in Fueling the Civil War,* paper 13, no. 3 (July 2001): 3, 7, <www.hrw.org/reports/2001/afghan2/> (13 July 2001).

4. United Nations, *Transcript of Press Conference by Secretary-General Kofi*

*Annan at Headquarters, 19 December 2000,* SG/SM/7668, New York, 20 December 2000.

5. United Nations Office for the Coordination of Humanitarian Affairs, *Vulnerability and Humanitarian Impact of UN Security Council Sanctions in Afghanistan,* New York, 17 August 2000, 5, <wwww.reliefweb.int> (5 September 2001).

6. United Nations Office of the UN Coordinator for Afghanistan, *Vulnerability and Humanitarian Implications of UN Security Council Sanctions in Afghanistan,* Islamabad, December 2000, §5, 36.

7. U.S. Department of State, "Taliban Fact Sheet," 20 December 2000, <www.state.gov/www/regions/sa/fact_sheet_taliban.html> (5 September 2001).

8. United Nations Office of the UN Coordinator for Afghanistan, *Vulnerability and Humanitarian Implications,* December 2000, §3.1, 28.

9. Saleem Shahid, "Afghanistan Facing Serious Economic Crisis," *Dawn* (Karachi), 19 November 1999, 18.

10. United Nations Office of the UN Coordinator for Afghanistan, *Vulnerability and Humanitarian Implications,* December 2000, §4.1, 33–34.

11. United Nations Security Council, *The Situation in Afghanistan and Its Implications for International Peace and Security: Report of the Secretary-General,* S/2001/384-A/55/907, New York, 19 April 2001, par. 35.

12. Christopher S. Wren, "Afghan Rulers to Let Women Carry Out a UN Survey," *New York Times,* 19 June 2001, A3.

13. United Nations Office of the UN Coordinator for Afghanistan, *Vulnerability and Humanitarian Implications,* December 2000, §2.1–2.2, 6–7.

14. Ibid., §1.4, 5–6.

15. United Nations, *The Situation in Afghanistan,* S/2001/384-A/55/907, par. 56.

16. United Nations Security Council, *Report of the Committee of Experts Appointed Pursuant to Security Council Resolution 1333 (2000), Paragraph 15(a), Regarding Monitoring of the Arms Embargo Against the Taliban and the Closure of Terrorist Training Camps in the Taliban-held Areas of Afghanistan,* S/2001/511, New York, 22 May 2001, par. 79.

17. Ibid., par. 78.

18. United Nations Security Council, *Security Council Resolution 1363 (2001),* S/RES/1363, New York, 30 July 2001, pars. 4(a), 4(b).

19. United Nations Security Council, *Report of the Committee of Experts,* S/2001/511, par. 32.

20. Ibid., par. 38.

21. Human Rights Watch, "Fueling Afghanistan's War" (Washington, D.C.: Human Rights Watch, 15 December 2000).

22. Barnett R. Rubin et al., *Afghanistan: Reconstruction and Peacemaking in a Regional Framework,* KOFF Peacebuilding Reports (Bern, Switzerland: Center for Peacebuilding, June 2001), 19.

23. Interview with Barnett R. Rubin by David Cortright and Linda Gerber, 14 June 2001, New York.

24. Ibid.

25. United Nations Security Council, *Report of the Committee of Experts,* S/2001/511, par. 56.

26. Ibid., pars. 57–58.

27. United Nations Security Council, *Security Council Ponders Establishment*

*of Sanctions-Monitoring Mechanism for Afghanistan*, SC/7069, New York, 5 June 2001, 9.

28. United Nations Security Council, *Report of the Committee of Experts*, S/2001/511, par. 59.

29. Rubin et al., *Afghanistan: Reconstruction and Peacemaking*, 27.

30. United Nations Security Council, *The Situation in Afghanistan*, S/2001/384-A/55/907, par. 56.

31. Rubin et al., *Afghanistan: Reconstruction and Peacemaking*, 12.

32. Ibid., 31.

# 4

# Success in the Making? The Evolution of UN Sanctions in Angola

For forty years, the government of Angola and the National Union for the Total Independence of Angola (UNITA) have been locked in a bitter armed struggle that has been described as "the world's deadliest war."[1] Both sides have been responsible for horrendous human rights abuses. Each has been able to finance continued war with commodity exports— oil for the government and diamonds for UNITA. Civilians have been and continue to be the primary victims of this gruesome conflict, with nearly 1 million dead out of a population of 12.5 million, more than 3 million driven from their homes, and the highest child mortality rate in the world.

Government forces gained the upper hand with a series of military offenses that by 2000 had driven UNITA from major military bases in the central highlands and shattered much of the rebel movement's conventional war capacity.[2] UNITA remained active militarily, however, and shifted to guerrilla warfare, "attacking mostly civilian targets, destroying infrastructure, killing innocent people, and laying land mines," according to United Nations (UN) monitors.[3] In February 2002, Angolan army units tracked down and killed UNITA's longtime leader Jonas Savimbi, dealing a further devastating blow to the rebel movement.

The UN has attempted to end the war in Angola by deploying peacekeepers, encouraging negotiations, and imposing sanctions against UNITA. The first sanctions came in September 1993 (Security Council Resolution [SCR] 864), when the Security Council banned the sale of arms and petroleum products to the rebel group. When UNITA repeatedly violated the 1994 Lusaka Protocol, the Security Council strengthened the sanctions. In 1997, travel, aviation, and diplomatic sanctions

This chapter was coauthored by Erica Cosgrove.

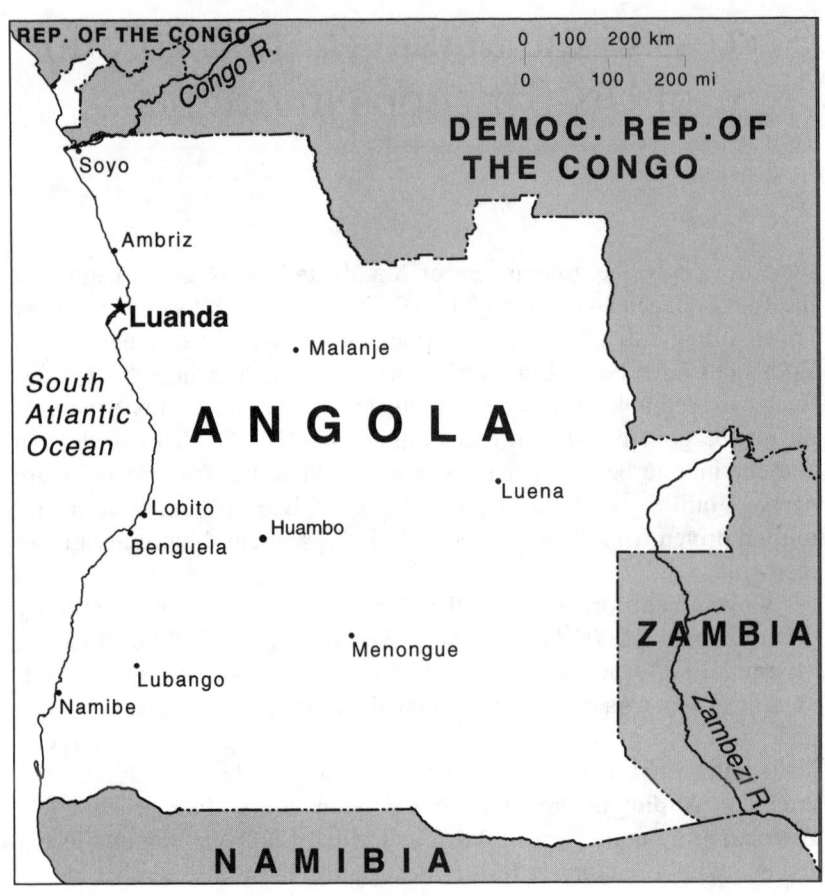

were added (SCR 1127), as were a diamond embargo and targeted financial sanctions in 1998 (SCR 1173). For a complete list of Security Council sanctions on Angola/UNITA, see the box on page 64. The imposition of tougher sanctions reflected a trend in UN policy against UNITA and toward more explicit support for the Luanda government. The goal of UN policy shifted from attempting to broker a negotiated agreement to using sanctions as a means of isolating the rebels politically and helping the government gain the upper hand militarily.[4]

The Council not only imposed stronger measures but took significant steps to enhance monitoring and enforcement. Beginning with the 1999 mission of the Canadian permanent representative to the UN, Robert Fowler, and continuing with reports from the panel of experts and the subsequent monitoring mechanism, the Council broke new ground in "naming and shaming" the violators of sanctions and mobilizing international pressure for greater compliance. As a result, the sanctions became increasingly effective in hampering UNITA.[5] According to the report of the monitoring mechanism, "There is no doubt that the sanctions, together with the military operations carried out by the Angolan armed forces, . . . are hurting UNITA's ability to wage war."[6]

The war in Angola is linked to other political and military struggles in central and southern Africa. As with the other sanctions cases under review, the conflict in Angola is part of a broader regional crisis. Both the Luanda government and the UNITA rebels have sought support among and intervened militarily in the affairs of other countries. The Angolan government helped to overthrow governments in Zaire and Congo-Brazzaville, in part because of their support for UNITA. UNITA has supported separatists in Namibia in reaction to that country's alliance with Angola and reportedly has cooperated with rebels in eastern Congo.[7] Apart from this direct military involvement, UNITA has received support from government leaders in Togo and Burkina Faso and from diamond dealers and arms traffickers in a dozen or more countries.

The prospects for an end to the war increased after the death of Savimbi and a subsequent decision by the Luanda government to halt military operations against UNITA. In March 2002 UNITA and government leaders signed a preliminary cease-fire, moving the country an important step closer to peace. Sanctions remained in place, however, at least for the time being, as international leaders maintained pressure on UNITA to respect the cease-fire and accept a political settlement.

# ANGOLA, Security Council Resolutions

| Resolution Number | Action |
|---|---|
| 864 | **15 September 1993**<br>Imposed an arms embargo on UNITA<br>Imposed a petroleum embargo except through ports of entry designated by the Angolan government<br>Created the sanctions committee |
| 1127 | **28 August 1997**<br>Imposed travel sanctions banning travel of senior UNITA officials and prohibiting flights to and from UNITA-held territory<br>Imposed diplomatic sanctions closing official UNITA offices<br>Enacted stronger sanctions in October 1997 |
| 1173 | **12 June 1998**<br>Froze UNITA financial assets<br>Banned all financial transactions with UNITA<br>Imposed an embargo on diamond imports not certified by the Angolan government<br>Banned any form of travel to UNITA-controlled territories |
| 1237 | **7 May 1999**<br>Established a panel of experts with six-month mandate to collect information and make recommendations |
| 1295 | **18 April 2000**<br>Established a monitoring mechanism with a six-month mandate to investigate relevant leads initiated by the panel of experts |
| 1336 | **23 January 2001**<br>Extended the mandate of the monitoring mechanism for a three-month period |
| 1348 | **19 April 2001**<br>Extended the mandate of the monitoring mechanism for an additional six months |

Whether these hopeful developments will finally put an end to Angola's agony remains to be seen.

## The Fowler Mission

With the exception of the sanctions against Iraq, the Security Council sanctions against UNITA have been the longest running of any current case. They have also been the most comprehensive, again with the exception of those against Iraq. Applied against UNITA-held territory, they targeted the lifeblood of the rebel movement's operations: arms, fuel, travel, diplomatic representation, diamonds, and finances. Until 1999, however, the sanctions existed mostly on paper and had little or no effect on the military capabilities of UNITA. Under sanctions, UNITA assembled an army of roughly 60,000 fighters, which became one of the most formidable military forces on the African continent. Savimbi felt sufficiently confident of the military forces at his disposal to launch a new round of military attacks against the government in 1998 and 1999.

The impact of the sanctions began to change when Robert Fowler assumed the chair of the Angola sanctions committee in 1999. In keeping with the activist vision of Canadian foreign minister Lloyd Axworthy, Fowler adopted a new and innovative approach to the role of UN sanctions committees. Previously, these committees had played a relatively minor and passive role, receiving desultory reports from member states on sanctions compliance and reviewing applications for exemptions. Fowler brought to his chairmanship a new conception of the role of sanctions committees. He instituted a more assertive monitoring and enforcement role for his committee. He engaged other governments, UN officials, nongovernmental experts, international institutions, and members of the private sector in a wide-ranging effort to strengthen compliance. In May 1999, Fowler embarked on a seventeen-day mission to central and southern Africa for discussions with government and private officials in the region. In July 1999, he traveled to Europe and Algeria (for a meeting of the Council of Ministers of the Organization of African Unity) to continue his consultations on strengthening sanctions implementation. Fowler met with experts in the areas of arms, petroleum, aviation, diamonds, and finance to seek suggestions on the most effective ways to enhance sanctions monitoring and enforcement.

The reports of Fowler's mission, issued in June and July 1999, contained nineteen recommendations for improving the implementation of sanctions.[8] The reports also reviewed Fowler's interactions with governments and private groups and the many commitments of cooperation he had been given. The very fact that the chairman was asking questions and seeking commitments injected a greater degree of seriousness into the sanctions and encouraged the various affected parties to acknowledge and pay more attention to the sanctions. This is not to suggest that the impact of the Fowler mission and subsequent investigative panels was immediate and dramatic. The process was more gradual and subtle, but the effect was nonetheless real. By focusing a spotlight on compliance issues, Fowler transformed the previously ineffective sanctions committee into a positive force for change. Fowler's efforts were explicitly noted with appreciation by the Security Council in SCR 1295 (2000).

## The Panel of Experts

One of the most important recommendations of Fowler's mission was that the Security Council establish panels of experts to conduct in-depth investigations of sanctions violations and recommend the best practices for enhancing compliance. In SCR 1237 (1999), the Council created two independent panels to examine and make recommendations on the sanctions against UNITA. The first was to investigate UNITA's finances, with particular focus on the diamond trade, and the second was to focus on arms trafficking and the sources of UNITA's continued supply of weapons and mercenaries.[9] At their first meeting, the panels decided to amalgamate and function as a single unit. Under the chairmanship of Swedish ambassador Anders Möllander, the ten-member panel visited nearly thirty countries, meeting with representatives of government, private industry, and nongovernmental groups. The panel drew heavily from videotaped interviews with senior defectors from UNITA. It considered information reliable only if it was corroborated by more than one source.

The panel of experts report, released in March 2000, was a bombshell. It shattered the UN's normal diplomatic niceties by specifically identifying governments, companies, and individuals responsible for violating Security Council sanctions. The report pulled no punches. It named names and identified specific violations. The panel implicated President Gnassingbe Eyadema of Togo in numerous violations of the sanctions. The report alleged that Eyadema received a "passport-sized" packet of diamonds on behalf of Savimbi in exchange for allowing

Savimbi's children to live in Togo.[10] Togo was also charged with importing military equipment for transshipment to UNITA and supplying passports to senior UNITA officials.[11] The panel released similarly damaging information about Blaise Compaorè, president of Burkina Faso. It described Compaorè as "Savimbi's closest and most genuine friend among African leaders" and reported allegations of "direct personal payments by Savimbi to Compaorè."[12] According to the panel, Burkina Faso also assisted with the supply of weapons, the smuggling of diamonds, and the issuance of false passports.

Many other governments and private actors were identified in the panel's listing of sanctions violators. It singled out Bulgaria as a country willing to sell weapons "with little or no regard for where those arms would actually end up."[13] Bulgarian flights ferried military equipment to UNITA's stronghold at Andulo, often after transiting through Togo. UNITA personnel, disguised as Zairians, received military training in Bulgaria.[14] The report also identified other Eastern European countries, including Ukraine, Belarus, and Russia, as possible sources of weapons and military support services. The diamonds to pay for these military purchases were traded on the diamond exchange in Antwerp, Belgium. The report described a "lax regulatory environment" in Antwerp and a failure to establish import control systems.[15] The panel issued thirty-nine recommendations for improving sanctions compliance.

The panel of experts report touched off a heated debate in the Security Council. A dozen African and European nations challenged the report's conclusions and methods.[16] Togo's UN representative dismissed the report as "rumor, hearsay, and scraps." The representative of Burkina Faso described it as a "report built on illusions rather than on certainties."[17] Some countries questioned the panel's reliance on UNITA defectors, but panel members replied that the defectors only confirmed evidence gathered from other sources.

Although countries named in the report denied allegations of wrongdoing, they also pledged to work with the Security Council in preventing violations and closing loopholes.[18] On the day of the report's release, South Africa announced steps to prevent its citizens from supporting UNITA. The week before, Belgium issued new rules to prevent the import of UNITA diamonds. Bulgaria, Ukraine, and other countries announced their intention to tighten controls on arms exports. Despite the controversy generated by the report—perhaps even because of it—the work of the panel of experts produced results.

Using independent panels of experts has become an innovative way for the Security Council to apply pressure on sanctions violators. Because of diplomatic protocol, the Security Council and its sanctions committees cannot be as blunt and direct as circumstances often warrant. The presence of an independent panel of experts, one step removed from the Council, provides some distance and allows UN representatives to dissociate themselves from the panel's findings. The panel reports serve as vehicles for identifying and implicating violators. The incriminating information has the same impact as if it were presented directly by the Council, but the representatives of member states do not have to confront one another. They are able to continue working together to search for diplomatic solutions.

## The Monitoring Mechanism

As recommended by the panel of experts, the Security Council decided in April 2000 (SCR 1295) to establish a monitoring mechanism to investigate leads on reported violations and develop means for improving the effectiveness of the sanctions.[19] The Council did not act on the thirty-eight other recommendations in the panel report. It ignored the panel's first and most important suggestion, that the Council apply sanctions against leaders and governments found to be deliberately violating sanctions. Given the controversy over the release of the panel of experts report, diplomatic sensitivity was too great to even consider such an option. Instead, Council members decided to seek further documentation and additional recommendations.

The decision to create a monitoring mechanism meant continued reliance on public exposure and education as a way of encouraging compliance. The mechanism specifically mentioned the mandate "to sensitize international public opinion."[20] The monitoring mechanism also served as a means of maintaining dialogue with neighboring states on sanctions compliance. By creating an entirely new body distinct from the panel of experts, the Council was able to continue discussions with officials in Togo, Burkina Faso, and other key countries. In the process, the Council received numerous assurances of a willingness to comply. One of the functions of the mechanism was "to put to the test the spirit of cooperation that has been voiced to us."[21] The monitoring mechanism thus combined public exposure and quiet diplomacy to mobilize international sanctions compliance. Systematic outreach to countries of the region became "the most effective diplomatic means" to win support for the isolation of UNITA.[22]

The monitoring mechanism examined violations of the arms, travel, diamonds, and financial sanctions. The work of the mechanism for the most part corroborated the findings of the panel of experts. Unlike the panel, however, it did not single out heads of state. It chose not to name names. It wanted to avoid stirring up resentment among affected political leaders. The results of its investigations were no less hard-hitting, though. It documented the role of Togo and Burkina Faso in supplying arms, smuggling diamonds, issuing travel documents, and providing financial assistance to UNITA. Through forensic analysis, the mechanism confirmed that the documents used to ship weapons from Bulgaria were forgeries.[23] The mechanism report also identified specific arms brokers and air transport companies involved in systematic violations of sanctions.

The final report of the monitoring mechanism presented twenty-two recommendations for improving sanctions monitoring and enforcement. The first of these, reiterating the primary suggestions of the Fowler mission and the panel of experts, was that the Security Council consider applying sanctions against governments found to be violating other sanctions.[24] Its last recommendation called on the Security Council to maintain the continuity of the monitoring process. It concluded that, although sanctions were having an impact on UNITA's military abilities, it was necessary to increase the pressure.

## Extending the Monitoring Mechanism

Recognizing the benefits of continuing the investigations into sanctions violations and the means to overcome them, the Security Council extended the work of the monitoring mechanism. In January 2001, the Council approved SCR 1336, continuing the mechanism's work for three months. In April 2001, it extended the mechanism's mandate for six more months (SCR 1348) and in October 2001 did the same for another six months (SCR 1374). These decisions indicated a recognition that the ongoing process of investigation and dialogue kept the pressure on sanctions violators and engaged an ever-widening network of international players in the enforcement of sanctions.

The addendum report of the monitoring mechanism, issued in April 2001, provided further documentation on arms smuggling, with an emphasis on the role of private arms brokers. The need to tighten the regulation of these brokers "has become urgent," the report said. It also recommended the establishment of an international register of "dubious" companies involved in sanctions busting.[25]

According to the report, the constant emphasis on enforcement of the travel sanctions was starting to produce results. "Some of the countries that have been . . . providing safe havens to senior UNITA officials and their family members are beginning to distance themselves from the organization," the report said.[26] The government of Côte d'Ivoire announced that, as of July 2001, passports would no longer be issued to UNITA officials. The October 2001 supplementary report of the monitoring mechanism confirmed Côte d'Ivoire's decision on UNITA passports. It also noted the government's efforts to ensure that only UNITA officials who refrained from active involvement with the rebel movement would be permitted to remain in the country.[27] These changes were potentially significant, given the important role in the past that Côte d'Ivoire had played as a base for the rebel movement. Nonetheless, UNITA officials continued to travel extensively in Africa, Europe, and North America. Unofficial UNITA representatives even met with members of the incoming Bush administration in the early months of 2001.[28]

The addendum report emphasized the positive contributions of sanctions in pressuring UNITA: "The Mechanism's overall assessment is that sanctions continue to play an important part in the effort to resolve the Angolan conflict. With no fixed arms supply lines and diminishing revenue from diamonds, UNITA's military capacity has been significantly reduced."[29] The supplementary report of the monitoring mechanism confirmed that arms deliveries to UNITA were "drastically reduced."[30] The combination of military setbacks and increasing sanctions pressure tilted the political balance against UNITA. According to the addendum report, increasing calls by UNITA for lifting the sanctions were signs that "the sanctions [were] hurting."[31]

One of the most important indications of the rebel movement's declining fortunes has been the dramatic drop in its revenues from diamond exports. The sanctions provided the impetus for the creation of a system of "worldwide controls on diamonds" and have made it more difficult for UNITA to market diamonds. The addendum report offered an estimate of UNITA diamond income in 2000 of "at least $100 million." It was a sizable amount but was also a major decrease from UNITA's previous diamond income of $300 million in 1999.[32] The principal factor accounting for the reduction of income was the loss of diamond-producing territory under UNITA control as a result of battlefield reverses. But the diamond sanctions also played a role and "have driven UNITA diamond trading deeper underground."[33]

Despite the decline in UNITA diamond exports, the overall problem of diamond smuggling from Angola has remained huge—amounting to an estimated 5 percent of the world's rough diamond supply. UNITA accounted for 25 to 30 percent of these illegal sales in 2000. The estimated income, according to the supplementary report, was in the range of $105 to $126 million.[34]

In another sign of the tightening of sanctions pressure against UNITA, governments in the region have taken various steps to improve the enforcement of Security Council sanctions. In December 2000, police chiefs from southern Africa met in Luanda to exchange intelligence information and coordinate their efforts in sanctions implementation. Representatives of the Southern African Development Community (SADC) participated in efforts to prevent the export of UNITA diamonds and monitor the movement of petroleum fuels into Angola. They also approved a project on mobile radar systems to monitor air traffic in the region.[35] In February 2001, Angola, Namibia, and Zambia reached a tripartite agreement to improve security along their common borders and strengthen the implementation of sanctions against UNITA. All these actions added weight to the sanctions and increased the pressure on UNITA.

## Creating Sanctions Success

Beneath the myriad details provided in the panel of experts and monitoring mechanism reports is a remarkable story of increasing sanctions effectiveness. For many years, the sanctions against Angola were considered among the least effective of UN policies. Not only was the Security Council reluctant to adopt more forceful sanctions, but it made little effort to monitor and enforce the measures in place. In our earlier assessment in *The Sanctions Decade,* we judged the Angola sanctions a failure.[36] We noted the beginnings of a stronger implementation effort in 1999 but offered little hope that these steps would improve overall effectiveness. We repeated this pessimistic assessment at the sanctions symposium sponsored by the German government in Berlin in December 2000. When colleagues questioned our analysis, we reexamined the data and, after reviewing the most recent UN reports, decided to change our assessment. Sanctions that began as halfhearted measures without teeth were becoming increasingly effective in isolating and exerting pressure on UNITA.

This transformation of the UN mission in Angola is one of the most important developments in sanctions policy in recent years. It resulted from a relatively modest investment in sanctions monitoring, initially by the government of Canada and subsequently by many other states and UN investigative panels. A few dozen researchers, backed by the authority of the Security Council and aided by the efforts of UN diplomats, uncovered the networks of deceit and criminality that sustained UNITA's rebellion and prolonged the war in Angola. By relentlessly exposing these operations to public scrutiny and by quietly engaging affected governments in the process of implementation, UN officials significantly tightened the pressures against the rebel movement. The battlefield defeats suffered by UNITA were the most important factor in its declining fortunes, but the improvement in sanctions monitoring also played a part.

There are important lessons in this story of sanctions improvement. The first is that monitoring is the key to success. As we and other analysts have repeatedly emphasized, sanctions are meaningless without an effective monitoring and enforcement effort. Security Council officials recognize this fact and have increasingly established monitoring mechanisms as a regular feature of sanctions policy.

Another lesson is that public exposure and quiet diplomacy can combine to exert effective pressure for change. Togo, Burkina Faso, and other governments have been encouraged to distance themselves from UNITA. There have been recent signs of progress in this direction. As noted earlier, Côte d'Ivoire has taken steps to comply with travel sanctions against UNITA. Togo has also shown signs of "coming into compliance," according to a U.S. State Department official.[37] The supplementary report of the monitoring mechanism noted that Togo became less important to UNITA "as a result of international pressure."[38] These were positive steps toward more effective sanctions implementation.

## Endgame or Stalemate?

The demise of Savimbi fundamentally transformed the Angola conflict. It further weakened UNITA, which was already suffering from the consequences of military setbacks and continuing sanctions, and raised doubts about the future of the rebel movement. As the monitoring mechanism addendum report warned, "UNITA has experienced serious military setbacks in the past which it has succeeded in overcoming; it should not be taken for granted that all the possibilities for UNITA rearmament have been exhausted."[39] UNITA still has thousands of armed fighters and tens of millions of dollars in annual income with which to carry out its campaign of violence and destruction against government-controlled territory. With its recent shift in military tactics from conventional to guerrilla warfare, UNITA could conceivably sustain military operations for years. It has shown no compunction in launching deadly strikes against civilian targets, as evidenced by its attack against a train near Luanda in August 2001 that killed more than 200 people.[40]

UNITA is not the only obstacle to peace in Angola, however. The Angolan government has done little to inspire public confidence or support. Its administration has been characterized by what one observer called "grotesque" levels of corruption among political and military elites. This has undermined public support for the government and siphoned off revenues from the country's vast and increasing oil revenues.[41] Angolan forces have been responsible for policies of torture, summary executions, and the indiscriminate killing of civilians. Media censorship remains pervasive. As government forces have extended state administration over areas taken from UNITA, police and military forces have killed civilians and gone on looting rampages. UN and Western diplomats generally have been quiet about these abusive policies. The UN is committed to the Luanda government as the legitimate victor in the 1992 elections, but it has been caught in a bind of supporting the lesser of two evils.

In the face of this conundrum, the UN has little choice but to encourage a bargaining process in which the Luanda government and UNITA try to find a negotiated political solution. For this purpose, continued sanctions may be extremely useful. UNITA forces have continued to wage war in part because they gain economic benefits from their control of diamond production. As the profits from these operations diminish and the costs of military resupply increase with the tightening of sanctions pressure, the rebel movement may become more amenable to a negotiated solution. To encourage a settlement, the government and its external supporters will have to offer incentives and security assurances.

If UNITA leaders and soldiers are to demobilize, they must have confidence that a negotiated peace will bring concrete benefits. They will need access to resources and economic opportunities.[42] Soldiers will need support for demobilization, including adjustment assistance and access to productive employment. The relatively successful demobilization efforts in Mozambique in the 1990s, funded through the World Bank, may offer a partial model for such assistance.

Angola has vast economic resources, which can be used to help finance a peace process. Its already considerable oil wealth will grow significantly in the years ahead as production expands. These oil revenues could be shifted from the funding of war to the financing of demobilization, providing economic opportunities for former UNITA soldiers and officials willing to abandon the military option. Doing so, however, will require rooting out rampant corruption, which can come only through the promotion of greater transparency and the use of oil resources for genuine national development. The International Monetary Fund has pressured the government in Luanda to become more transparent but has had only modest success so far. Continued efforts will be needed to encourage greater accountability on the part of the Angolan government.

External actors, particularly the United States, can play a major role in facilitating demobilization and national reconciliation. By using their leverage with the Luanda government to reduce corruption and improve respect for human rights and by maintaining ever tighter UN sanctions on UNITA, the major powers can encourage the parties to finally achieve a sustainable peace settlement.

## Notes

1. John Prendergast, "Angola's Deadly War: Dealing with Savimbi's Hell on Earth," special report (Washington, D.C.: United States Institute of Peace, 12 October 1999), 1.

2. United Nations Security Council, *Final Report of the Monitoring Mechanism on Angola Sanctions*, S/2000/1225, New York, 21 December 2000, par. 15.

3. United Nations Security Council, *Addendum to the Final Report of the Monitoring Mechanism on Sanctions Against UNITA*, S/2001/363, New York, 11 April 2001, par. 116.

4. We are grateful for this insight to William Reno, personal communication, 16 October 2001.

5. United Nations Security Council, *Interim Report of the Monitoring Mechanism on Angola Sanctions Established by the Security Council in Resolution 1295 (2000) of April 2000*, S/2000/1026, New York, 25 October 2000.

6. United Nations Security Council, *Final Report*, S/2000/1225, par. 250.

7. United Nations Security Council, *Addendum*, S/2001/363, par. 30.

8. See United Nations Security Council, *Letter Dated 4 June 1999 from the Chairman of the Security Council Committee Established Pursuant to Resolution 864 (1993) Concerning the Situation in Angola Addressed to the President of the Security Council*, S/1999/644, New York, 4 June 1999; and United Nations Security Council, *Letter Dated 28 July 1999 from the Chairman of the Security Council Committee Established Pursuant to Resolution 864 (1993) Concerning the Situation in Angola Addressed to the President of the Security Council*, S/1999/829, New York, 28 July 1999.

9. United Nations Security Council, *Security Council Resolution 1237 (1999)*, S/RES/1237, New York, 7 May 1999.

10. United Nations Security Council, *Report of the Panel of Experts on Violations of Security Council Sanctions Against UNITA*, S/2000/203, New York, 10 March 2000, pars. 33, 102.

11. Ibid., pars. 32, 137.

12. Ibid., par. 103.

13. Ibid., par. 51.

14. Ibid., pars. 41, 44.

15. Ibid., pars. 89, 90.

16. Barbara Crossette, "Diamonds-for-Arms Report Is Challenged in Security Council," *New York Times*, 16 March 2000, A12.

17. Ibid.

18. Ibid.

19. United Nations Security Council, *Security Council Resolution 1295*, S/RES/1295 (2000), 18 April 2000.

20. United Nations Security Council, *Interim Report*, S/2000/1026, 4.

21. Ibid., 14.

22. United Nations Security Council, *Supplementary Report of the Monitoring Mechanism on Sanctions Against UNITA*, S/2001/966, New York, 12 October 2001, par. 266.

23. United Nations Security Council, *Final Report*, S/2000/1225, par. 49.

24. Ibid., par. 224.

25. United Nations Security Council, *Addendum*, S/2001/363, par. 34.

26. Ibid., par. 39.

27. United Nations Security Council, *Supplementary Report*, S/2001/966, par. 51.

28. United Nations Security Council, *Addendum*, S/2001/363, par. 41.

29. Ibid., par. 10.

30. United Nations Security Council, *Supplementary Report*, S/2001/966, par. 11.

31. United Nations Security Council, *Addendum*, S/2001/363, par. 10.

32. Ibid., par. 54.

33. Ibid., par. 107.

34. United Nations Security Council, *Supplementary Report*, S/2001/966, pars. 141, 176.

35. Ibid., par. 254.

36. David Cortright and George A. Lopez, with Richard W. Conroy, "Angola's Agony," in Cortright and Lopez, *The Sanctions Decade: Assessing UN Strategies in the 1990s* (Boulder, Colo.: Lynne Rienner Publishers, 2000), 147–165.

37. According to an interview at the U.S. State Department conducted by David Cortright, George Lopez, and Linda Gerber, Washington, D.C., 11 June 2001.

38. United Nations Security Council, *Supplementary Report*, S/2001/966, par. 50.

39. United Nations Security Council, *Addendum*, S/2001/363, par. 34.

40. "UNITA—Down but Not Out," *The Economist*, 18 August 2001, 35.

41. Prendergast, "Angola's Deadly War: Dealing with Savimbi's Hell on Earth."

42. Ibid., 6.

# 5

## Sanctions and Regional Security:
## The Crisis in West Africa

The United Nations (UN) has made an enormous commitment to resolving armed conflict in Sierra Leone and, increasingly, in the entire West African region. As in Angola, a mission that experienced initial setbacks gradually began to show positive results. A combination of factors—battlefield reverses for the rebels of the Revolutionary United Front (RUF), the introduction of a large UN peacekeeping force and British troops, and the strengthening of UN sanctions—shifted the political balance in favor of the government and created conditions for a successful cease-fire. Although enormous security problems remain in Sierra Leone and armed conflict continues in neighboring Liberia and Guinea, the overall political situation has improved considerably, thanks in large part to the role of the United Nations.

The United Nations immersed itself deeply in the tortured affairs of Sierra Leone. The Security Council deployed the largest United Nations peacekeeping force in the world, the UN Mission in Sierra Leone (UNAMSIL), with an authorized strength of more than 17,000 troops. A disarmament, demobilization, and reintegration commission succeeded in demobilizing more than 46,000 combatants.[1] UN humanitarian agencies mounted major relief and refugee support operations in the region. A special criminal court was authorized to try RUF leaders for crimes against humanity. The Security Council imposed targeted sanctions on both the RUF and the Liberian government of Charles Taylor. Numerous UN envoys and assessment missions crisscrossed the region, monitoring humanitarian and security conditions; brokering cease-fires; and attempting to implement peace agreements, including a major disarmament, demobilization, and resettlement effort.

The goal of these efforts has been to end the armed conflict in Sierra Leone and bring about a settlement between the RUF and the elected government of Ahmed Tejan Kabbah within the general framework of the 1999 Lomé peace agreement. The RUF previously violated

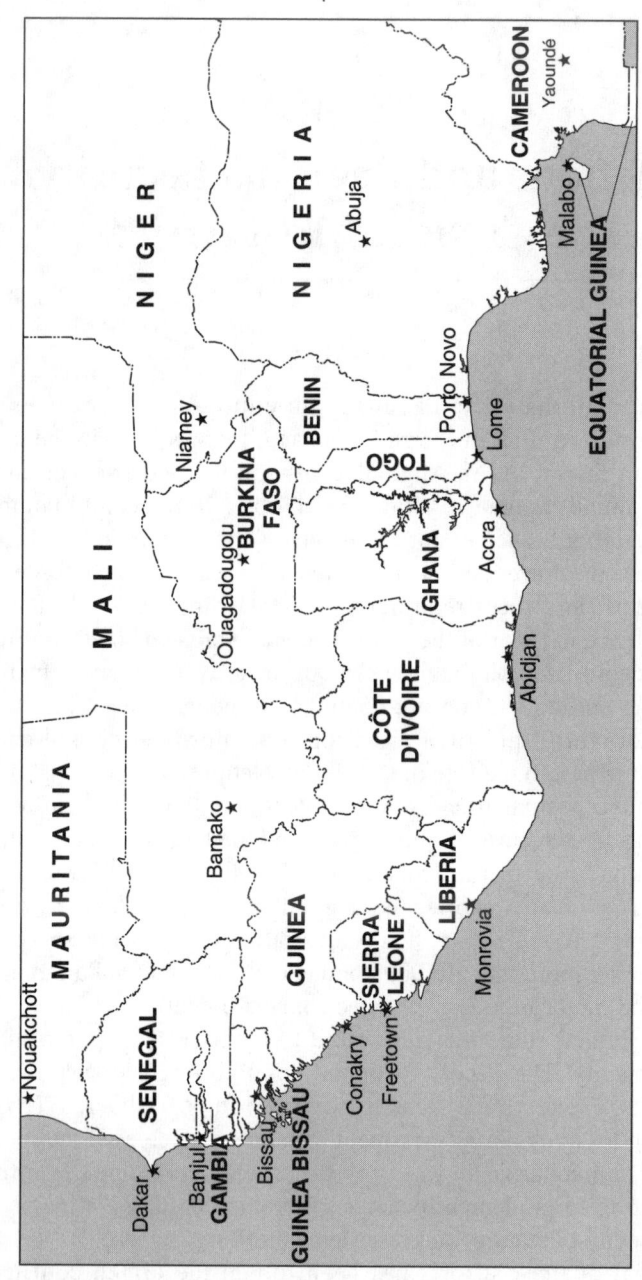

West Africa

the cease-fire and demobilization aspects of the agreement and in May 2000 even captured and killed UN peacekeepers. A May 2001 UN inter-agency mission to West Africa questioned whether the political aspects of the agreement, such as power sharing and the transformation of the RUF into a political party, could be reconciled with the fact that many RUF leaders were suspected of committing gross violations of human rights.[2] The International Crisis Group (ICG) termed the Lomé accord "utterly misguided" and described it as "a vain exercise motivated largely by political expediency . . . to elevate those responsible for the deaths of thousands of innocent civilians into statesmen."[3] With the recent changes in political and military conditions, however, the prospects for a more peaceful transition have improved.

As the UN has become steadily more involved, the crisis has spread and become increasingly regional. Within Sierra Leone itself, armed conflict has ebbed, following a November 2000 cease-fire (reaffirmed in May 2001), but fighting has spread to Guinea and Liberia. The two countries have mounted armed attacks and supported internal rebellions against the other. In the summer and fall of 2000, RUF and Liberian forces began crossing into Guinea's southeastern diamond region, and Guinean troops attacked RUF and Liberian army-controlled areas. Liberians United for Reconciliation and Democracy, a rebel group supported by Guinea, has engaged in armed skirmishes with Liberian government troops, bringing the fighting close to Monrovia in early 2002.

The crisis has threatened to spread its destabilizing influences even farther afield, to Côte d'Ivoire, Guinea-Bissau, and the Casamance region of Senegal.[4] The UN interagency mission to West Africa spoke of a possible "domino effect" that could engulf the entire region.[5] The ICG placed the crisis in Sierra Leone "at the heart of a series of conflicts that risk forming an arc of violence from southern Senegal to the Ivory Coast."[6] The conflict has developed into "a human tragedy of massive proportions that is rapidly becoming a security nightmare for all of West Africa."[7]

## The Role of Sanctions

Security Council sanctions have been a central part of the UN response to the crisis in West Africa. Sanctions have steadily become more sophisticated and far-reaching as the crisis has deepened. Sanctions

## SIERRA LEONE AND LIBERIA,
### Security Council Resolutions

Resolution
Number　　　Action

**SIERRA LEONE**
**1132**　　　　**8 October 1997**
　　　　　　　Imposed an oil embargo and an arms embargo
　　　　　　　Imposed travel sanctions on members of the AFRC
　　　　　　　　junta and their families
　　　　　　　Conditioned the lifting of sanctions on the junta relin-
　　　　　　　　quishing power
　　　　　　　Created the sanctions committee

**1156**　　　　**16 March 1998**
　　　　　　　Lifted the oil embargo

**1171**　　　　**6 June 1998**
　　　　　　　Confirmed the removal of sanctions on the govern-
　　　　　　　　ment
　　　　　　　Reimposed the arms embargo and travel ban on the
　　　　　　　　RUF and members of the former military junta

**1306**　　　　**5 July 2000**
　　　　　　　Imposed an embargo on all diamond exports not under
　　　　　　　　the control of the government
　　　　　　　Established the panel of experts

**LIBERIA**
**788**　　　　　**19 November 1992**
　　　　　　　Imposed a limited arms embargo (exempted
　　　　　　　　ECOMOG forces)

**985**　　　　　**13 April 1995**
　　　　　　　Created the sanctions committee

**1343**　　　　**7 March 2001**
　　　　　　　Demanded cessation of support for the RUF in Sierra
　　　　　　　　Leone
　　　　　　　Reimposed the arms embargo; imposed assets freeze,
　　　　　　　　travel ban, and diamond embargo after a two-month
　　　　　　　　grace period

were first imposed against Sierra Leone in response to the May 1997 overthrow of the Kabbah government by disgruntled members of the armed forces, with subsequent backing from the RUF. In October 1997, responding to a request from the Economic Community of West African States (ECOWAS), the Council approved Security Council Resolution (SCR) 1132, imposing an arms embargo, an oil embargo, and a travel ban on members of the Armed Forces Revolutionary Council (AFRC) military junta and their families. ECOWAS had imposed general trade sanctions, but the Security Council opted for more targeted and selective measures to avoid exacerbating an already severe humanitarian emergency. In March 1998, following the ouster of the military junta by ECOWAS forces, the Council adopted SCR 1156, lifting the oil embargo on the government. In June 1998, the Council approved SCR 1171, confirming the lifting of sanctions on the restored Kabbah government but reimposing the arms embargo and travel ban on the RUF and former members of the military junta. The decision to reimpose sanctions came in response to the continuing armed rebellion by the RUF and its allies. For a list of Security Council sanctions on Sierra Leone and Liberia, see the box on page 80.

In July 2000, following further armed attacks by the RUF and the capture of UN peacekeepers, the Council significantly increased the pressure on the rebels. Recognizing "the role played by the illicit trade in diamonds in fueling the conflict in Sierra Leone," the Council adopted SCR 1306, imposing an embargo on all diamonds originating in Sierra Leone.[8] The diamond embargo was to apply to all diamond exports from Sierra Leone until the government in Freetown created a certification system that would exclude diamonds originating from RUF-controlled areas.

As part of SCR 1306, the Council created a panel of experts to report on possible violations of the sanctions. The panel was also asked to examine the links between the diamond trade and arms trafficking and to assess the adequacy of air traffic control in the region. The panel report, issued in December 2000, confirmed that "diamonds have become an important resource for Sierra Leone's RUF in sustaining and advancing its military ambitions."[9] It also found "widespread breaking of the UN Security Council sanctions on both weapons and diamonds."[10] The panel report issued a number of policy recommendations for plugging the leaks in the sanctions regime and improving overall compliance. Its most important recommendation was the imposition of sanctions on Liberia.

## Pressuring Liberia

The RUF and the government of Charles Taylor in Liberia are closely linked. The RUF was essentially created by Taylor. It received indispensable support from Taylor's National Patriotic Front of Liberia (NPFL), and after 1997, following Taylor's election as president, from the government of Liberia. Taylor encouraged and supported RUF incursions into Sierra Leone, helping the rebel group establish a strong foothold in the alluvial diamond fields of the eastern Mano River region, which is shared by the two countries. RUF forces have since dominated the diamond fields, largely on behalf of Taylor. As a result, Liberia, a country with little previous diamond production, became a major diamond exporter. A very high portion of these diamonds originated in RUF regions of Sierra Leone, but some reportedly also came from territory in Angola controlled by the National Union for the Total Independence of Angola.[11]

Liberia's efforts to exploit diamond production have been at the heart of the conflict in Sierra Leone. As a report by Partnership Africa Canada concluded:

> There is little doubt that Liberia has become a major centre for massive diamond-related criminal activity, with connections to smuggling and theft throughout Africa and considerably further afield. In return for weapons, it has provided the RUF with an outlet for diamonds, and has done the same for other diamond producing countries, fueling war and providing a safe haven for organized crime.[12]

The Sierra Leone expert panel "found unequivocal and overwhelming evidence that Liberia has been actively supporting the RUF at all levels, in providing training, weapons and related matériel, logistical support, a staging ground for attacks, and a safe haven for retreat and recuperation."[13] The panel also found that "the bulk of RUF diamonds leave Sierra Leone through Liberia" and that this illicit trade "could not be conducted without the permission and the involvement of Liberian government officials at the highest level."[14] The panel concluded that "Charles Taylor is actively involved in fueling the violence in Sierra Leone."[15]

UN sanctions were first imposed on Liberia in 1992. In November of that year, the Security Council adopted SCR 788, which established an arms embargo. The Council acted in response to a request for UN sanctions from ECOWAS, which had intervened militarily in the Liberian war in an attempt to prevent Charles Taylor and the NPFL from taking power. The arms embargo was not enforced, however (more than two years elapsed before the Council even created a sanctions committee), and it played no role in limiting the NPFL insurgency. The arms embargo was kept in place after Taylor was elected president in 1997.

In March 2001, as evidence of Taylor's support for the RUF mounted, the Council approved new sanctions against Liberia. SCR 1343 reauthorized the arms embargo, imposed a travel ban on senior members of the government of Liberia and its armed forces and their spouses, and mandated that Liberia freeze the financial assets of the RUF. The resolution also placed an embargo on all diamond exports from Liberia. At the request of ECOWAS, implementation of the sanctions was delayed two months to give Liberia a chance to comply with UN demands. The Council judged the initial response from Monrovia to be inadequate and proceeded to enact the sanctions in May 2001. The implementing resolution called for the creation of a panel of experts to report on sanctions violations and recommend steps for enhancing compliance.

SCR 1343 represented the first time the Security Council imposed sanctions against one country because of its refusal to comply with sanctions against another country. The sanctions against Liberia were intended to strike at the source of the RUF rebellion. They were also a form of secondary pressure designed to persuade Liberia to cut off its support for the RUF.

The Sierra Leone panel of experts urged consideration of additional secondary measures. It suggested the extension of diamond sanctions to Côte d'Ivoire and Guinea, if these countries did not adopt a diamond certification system similar to that in Sierra Leone.[16] The panel also urged that restrictions on arms exports be placed on specific producer countries found to be violating the embargo on Sierra Leone.[17] It is unlikely that the Council will adopt these additional measures to resolve the conflict in Sierra Leone. Nonetheless, the decision to impose secondary measures against Liberia was a significant development, one that may lead to similar developments in other cases.

## Monrovia Replies

Liberia responded to the threat of sanctions with a series of gestures designed to demonstrate a willingness to comply with UN demands. In January 2001, the government announced that it was no longer supporting the RUF militarily or financially, that all persons associated with the RUF had been ordered to leave Liberia, that RUF financial assets in Liberian banks were frozen, that diamond imports from Sierra Leone were banned, and that Liberia's own diamond exports were being suspended for 120 days, pending the creation of an internationally acceptable certification system for Liberia. These announced concessions appeared to indicate that sanctions were having an immediate and powerful effect. A delegation from ECOWAS that visited Liberia in April 2001 reported that the government of Liberia "seemed serious in meeting the demands of the Security Council."[18] The ECOWAS mission found Liberia's announced plans to control diamonds "commendable."[19]

The ECOWAS delegation also found grounds for skepticism, however. It reported that known RUF leaders, including Sam Bockarie, were seen openly in the streets of Monrovia. Secretary-General Kofi Annan also seemed unconvinced. In his April 2001 report to the Security Council, the Secretary-General noted Liberia's announcements but observed that the UN "does not have the capacity to provide independent confirmation of the claims by the Government of Liberia."[20] Members of the Security Council in New York were clearly skeptical about Liberia's actions. ECOWAS had recommended an observation mission to determine if Taylor's announcements were genuine, but members of the Security Council demurred. The Council refused to consider any further delay and duly enacted the sanctions in May 2001 at the conclusion of the previously agreed sixty-day waiting period.

Liberia's initial response to the threat of Security Council action appeared to indicate a real concern about the potential impact of sanctions. As West African officials told the UN interagency mission, "The threat of such sanctions might be more effective than their actual imposition."[21] The very fact that the gestures were made was a sign of sanctions impact. The threat of sanctions altered the Monrovia government's policy calculations. Before the adoption of SCR 1343, Liberia had little regard for the importuning of the Security Council and certainly had no reason to fear the mostly forgotten and ignored arms embargo, originally established in 1992. Once the Security Council became serious about imposing more effective sanctions, however, the Taylor regime began to take notice and mounted a diplomatic effort to give the appearance of cooperation.

This pattern of initial response to the threat of sanctions was also evident in the case of Sierra Leone. When ECOWAS and UN sanctions were imposed against the military junta in Freetown in 1997, coup leaders agreed to enter into negotiations. Just fifteen days after the Security Council adopted SCR 1132 in October 1997, the junta signed an agreement in Conakry pledging to restore the elected government of Sierra Leone within six months. It took military action from ECOWAS, however, to enforce this pledge. As noted in Chapter 1, a similar pattern of targeted regimes responding to the threat or initial imposition of sanctions occurred in several other cases, including Somalia, Libya, Haiti, and Afghanistan. This general pattern of an initial response to sanctions is noteworthy.

## Social Impacts

Humanitarian conditions in Sierra Leone, already among the worst in the world, have continued to deteriorate in recent years, according to the reports of the Secretary-General.[22] Sierra Leone and Liberia rank near the bottom of the UN Development Programme's Human Development Index. The wars and political turmoil of the past decade have pushed people in the two countries ever deeper into poverty and misery. Estimates of the number of people killed over the past decade in Sierra Leone range from 43,000 to 75,000.[23] In Liberia, the eight-year war resulted in an estimated 200,000 deaths before finally coming to an end in 1997.[24] Only 37 percent of adult Liberians are considered literate, and 80 percent of the population lives in poverty, on less than U.S.$1 a day.[25] Sierra Leone has experienced one of the worst refugee crises in the world. Some 2 million people, almost half the country's population, have been forced to flee their homes.[26] In 2001, Guinea was hosting 300,000 refugees from Sierra Leone and 120,000 from Liberia.[27] The huge numbers of refugees and internally displaced persons in the region have created acute problems of overcrowding in UN camps and transit centers.

The horrendous social conditions within Sierra Leone and Liberia have resulted not from sanctions but from war, impoverishment, and corruption. The ECOWAS trade sanctions in 1997 hindered food shipments and relief efforts in Sierra Leone, according to a 1998 assessment by the UN Office for the Coordination of Humanitarian Affairs,[28] but these effects were relatively short-lived. UN sanctions, in contrast, were intentionally designed to avoid adverse consequences for the general population. The embargoes on weapons imports and the travel bans on designated RUF and Liberian government leaders were selective measures that avoided broader social impacts.

There is no evidence of social impacts from the embargo on diamond exports. The UN's October 2001 assessment of humanitarian consequences in Liberia made no mention of the diamond sanctions. In Sierra Leone, the workers who dig and pan through the mud of the alluvial diamond fields have continued to mine precious stones. By 2000, the Sierra Leone government and UNAMSIL were in control of most of the mining areas. Diamond traders were able to maintain their operations, provided they obtained government-approved certificates of origin. In Liberia, the diamond sanctions could affect the intermediaries who illegally bring diamonds from Sierra Leone to market, but denying enrichment opportunities for these smugglers and the political leaders who support them is precisely the point of the sanctions.

The social impact of possible future sanctions on the Liberian timber industry could be severe. According to the October 2001 UN humanitarian assessment, a ban on Liberian timber exports could result in the loss of up to 10,000 relatively well-paid jobs.[29] In a country that averages nine dependents for each employed person, this change could mean a loss of primary means of support for approximately 90,000 people. Timber exports also provide about 9 percent of Liberian government revenues, and they constitute the predominant commercial activity at three of the country's four ports.[30] A timber embargo thus could have far-reaching economic and social consequences. In a Security Council briefing on the report, representatives of Global Witness challenged the accuracy of the UN's humanitarian assessment, claiming that the figures for employment and economic impact were exaggerated.[31] A number of Council members expressed opposition to timber sanctions, however, for political and economic reasons as well as because of humanitarian concerns, and it appeared unlikely that such measures would be adopted.

## Policy Impacts?

UN sanctions have had positive impacts. RUF forces and their Liberian supporters have faced shortages of arms and money. They have shown a new readiness to accept a negotiated peace settlement. These trends became evident following the tightening of sanctions in Sierra Leone in 2000 and their imposition in Liberia in 2001. The RUF signed an unconditional cease-fire in November 2000 and affirmed this agreement in May 2001. In March and April 2001, less than a year after they mounted armed attacks against UN peacekeepers, RUF officials invited

UNAMSIL forces to begin deploying in rebel-controlled territory. An analysis in *The Economist* traced the RUF truce in part to the imposition of UN sanctions against Liberia.[32]

These shifts in RUF/Liberian policy may have been partially a response to sanctions pressures, but they also resulted from changes in battlefield conditions.[33] Hundreds of troops from the United Kingdom intervened in May 2000 to help free UN peacekeepers. They remained in the country to train the armed forces of Sierra Leone, thereby increasing military pressure on the RUF. Military attacks from Guinea also played a role. Guinean forces carried out armed attacks and bombing raids against RUF and Liberian territory, ostensibly in retaliation for raids against towns and villages in Guinea. Clashes occurred in September 2000 and continued into 2001.

The political and military effects of the Guinean attacks on RUF and Liberian forces were "devastating," according to a BBC report.[34] One of the reasons the RUF accepted the deployment of UN peacekeepers was to obtain help in fending off further military incursions from Guinean forces. The combination of military pressure from Guinea, the presence of UK troops, the growing deployment of UNAMSIL, and the strengthening of Security Council sanctions fundamentally changed the dynamics of the struggle.

The specific role of sanctions in helping to bring about these changes cannot be determined precisely, but it is likely that the imposition of diamond sanctions and increased international attention to the role of Liberia made it more difficult for the RUF to rely on cross-border assistance from the Taylor regime. The pressures were as much psychological as economic. The tightening of sanctions, like the expansion of UNAMSIL, was a sign of increased pressure on Liberia and the RUF. The fact that sanctions were now being applied to Liberia as well as the RUF undoubtedly had a sobering impact in Monrovia. More than the actual impact of sanctions themselves, it was probably the threat of sanctions and what they implied for the future that had the greatest impact on the policy calculations of Taylor and the RUF commanders.

### The Way Forward: Coercion or Persuasion?

In West Africa, as in Angola, the United Nations has gradually shifted from a more traditional stance of neutrality and the pursuit of negotiations toward a more coercive role of increasing pressure on the RUF and its Liberian patrons. The UN interagency missions to West Africa found substantial support in the region for strengthening the UNAMSIL mandate from neutral peacekeeping to more assertive peace enforcement.[35] The April 2001 report from the ICG called for abandoning further negotiations with the RUF and pursuing instead a strategy of military attack and coercive sanctions to defeat the RUF. According to the report, "There should be no more negotiations with the . . . RUF other than for its complete disarmament and demobilization."[36] The former U.S. ambassador to Sierra Leone, John Hirsch, likewise argued that "the war should be brought to an end not by further protracted negotiations, but by RUF's surrender."[37]

Many within the UN and in Africa have been skeptical of or opposed to a more aggressive strategy. Some UN and ECOWAS officials have continued to support a more conciliatory approach, attempting to persuade rather than coerce RUF commanders into accepting UNAMSIL deployment and adhering to the Lomé accord as a basis for political settlement. ECOWAS played a major role in the past in attempting to resolve the crisis, but its largest member, Nigeria, has been reluctant to intervene again militarily. Although ECOWAS has remained involved and its military contingents have served in UNAMSIL, the organization has remained divided between supporters of the Kabbah government (Nigeria, Côte d'Ivoire, and Ghana) and supporters of the RUF (Liberia and Burkina Faso).

For the UN, a militarily assertive strategy in West Africa presents fundamental difficulties. The prospects of UNAMSIL or any other UN peacekeeping force mounting military enforcement efforts successfully are practically nil. As the August 2000 Brahimi Report convincingly argued, UN peacekeeping missions have been fundamentally incapable of applying sustained, effective combat pressure.[38] The UN has repeatedly failed in attempts to project credible force. The embarrassing debacle of RUF forces capturing UNAMSIL troops in May and June 2000 only confirmed the ineptitude of UN peacekeeping when confronted with hostile force.

In Sierra Leone, the function of military enforcement has been performed by British troops and military advisers, who arrived in June 2000 to rescue UN peacekeepers and remained to train and shape the Sierra Leone army. Unlike UN peacekeepers, British troops were more heavily armed and operated with rules of engagement that permitted the use of coercive force, which allowed the growing forces of UNAMSIL to preserve a largely neutral presence. UNAMSIL expanded into a very large force, but it functioned primarily in the traditional mold of UN peacekeeping, lightly armed and lacking robust rules of engagement.

UN peacekeepers served as tacit partners of the British troops, notwithstanding some tensions between the two forces.[39] British troops provided the coercive presence that convinced some RUF forces to surrender their arms and seek the protection of UN peacekeepers.

Security Council sanctions have played a key role in this increasingly assertive strategy by applying coercive pressure on both the RUF and the Liberian government. The sanctions have deprived the RUF and the Taylor government of income, arms, and travel opportunities. They have signaled international determination to isolate and pressure the RUF and the government in Monrovia. Through continuing and more vigorous efforts to enforce the sanctions, and with the continued presence of both peace enforcement and peacekeeping troops, the international community may eventually succeed in bringing peace to Sierra Leone.

## Notes

1. Communiqué issued by the Joint Government of Sierra Leone/ Revolutionary United Front/UNAMSIL Committee on Disarmament, Demobilization and Reintegration, 17 January 2002, <http://www.sierra-leone.org/ jointcommittee011702.html> (25 February 2002).

2. United Nations Security Council, *Towards a Comprehensive Approach to Durable and Sustainable Solutions to Priority Needs and Challenges in West Africa: Report of the Inter-Agency Mission to West Africa*, S/2001/434, New York, 2 May 2001, par. 85.

3. International Crisis Group, *Sierra Leone: Time for a New Military and Political Strategy*, Freetown/London/Brussels, 11 April 2001, 3.

4. United Nations Security Council, *Towards a Comprehensive Approach*, S/2001/434, par. 13.

5. Ibid.

6. International Crisis Group, *Sierra Leone*, ii.

7. Ibid.

8. United Nations Security Council, *Security Council Resolution 1306 (2000)*, S/RES/1306, New York, 5 July 2000.

9. United Nations Security Council, *Report of the Panel of Experts Appointed Pursuant to Security Council Resolution 1306 (2000), Paragraph 19, in Relation to Sierra Leone*, S/2000/1195, New York, 20 December 2000.

10. Ibid., par. 17.

11. Ian Smillie, Lansana Gberie, and Ralph Hazleton, *The Heart of the Matter: Sierra Leone, Diamonds and Human Security* (Ottawa, Ontario, Canada: Partnership Africa Canada, January 2000), 47.

12. Ibid., 48.

13. United Nations Security Council, *Report of the Panel of Experts Appointed Pursuant to Security Council Resolution 1306 (2000), Paragraph 19, in Relation to Sierra Leone*, S/2000/1195, par. 20.

14. Ibid., par. 2.

15. Ibid., par. 23.

16. Ibid., par. 8.

17. Ibid., par. 39.

18. As reported in United Nations Security Council, *First Report of the Secretary-General Pursuant to Security Council Resolution 1343 (2001) Regarding Liberia*, S/2001/424, New York, 30 April 2001, par. 37.

19. Ibid., par. 33.

20. Ibid., par. 7.

21. United Nations Security Council, *Towards a Comprehensive Approach*, S/2001/434, par. 114.

22. United Nations Security Council, *Eighth Report of the Secretary-General on the United Nations Mission in Sierra Leone*, S/2000/1199, New York, 15 December 2000, par. 55.

23. *The Economist* reported "some 43,000" killed in Sierra Leone in the past ten years. See "Sierra Leone: The Spreading Battleground," *The Economist*, 7 April 2001. According to a 1999 report by Human Rights Watch, between 50,000 and 75,000 died from 1991 to 1999. See Human Rights Watch, *Getting Away with Murder, Mutilation and Rape: New Testimony from Sierra Leone* (New York: Human Rights Watch, June 1999), 1.

24. U.S. Department of State, "Liberia Country Report on Human Rights Practices for 1997" (Washington, D.C.: U.S. Government Printing Office, 30 January 1998).

25. United Nations Security Council, *Report of the Secretary-General in Pursuance of Paragraph 13(a) of Resolution 1343 (2001) Concerning Liberia*, S/2001/939, New York, 5 October 2001, par. 19.

26. "Sierra Leone: The Spreading Battleground," 48.

27. Norimitsu Onishi, "Guinea in Crisis as Area's Refugees Pour In," *New York Times*, 24 February 2001, A1.

28. United Nations Office for the Coordination of Humanitarian Affairs, *Sierra Leone Humanitarian Situation Report, 21 January–12 February 1998*, 98/0016, New York, 17 February 1998.

29. United Nations Security Council, *Report of the Secretary-General in Pursuance of Paragraph 13(a)*, S/2001/939, par. 34.

30. Ibid., pars. 36, 38.

31. Global Witness, "The Real Price of Sanctions on Timber," 17 October 2001, supplement to the report, *Taylor-Made: The Pivotal Role of Liberia's Forests and Flag of Convenience in Regional Conflict*, Global Witness, London, September 2001, <www.oneworld.org/globalwitness/liberia/taylormade2.pdf> (25 October 2001).

32. "Sierra Leone: The Spreading Battleground," 48.

33. Lansana Gberie, "Analysis: Rebels Without a Future," *BBC Online*, 21 May 2001, <news.bbc.co.uk/hi/english/world/africa/newsid_1343000/1343113.htm> (9 September 2001).

34. Ibid.

35. United Nations Security Council, *Towards a Comprehensive Approach*, S/2001/434, par. 31.

36. International Crisis Group, *Sierra Leone*, ii.

37. John L. Hirsch, "War in Sierra Leone," *Survival* 43, no. 3 (Autumn 2001): 145–162.

38. Lakhdar Brahimi et al., *Comprehensive Review of the Whole Question of Peacekeeping Operations in All Their Aspects: Identical Letters Dated 21 August*

*2000 from the S-G to the President of the General Assembly and the President of the Security Council,* A/55/305-S/2000/809, New York, 21 August 2000 (also known as the "Brahimi Report").

39. These observations are based on personal observation in Sierra Leone during the summer of 2001 by William Reno; personal communication from William Reno, October 2001.

# 6

# Following the Money Trail: Targeted Financial Sanctions

Waging war or maintaining a terrorist network costs money, lots of it. The armed conflicts that the United Nations seeks to prevent and control around the world are sustained by complex financial networks. If these networks can be discovered and penetrated, a target group's ability to violate international norms will be significantly affected. Tightening international controls on the financing of war and criminal activity is one of the most effective tools available for upholding the principles of the UN.

Because they have numerous advantages over general trade sanctions, targeted financial sanctions have grown in significance in UN circles. They focus coercive pressures on decisionmaking elites rather than innocent or vulnerable populations. They avoid the humanitarian hardships that can result from broader trade sanctions. The costs of enforcing targeted financial sanctions, although not inconsiderable, are less than the challenges of attempting to block commercial trade. Targeted financial sanctions represent a more focused form of sanctions that can minimize unintended adverse consequences and achieve greater effectiveness.

The record of success for financial sanctions is uneven, however. When assessing their effectiveness, it is hard to know whether the glass is half full or half empty. Despite the progress that has been achieved in refining the methods of financial control, political despots and money launderers continue to operate in a vast netherworld of unofficial and illegal finance. The costs of money laundering may have increased in recent decades because of stronger international enforcement efforts, but the profits and benefits involved are more than sufficient to absorb those costs.[1] The struggle against illegal financing is like a race through a maze to which there seems no end. International regulators constantly strive to overtake criminals and political pariahs, but regulators always remain a step or two behind their resourceful targets.

Yet there is reason for hope. The cooperative efforts of developed countries to strengthen international financial regulation and control have created significant new tools of enforcement. The Security Council has acquired valuable experience in administering targeted financial sanctions. The Council has broadened the reach of assets freezes to include individuals as well as governments, and it has strengthened monitoring by creating investigative panels and, in the Angola case, hiring a private security firm. Taken together, these advances have slowly but steadily improved the ability of the Security Council to utilize targeted financial sanctions.

In this chapter, we focus on the most frequently employed form of financial sanction, the freezing of assets. We do not address such measures as withholding credits and loans or blocking nonhumanitarian foreign assistance. These actions are not within the purview of the Security Council. Moreover, such measures can have broad economic effects that are similar to those associated with general trade sanctions. The attention of the UN, the European Union (EU), and other major players has been on targeted financial sanctions that seek to block the transactions and freeze the assets of specific individuals and groups responsible for objectionable behavior. In these pages, we examine recent cases of multilateral financial sanctions, review the many obstacles to more effective enforcement, consider international efforts to combat money laundering, and assess the most important requirements for strengthening targeted financial sanctions as tools of Security Council policy.

## A Review of Cases

Targeted financial sanctions have been relatively rare historically. Of the 116 sanctions episodes examined in the 1990 Institute for International Economics study, only thirteen involved freezing financial assets. All the assets freezes were imposed during times of war or major international crisis, and most were in combination with other coercive economic measures. Since 1990, with the increase in the frequency and diversity of Security Council sanctions, targeted financial sanctions have become more prevalent. Of the fourteen cases of Security Council sanctions since 1990, six have included targeted financial sanctions. The EU sanctions imposed against the Federal Republic of Yugoslavia in 1998 also included a financial assets freeze. A review of these cases, along with a review of the financial pressures that helped to bring down the apartheid regime in South Africa, can identify the factors that contribute to the success or failure of financial sanctions.

## South Africa

The international sanctions against South Africa during the 1970s and 1980s included a unique, bottom-up citizens' divestment campaign to withdraw financial support from the apartheid regime. In 1962, the UN General Assembly adopted a resolution urging countries to ban all trade with South Africa, but this measure was nonbinding, and few countries complied. The Security Council imposed a mandatory arms embargo in 1977 but could not agree on more forceful economic or financial measures.[2] The most effective action against apartheid came from civil society groups in North America, Europe, and elsewhere in the world. Local governments, religious bodies, universities, foundations, labor unions, and other private institutions launched a massive transnational movement to sever financial ties with the apartheid government. This movement led to the withdrawal of some $20 billion in assets from firms and banks doing business in South Africa.[3] These measures, combined with steadily intensifying sanctions pressure from individual governments and international organizations, undermined business confidence in the apartheid government and provided political and moral encouragement to the black majority population represented in the opposition African National Congress (ANC).

The mounting international isolation of South Africa and the widespread domestic resistance of the majority population posed increasingly unacceptable risks to investors. In 1985, the country experienced a credit squeeze when major U.S. banks decided to roll over South Africa's external debt short term rather than long term. The bankers based this decision on purely economic considerations, but their perception of financial risk was strongly influenced by the regime's mounting political problems at home and abroad. As the country became increasingly ungovernable and financial difficulties mounted, business and government leaders initiated a dialogue with Nelson Mandela and the ANC, which led to elections and the transition to majority rule.

The grassroots antiapartheid movement put substantial economic and financial pressure on the government of South Africa. In no other case before or since have citizen groups and private actors played such an important role in sanctioning an abusive regime.[4] The pressures generated were general rather than targeted, often affecting the oppressed African majority more than the white elites responsible for apartheid. The sanctions enjoyed the support of the ANC, however. The ANC urged stronger and more comprehensive international pressures against the Pretoria government as an essential part of its strategy for ending apartheid. Better to suffer the hardships of sanctions, the ANC said, than the brutalities of racial repression. In the end, the combination of international pressure and domestic resistance succeeded in bringing about political change. The bottom-up financial sanctions of the anti-apartheid movement played an important role in achieving this success.

Assets freezes have been included in several of the most important sanctions regimes imposed by the UN Security Council since 1990. These regimes include Iraq, Yugoslavia (1992–1995), Libya, Haiti, Angola, and Afghanistan.[5] In all these cases, the Security Council imposed a freeze on the assets of the targeted government or, in the case of Angola, the National Union for the Total Independence of Angola (UNITA) rebel movement. In three of the cases—Haiti, Angola, and Afghanistan—the Security Council also imposed sanctions on designated individuals. The EU and U.S. sanctions against the government of Yugoslavia in 1998 to 2000 included a freeze on the assets of the Belgrade regime as well as designated individuals. (The sweeping financial sanctions included in the Security Council resolution [SCR] to counter terrorism, SCR 1373 [2001], are addressed in Chapter 7.) Broadening the scope of financial sanctions is a means of exerting stronger and more targeted pressure on the decisionmaking elites who are responsible for abusive practices and who can influence government policy. Table 6.1 summarizes the recent multilateral cases and the trend toward freezing both individual and government assets.

## Iraq (1990–)

The Security Council sanctions imposed against Iraq in August 1990 (SCR 661) included a freeze on the assets of the governments of Iraq and Kuwait. The Council instructed UN member states to prevent the removal of any Iraqi or Kuwaiti funds or financial resources.[6] Even before the enactment of these Security Council sanctions, the U.S. government acted swiftly to freeze Kuwaiti assets held in U.S. banks, thus preventing the Baghdad regime from gaining access to Kuwait's huge foreign reserves, estimated at nearly $100 billion.[7] The financial sanctions on Iraqi government assets had little apparent economic or politi-

**Table 6.1  Multilateral Financial Sanctions, 1990–2001**

| Case | Sanctioning Authority | Targeted Against Assets of Government | Targeted Against Assets of Designated Individuals |
|---|---|---|---|
| Iraq, 1990– | | | |
| S/RES/661 (1990) | UN Security Council | Yes | No |
| Yugoslavia (Serbia and Montenegro), 1992–1995 | | | |
| S/RES/757; S/RES/787 (1992) | UN Security Council | Yes | No |
| S/RES/820 (1993) | UN Security Council | Yes | No |
| Libya, 1993–1999 | | | |
| S/RES/883 (1993) | UN Security Council | Yes | No |
| Haiti, 1993–1994 | | | |
| S/RES/841 (1993) | UN Security Council | Yes | No |
| S/RES/917 (1994) | UN Security Council | Yes | Yes |
| Angola, 1998– | | | |
| S/RES/1173 (1998) | UN Security Council | Yes | Yes |
| Yugoslavia, 1998–2000 | | | |
| 98/240/CFSP (1998) | European Union | Yes | No |
| 1295/98 (1998) | European Union | Yes | No |
| 1999/318/CFSP (1999) | European Union | Yes | Yes |
| Afghanistan, 1999– | | | |
| S/RES/1267 (1999) | UN Security Council | Yes | No |
| S/RES/1333 (2000)[a] | UN Security Council | No | Yes |

Note: a. Measures from S/RES/1333 entered into force on 19 January 2001.

cal impact. The total amount of assets frozen has been estimated at approximately $4 billion to $5 billion, scattered in holdings in some thirty countries.[8] The financial sanctions against Iraq never included a freeze on the assets of Saddam Hussein and his family and close associates. Even when Iraq openly defied UN weapons inspectors in the late 1990s and when published reports suggested that Saddam Hussein and his family had amassed billions of dollars through illegal oil sales and the diversion of resources from the oil for food program, the Security Council refused to consider an assets freeze against the Iraqi leader.[9] The general backlash against and exhaustion with sanctions in Iraq prevented the Council from taking additional measures to impose targeted pressure on the regime.

## Yugoslavia (1992–1995)

The financial sanctions against the former Yugoslavia during the war in Bosnia were more effective than those against Iraq. The initial UN sanctions imposed in SCR 757 (1992) included a general trade embargo and a freeze on the assets of the Yugoslav government. The sanctions were strengthened in April 1993 with the adoption of SCR 820, whereby the Security Council broadened the assets freeze to cover all commercial and industrial entities controlled by Belgrade and all Yugoslav resources within other countries.[10] The assets freeze seriously depleted Belgrade's financial reserves. The total amount of Yugoslav financial assets frozen during this period was estimated at approximately $2.8 billion.[11] The Belgrade government initially hid some of its financial assets in a network of front companies and also continued to do business with firms in Russia. But these efforts were not sufficient to offset the impact of the assets freeze and the denial of access to financial markets in Europe and the United States. The UN sanctions and assets freeze had serious costs for Yugoslavia. Slobodan Milosevic, a former banking official, recognized the crippling impact that financial sanctions would have on Yugoslavia's prospects for achieving currency convertibility and attracting international investment. Over time, UN sanctions contributed to Milosevic's willingness to negotiate for peace.

## Libya (1993–1999)

In the case of Libya, the initial Security Council sanctions imposed in March 1992 by SCR 748 did not include an assets freeze. Financial sanctions were added in SCR 883, adopted in November 1993, to intensify pressure against the government for its refusal to comply with UN demands. SCR 883 mandated a freeze on all funds or other financial resources owned or controlled by the government of Libya or any other official Libyan entity. The language of SCR 883 specified that the assets freeze was to apply not only to Libyan government funds but also to all commercial, industrial, or public utilities owned or controlled by the Tripoli government.[12] The Security Council vitiated the potential impact of the financial sanctions, however, by exempting funds or financial resources derived from Libyan oil sales. This was a concession to European countries, which depended heavily on Libyan oil and did not want to risk a disruption of oil imports. The exemption of oil revenues made the financial sanctions meaningless. The financial sanctions thus played little or no role in pressuring Libya to cooperate with UN demands.

## Haiti (1993–1994)

The Security Council imposed financial sanctions on Haiti as part of the initial oil and arms embargo authorized in SCR 841 (1993). The Council froze the funds of the military-controlled government of Haiti and any entities controlled by that regime. The following year, after the military junta reneged on its pledge to permit the return of elected president Jean-Bertrand Aristide, the Council strengthened the sanctions by adopting SCR 917 (1994). It was the first time that the Council froze the assets of designated individuals, including officers of the Haitian military and police and their immediate families.[13] A list of targeted individuals was subsequently published by the Haiti sanctions committee. These targeted sanctions were not legally binding, however. SCR 917 did not use the language "decides" but merely "strongly urges." This wording meant that states were not legally obligated to comply. The United States imposed a partial freeze on the assets of eighty-three individuals and thirty-five companies, but few other countries followed suit.[14] In any case, the financial sanctions and other measures imposed by the Security Council did not have a chance to work. U.S. military pressure forced the junta to step down in September 1994.

## Angola (1998–)

Security Council sanctions were initially imposed against the UNITA rebel movement in Angola in 1993 with the adoption of SCR 864. They were strengthened in 1997 through SCR 1127 and again in 1998 with the adoption of SCR 1173. Resolution 1173 directed UN member states to freeze the funds and financial resources of UNITA as an organization. This resolution also imposed an assets freeze on designated senior officials of UNITA and adult members of their immediate families.[15] The Council specified that the assets freeze would apply to the same list of UNITA officials and adult members of their immediate families whose travel was banned by SCR 1127 (1997). It was the first time that the Council imposed both a mandatory assets freeze and a travel ban on the same list of individuals. The Angola sanctions committee subsequently issued a list of 153 senior UNITA officials and their adult immediate family members.[16] The list has been progressively updated and refined ever since, as UN officials attempt to keep pace with changes in the UNITA leadership despite the group's various evasion techniques.

The Security Council has had great difficulty in attempting to locate and freeze the financial assets of UNITA and its leaders. UNITA accounts have been found in Portugal and five other countries.[17] The freezing of these funds has not impounded very much money.[18] Most UNITA assets are in the form of diamonds, which are used in packets as a medium of currency and exchange. According to the December 2000 report of the Angola monitoring mechanism, UNITA responded to financial sanctions by moving its assets away from high-profile individual leaders to lower-level officials.[19] UNITA also transferred its funds electronically to safe havens in unregulated offshore banking centers. In an attempt to trace UNITA's financial resources, the Security Council made the unprecedented decision of employing a private investigative agency. In April 2001, the Council announced that Kroll Associates was being hired on a sixteen-week contract to trace assets and gather information on UNITA's finances.[20] The investigation was commissioned in an attempt to uncover UNITA's financial networks and strengthen the ability of UN member states to locate and freeze the assets of the rebel movement. The hiring of Kroll Associates was another sign of the increasing seriousness of Security Council attempts to use targeted financial sanctions.

### Yugoslavia (1998–2000)

One of the most interesting recent examples of multilateral financial sanctions involved not the UN but the EU. Acting under its new Common Foreign and Security Policy, the EU imposed a series of sanctions against the Milosevic regime in Yugoslavia because of its repressive policies in Kosovo. The EU sanctions included an arms embargo, travel sanctions, an oil embargo, an investment ban, and financial sanctions. The United States adopted parallel measures. The EU sanctions were originally intended to end Serbia's repression and use of force in Kosovo. Later, the objectives changed to promoting democracy and human rights and encouraging a change of regime in Belgrade.

The EU financial sanctions against Yugoslavia began with a March 1998 prohibition against financial support for trade or investment in Serbia. A ban was also imposed on European government financing of the privatization of state-owned companies in Serbia. These measures were intended to deny income to the government of Serbia. In June 1998, the EU Council strengthened the sanctions by ordering a freeze on the assets of the governments of Yugoslavia and Serbia. In the spring of 1999, as the conflict in Kosovo raged, the EU Council went further and broadened the assets freeze to include persons acting on behalf of the Serbian government. Financial sanctions were thus applied to individuals as well as the government. The list of individuals whose assets were to be frozen was the same as the list of those whose travel was banned. That list, regularly updated, grew from ten persons in the spring of 1998 to more than 200 a year later and eventually to almost 800 names by the summer of 2000.[21] It included persons who supported the Milosevic regime politically, financially, or in both ways; leaders of the military and other security forces; and persons indicted for crimes by the International Criminal Tribunal on Yugoslavia. These people were denied access to hard currency trading and were unable to travel to conduct business or engage in professional activities.[22] The targeted financial sanctions, in addition to various other sanctions, exerted effective pressure on those responsible for the repressive policies of the Milosevic regime. Combined with incentives and aid provided to opposition groups, these financial sanctions helped topple Milosevic.

### Afghanistan (1999–)

The initial Security Council sanctions against the Taliban regime in Afghanistan, SCR 1267 (1999), included a freeze on the funds and financial resources of the Taliban or any entity owned or controlled by it. These measures were strengthened a year later with the adoption of SCR 1333 (2000), which imposed the assets freeze on a list of designated individuals as well as the Taliban organization. The list targeted Usama bin Laden and individuals connected with him, particularly those associated with the al-Qaida organization.[23] Following the precedent set in the Angola case, a mandatory assets freeze and visa ban were applied to the same list of designated leaders. The UN Secretariat subsequently issued a list of forty-five Taliban officials whose travel was to be banned and whose assets were to be frozen.[24] As we describe in Chapter 7, the global freeze on Taliban assets netted considerable sums and contributed to the economic and political isolation of the Taliban regime.

## Requirements for Effective Financial Sanctions

Determining whether financial sanctions will work requires an assessment of a target's potential vulnerability to such measures. In some circumstances, a regime or its leadership may be so poor or so isolated from international financial markets as to be largely immune from financial sanctions. The degree of state control over financial markets also influences vulnerability. Centralized economies may be better able to manage the economic shocks that result from sanctions, in part by shifting the economic burden from decisionmaking elites to vulnerable populations or opposition constituencies. The degree of secrecy and information control in a target regime is also a factor. It is more difficult to identify and trace assets in a closed society than in an open one. All these factors need to be weighed in evaluating whether and how financial sanctions might be able to achieve UN objectives.

The effectiveness of financial sanctions also depends on a range of practical policy considerations—the ability of sanctioning authorities to act swiftly, the institutional capacity of the UN and its member states to implement such measures, and the degree of cooperation among major financial powers. These and other challenges to sanctions implementation are examined in the following pages.

When sanctions are imposed, those who are targeted inevitably seek to avoid coercive pressures. When the object being sanctioned is money, the most fungible and precious of all resources, the strategies and techniques of evasion are highly evolved. The recent cases of multilateral financial sanctions have illustrated many of these methods, such as moving funds to unregulated offshore havens, obtaining funds through illicit transactions, and utilizing fronts and aliases. Other circumvention schemes include back-to-back loans in countries with weak regulatory controls, asset pledges and swaps, and the triangulation of goods and funds through a series of countries.[25] Apart from the evasion strategies of targets, financial sanctions are also hampered by a lack of enforcement capability at the UN and within many member states and by the reluctance of private bankers to accept greater public regulation of international finance. Evaluating these challenges is part of the process of making financial sanctions more effective.

Considerable progress has been achieved in recent years in developing an agenda to improve financial sanctions. The government of Switzerland took the lead by sponsoring two international seminars on UN financial sanctions in Interlaken in 1998 and 1999. Financial regulators, UN officials, private bankers, lawyers, and scholars from more than twenty countries gathered to find ways of enhancing the effectiveness of targeted financial sanctions.[26] Under the leadership of Swiss ambassador Rolf Jeker, the Interlaken seminars developed concrete proposals for improving technical capacity, strengthening UN and member state implementation efforts, and clarifying the language and technical terms employed in Security Council resolutions. The Watson Institute for International Studies at Brown University contributed to this process by sponsoring a series of roundtable discussions with the Council on Foreign Relations in New York in May and June 1998. In May 2000, the Watson Institute convened a financial sanctions simulation exercise, conducted in cooperation with the Naval War College in Rhode Island.[27] The Watson Institute roundtables and simulations exercise brought together bankers, lawyers, scholars, and policymakers to explore further options for improving targeted financial sanctions. In cooperation with the government of Switzerland and the UN Secretariat, the Watson Institute convened a July 2001 workshop on financial sanctions for Security Council members in New York. In October 2001, it published a manual on financial sanctions to assist member states in implementing such measures.[28] Out of these various initiatives have come practical proposals, many of which are outlined below, for overcoming the obstacles to effective implementation of targeted financial sanctions.

## Moving Quickly

Speed and decisiveness are necessary to freeze assets before they can be moved to safe havens. The political decisionmaking process at the UN, however, tends to be plodding. The debate and political maneuvering needed to achieve consensus on financial sanctions usually provide ample warning to potential targets, allowing them to move and shelter assets and thereby mute the impact of financial sanctions. Once sanctions are imposed, international officials may need additional time to collect information on the finances of a targeted government and the individuals who influence it. The ease with which funds can be electronically transferred from one account to another stands as a huge obstacle to the effectiveness of financial sanctions. By the time financial sanctions are adopted and the potential targets are identified, it may be too late to locate and freeze the targeted assets.

A related complication is the rapid development of nonbank financial transactions and the development of cybercurrency and other new forms of financing. Banks are no longer the sole players in international finance. Insurance companies, brokerage firms, and other institutions are expanding into the banking business. New electronic forms of money such as smart cards have made the task of financial monitoring and control more difficult. Traditional financial institutions are being replaced by direct seller-to-buyer transactions via the Internet and other electronic means. This situation has eroded the ability of governments to control financial markets.[29]

The requirement for rapid and decisive action to freeze financial assets runs counter to the Security Council's practice of delaying the implementation of sanctions to give targeted authorities an opportunity to comply with UN demands. When the Security Council approved an assets freeze and other strengthened sanctions against UNITA in Angola in 1998 (SCR 1173), it delayed imposition of the additional measures for two weeks. When the Council adopted financial sanctions against the Taliban in Afghanistan, it delayed implementation for thirty days. The practice of offering targets an opportunity to cooperate before enacting coercive measures is intended to encourage compliance or at least to initiate a bargaining process. This approach can be an effective means of prompting concessions from a target, but it makes it impossible for the Council to move with the requisite speed in freezing assets.

A possible solution to the challenge of moving quickly was discussed at the second Interlaken seminar and at the financial sanctions simulation sponsored by the Watson Institute. When imposing financial sanctions, the Security Council could decide to freeze all assets immediately, then roll back these measures after a short period, when sanctions would be lifted on all accounts and transactions except for those of the targeted government and designated individuals. The specific proposal considered at the sanctions simulation was "to impose a general financial sanction on the entire population, followed by its immediate release on the overwhelming majority of the population" within two weeks.[30] The Security Council would offer to release all accounts, including those of the government and targeted individuals, if the targeted authorities complied with UN demands. This general lockdown approach would enable sanctioning authorities to move quickly enough to catch targeted assets before they were transferred. The short duration of the general sanction would avoid potential humanitarian harm that could result from a prolonged financial lockdown. The interim period would provide a window for obtaining compliance or negotiating a settlement. This approach deserves further consideration as at least a partial response to the need for speed in freezing financial assets.

## Building Capacity

The most important requirement for the success of sanctions, financial or otherwise, is a strong capacity for implementation at the UN and among UN member states. Although the Security Council has gained valuable experience with financial sanctions in recent years, the capacity of the UN Secretariat to monitor and enforce these measures remains woefully inadequate. The functioning of the UN depends on the cooperation and the capacity of its member states. If members do not have the legal authority or institutional means to implement Security Council resolutions, UN sanctions will have little or no impact. It has been estimated that only about a dozen countries have the means for properly enforcing financial sanctions.[31] Where such capacity does exist, particularly in the United States and Western Europe, variations in legal and administrative systems impede effectiveness.

In the private sector, there is a reluctance to enforce UN-mandated financial sanctions. Banks generally resist as much government regulation as they can. Many chafe at the demanding financial disclosure rules and inspection requirements that are part of the emerging system of international financial regulations. These requirements run counter to the tradition of bank secrecy, which many financial officers consider vital to their ability to attract business.[32] Despite these misgivings, however, in recent decades bankers have had to accept greater government control of their affairs, as nations attempt to prevent money laundering and other financial crimes. Codes of secrecy are being replaced by the norm of "know your customer" and an emphasis on the virtues of transparency.

The United States has the most highly developed capacity for implementing financial sanctions.[33] U.S. law explicitly authorizes and empowers financial institutions to comply with multilateral financial sanctions. The Office of Foreign Assets Control (OFAC) in the U.S. Treasury is the largest sanctions enforcement unit in the world, with a staff of more than fifty professionals and decades of experience in the implementation of sanctions. No other country can match the U.S. capability in this regard.

The OFAC implementation model includes intensive efforts to promote awareness of sanctions compliance requirements among banks and other financial institutions. Banks are on the front line of financial sanctions policy, and they need to be informed and supported in their implementation efforts. OFAC gives workshops and presentations to industry groups and fields thousands of telephone inquiries from banking officials. Banks in turn are required to screen financial transactions and to report on any blocked or rejected items.[34]

At the heart of the U.S. model is the ability to identify specific individuals and entities whose assets are to be frozen. This identification is essential to the success of targeted financial sanctions. In the United States, the persons and entities subjected to financial sanctions are identified as specially designated nationals (SDNs). OFAC is responsible for developing and maintaining the SDN list, which has more than 3,000 names, including those targeted by financial sanctions as well as individuals suspected of money laundering or other financial crimes.[35] Just because a person or entity appears on the SDN list does not necessarily mean that criminal or civil laws have been violated, although sometimes that is the case. The primary basis for designation is a suspected financial relationship with the target of a criminal or political enforcement action.

A continuous effort to track the activities of designated persons is crucial to the effectiveness of the SDN system. It involves cooperation among banking officials and law enforcement officers in many countries, especially the major financial centers. An accurate and up-to-date list of designated individuals and companies can be a valuable instrument in combating international financial crimes and applying effective financial sanctions.

In the 1990s, the UN Security Council acquired the capacity to develop lists of designated individuals. In the Angola and Afghanistan cases, the Security Council imposed financial sanctions on individuals as well as governments, and the Secretariat published lists of designated individuals. This significant trend reflected a growing ability to freeze the assets of individuals as well as governments.

Once a list of designated individuals is available, banks and other financial institutions can utilize special screening software to detect illegal or prohibited financial transactions. Name recognition software has been used in U.S. banks since the 1980s. It allows banking officials to identify and interdict transactions by targeted individuals or companies. All financial transfers are processed through name recognition programs, and any transactions associated with designated individuals or entities are automatically selected for further analysis and possible criminal enforcement action. To date, the use of screening software is largely confined to the United States. Greater use of such software by financial institutions in other countries would help to strengthen multilateral sanctions enforcement.

Effective enforcement also requires locating the designated assets. Where are the targeted assets, and how can they be traced and interdicted? Answering these questions can be enormously difficult. The tradition of bank secrecy and the easy availability of offshore financial havens provide ample opportunities for hiding assets. The UN, lacking independent intelligence or enforcement capabilities, is handicapped in this regard. In the case of Angola, the Security Council created an investigative panel and a monitoring mechanism to help uncover

UNITA's financial assets. UN investigative panels can perform a useful service in "naming and shaming" those who violate sanctions, but their utility in locating assets has been limited to date.

An innovative proposal for strengthening the UN's ability to identify and trace assets was developed at the financial sanctions simulation sponsored by the Watson Institute. The proposal called for retrospective reporting. States would be required to report to the Security Council on all financial transactions carried out for or on behalf of those targeted by sanctions.[36] Information on the recent financial activity of targeted governments and individuals would offer clues on evasion methods and the likely locations of transferred targeted funds, helping the Security Council and any investigative panels it might establish to trace assets, detect sanctions violations, and develop appropriate interdiction strategies. A requirement for the retrospective reporting of all recent financial transactions with targeted governments and individuals could be a useful addition to SCRs that impose financial sanctions.

Unlike general trade embargoes, which require broad multinational participation, financial sanctions can succeed with the cooperation of a smaller number of countries. The success of financial sanctions depends primarily on the cooperation of the world's most important financial centers in the United States, Europe, and Japan. The support and participation of the member countries of the Organization for Economic Cooperation and Development (OECD) may be sufficient in most cases to ensure the effectiveness of financial sanctions. The approval of the UN Security Council is still important to achieve political legitimacy and support, but the implementation and enforcement of financial sanctions depend on the OECD countries. The greater the cooperation among these countries, the more effective the enforcement of UN financial sanctions.

These international enforcement efforts could be strengthened through greater harmonization of the domestic legislative and administrative systems of OECD countries. The Interlaken seminars emphasized the importance of common legal definitions and administrative procedures for effective sanctions enforcement. Banking institutions in the United States, Japan, and Europe have differing legislative mandates, legal definitions, and administrative procedures for implementing sanctions. Following the Interlaken seminars, progress has been made in narrowing these differences. Researchers at the Watson Institute surveyed the legal systems of the six most important financial centers—the United States, the United Kingdom, France, Germany, Switzerland, and Japan—and drafted a model law identifying the principal measures needed to harmonize and strengthen domestic legal and administrative systems.[37] Within the EU, steps have already been taken toward creating more uniform standards for sanctions enforcement. These efforts will enhance cooperation and improve sanctions effectiveness.

## The Battle Against Money Laundering

Important lessons for improving financial sanctions can be gleaned from international efforts to combat money laundering. The problem of drug trafficking is huge. Michel Camdessus, managing director of the International Monetary Fund, estimated in 1998 that drug trafficking and the accompanying money laundering account for 2 to 5 percent of global gross domestic product, equivalent to between $800 billion and $2 trillion per year.[38] Financial crime and money laundering are major threats to financial integrity and social stability.

Since the 1980s, the international community has devoted substantial effort to combating financial crime. In 1988, the UN adopted the Vienna Convention Against Illicit Traffic in Narcotic Drugs and Psychotropic Substances, thereby criminalizing the laundering of profits from narcotics trafficking.[39] At the Group of Seven/Group of Eight (G7/G8) economic summits, world leaders have approved a number of programs designed to strengthen international efforts against money laundering. One of the most important was the Financial Action Task Force (FATF) created at the Paris summit in 1989. FATF has become a leading force in combating money laundering. Comprising experts from government, law enforcement, and bank regulation, FATF has worked to strengthen the legal and administrative capacity of its twenty-nine member countries.[40] At the G7 summit in Okinawa in July 2000, world leaders expanded the mandate of FATF by authorizing it to take on the task of improving financial regulation in nonmember countries.[41] These continuing efforts to enhance international cooperation against money laundering augur well for the prospects of enhancing the effectiveness of multilateral financial sanctions. Many of the enforcement tools used in the battle against money laundering can be applied to enforcing UN financial sanctions.

Complementing the work of FATF is the Financial Crimes Enforcement Network (FinCEN), established by the United States in 1990 to assist in the enforcement of anti-money-laundering laws. With a staff of more than 160, FinCEN has become the U.S. Treasury Department's leading agency for collecting intelligence data and enhancing law enforcement efforts against financial crime. It has assisted dozens of countries in developing financial intelligence units and has also provided technical assistance for strengthening anti-money-laundering laws and institutions.[42] More than fifty financial intelligence units now exist in different countries, and they have formed their own association, the Egmont Group, to enhance cooperation in intelligence gathering and law enforcement against financial crimes.[43]

The EU has made a significant commitment to controlling money laundering. A 1991 *Directive on the Prevention of the Use of the Financial System for the Purposes of Money Laundering* required all EU banking institutions to report suspicious transactions and take measures to control and prevent illegal financial activity.[44] In Latin America as well, countries have strengthened efforts to criminalize money laundering. The 1995 Summit of the Americas Ministerial Conference on Money Laundering committed the thirty-four participating governments to enact laws against money laundering, modify bank secrecy laws, and establish mechanisms for strengthening law enforcement efforts.[45] These and other efforts to combat money laundering have improved the means available for enforcing targeted financial sanctions.

One of the most important battles in the war against financial crime is the campaign to rein in offshore financial havens. The existence of unregulated financial centers is a major obstacle to the enforcement of financial sanctions and laws against money laundering. In the United States and other OECD countries, banks generally comply with government regulations and oversight laws. In jurisdictions such as the Cayman Islands, the Bahamas, and Cyprus, however, banks are intentionally structured to avoid regulation and legal scrutiny. These offshore centers operate as havens not only for avoiding or minimizing taxes but for sheltering illicit profits. The centers are a refuge for political despots seeking to avoid international sanctions. The scale of the offshore banking business is vast. The U.S. government estimated in 1996 that 20 percent of the world's mutual funds are channeled through offshore centers.[46] Grand Cayman Island is home to a huge offshore banking industry, serving as the address of record for more than 26,000 companies.[47] Its banking assets exceed $670 billion.[48]

The problem of offshore banking centers has grown in recent years, owing to globalization and advances in electronic banking technology. In the 1990s, a number of Pacific Island nations established rogue banking operations. Nauru, Niue, and Vanuatu became favored addresses for those seeking to avoid financial scrutiny. Much of the capital spirited out of Russia in recent years, for example, went to accounts in Nauru.[49]

Similar financial havens have emerged on small Caribbean islands, including Dominica, Antigua and Barbuda, and Barbados. Gaining greater international control over these offshore financial centers is crucial to curbing international money laundering and making UN financial sanctions more effective.

It may be easy for a criminal or political pariah to move assets to offshore financial havens, but attempting to use those assets in the future can be difficult. Funds that are stashed away in Pacific or Caribbean islands eventually have to reenter the financial mainstream if they are to have maximum use value. The most important commodities and manufactured goods are traded in hard currency, often in dollars. These transactions are cleared through banks in New York and other major financial centers, exposing them to regulation and potential interdiction. Attempting to use sheltered assets thus involves risk. This fact suggests that, although financial sanctions may not be able to prevent the flight of assets to safe havens, they may nonetheless prevent or make more difficult the use of those assets in the future.[50]

Offshore financial havens have come under greater pressure in recent years to ease bank secrecy and cooperate with international law enforcement. The expansion of the mandate of FATF is a part of this process. The Offshore Group of Banking Supervisors has agreed to work with FATF in evaluating the compliance of its members with the Vienna Convention and laws against drug money laundering. In June 2000 FATF issued a report identifying more than two dozen jurisdictions that were either "non-cooperative" or "deficient" in bank regulation practices.[51] The finance ministers of the G7 countries subsequently advised their domestic financial institutions to be wary of transactions with banks in these jurisdictions. They also warned that enforcement measures might be forthcoming if the listed jurisdictions did not cooperate with international efforts to prevent financial crime.[52]

To strengthen international law enforcement against financial crime, the United States has signed a series of mutual legal assistance treaties with dozens of countries. These bilateral agreements permit the exchange of information and criminal evidence in money laundering and assets forfeiture cases. Treaties have been negotiated with the Cayman Islands, Panama, and other countries that host offshore financial institutions. These agreements have proved effective in criminal investigations of money laundering.[53]

Some nations that host unregulated financial centers are also recipients of substantial bilateral and multilateral economic assistance. Conditioning such aid on compliance with international financial regulations and enforcement of Security Council sanctions could encourage greater cooperation. Compliance with Security Council sanctions and money-laundering controls could be incorporated into the World Bank's "good governance" framework as a criterion for receiving loans and grants. At their July 2000 summit, the G7 finance ministers indicated their support for such an approach. The final statement of the Okinawa summit declared that

> the G-7 are willing . . . to take measures against [uncooperative jurisdictions,] including the possibility to condition or restrict financial transactions with those jurisdictions and to condition or restrict support from international financial institutions to them.[54]

Doing so could be another important step toward regulating offshore financial centers and improving the effectiveness of Security Council financial sanctions.

## Conclusion

In many ways, UN targeted financial sanctions now stand at a crossroads. Beginning with the bottom-up global sanctions on South Africa and developing further refinements in multiple cases, the UN now has gained sufficient experience that it can make sound judgments about the conditions for the success of targeted financial sanctions. The Interlaken process and the Watson Institute manual for design and implementation provide states and banks useful templates and decisionmaking tools for achieving effectiveness in a timely manner.[55] This technical assistance will prove invaluable as targeted financial measures are crafted and blended into the new counterterrorism program authorized in SCR 1373.

U.S. leadership in financial sanctions has been crucial in the past decade, and it remains vital if the current efforts at reform are to achieve results. The administration of President George W. Bush initially expressed reservations about multilateral financial regulations, but the mood in Washington changed dramatically on these issues after the attacks on 11 September 2001. The United States encouraged passage of SCR 1373 and mobilized an intensive worldwide campaign to impose financial sanctions on terrorists and those who support them. A continued commitment from the United States and other major financial powers will enable the international community to make further progress in the struggle to prevent financial crime and to apply these sanctions in the search for security against international terror networks.

# Notes

1. David A. Andelman, "The Drug Money Maze," *Foreign Affairs* 73, no. 46 (July–August 1994): 108.

2. Jennifer Davis, "Sanctions and Apartheid: The Economic Challenge to Discrimination," in David Cortright and George A. Lopez, eds., *Economic Sanctions: Panacea or Peacebuilding in a Post–Cold War World?* (Boulder, Colo.: Westview Press, 1995), 173–184.

3. Ibid., 178.

4. This strategy of citizen-driven change and challenge to the apartheid system is profiled in Janice Love, *The U.S. Anti-Apartheid Movement: Local Activism in Global Politics* (New York: Praeger, 1985).

5. Not included in this list are any financial sanctions against the Revolutionary United Front (RUF) in Sierra Leone or Liberia. The Security Council sanctions against Sierra Leone, SCR 1171 (1998) and SCR 1306 (2000), imposed an arms embargo, a travel ban, and a diamond embargo on the RUF but made no mention of any financial restrictions. The sanctions against Liberia, SCR 1343 (2001), included an arms embargo, a travel ban, and a diamond embargo but not an assets freeze. However, par. 2(d) of SCR 1343 demanded that the Liberian government "freeze funds or financial resources that are made available by its nationals or within its territory . . . for the benefit of the RUF." Because this was not an obligation on UN member states, it is not listed as an example of Security Council financial sanctions.

6. United Nations Security Council, *Security Council Resolution 661 (1990)*, S/RES/661, New York, 6 August 1990, par. 4.

7. U.S. News and World Report, *Triumph Without Victory: The History of the Persian Gulf War* (New York: Random House, 1992), 38–39.

8. Sarah Graham-Brown, *Sanctioning Saddam: The Politics of Intervention in Iraq* (London: I. B. Taurus, 1999), 77.

9. In June 2000, *Forbes* magazine estimated Saddam Hussein's net worth to be approximately $7 billion. Arik Hesseldahl, "How Dictators Manage Their Billions," *Forbes Magazine*, 22 June 2000, <www.forbes.com/2000/06/22/feat.html> (30 March 2001).

10. United Nations Security Council, *Security Council Resolution 820 (1993)*, S/RES/820, New York, 17 April 1993, par. 21.

11. Stephen Engelberg, "Conflict in the Balkans: UN Steps Said to Dry up Serbs' Cash," *New York Times,* 13 May 1993, A8.

12. United Nations Security Council, *Security Council Resolution 883 (1993)*, S/RES/883, New York, 11 November 1993, pars. 3–4.

13. United Nations Security Council, *Security Council Resolution 917 (1994)*, S/RES/917, New York, 6 May 1994, pars. 3–4.

14. Paul Richter, "Clinton Freezes U.S. Assets of Haitian Leaders," *Los Angeles Times,* 19 October 1993, A1.

15. United Nations Security Council, *Security Council Resolution 1173 (1998)*, S/RES/1173, New York, 12 June 1998, par. 11.

16. United Nations Security Council, *Final Report of the Monitoring Mechanism on Angola Sanctions*, S/2000/1225, New York, 21 December 2000, annex A.

17. United Nations Security Council, *Supplementary Report of the Monitoring Mechanism on Sanctions Against UNITA*, S/2001/966, New York, 12 October 2001, par. 223.

18. United Nations Security Council, *Final Report of the Monitoring Mechanism on Angola Sanctions,* S/2000/1225, par. 214.

19. Ibid., section Q, par. 217.

20. "UN Asks U.S. Firm to Follow the Money in Angola," Reuters, 18 April 2001.

21. Anthonius W. de Vries, "European Union Sanctions Against the Federal Republic of Yugoslavia from 1998 to 2000: A Special Exercise in Targeting," in David Cortright and George A. Lopez, eds., *Smart Sanctions: Targeting Economic Statecraft* (Lanham, Md.: Rowman and Littlefield, 2002).

22. Robert Black and Neil King Jr., "Milosevic's Cronies Struggle for Removal from West's Black List," *Wall Street Journal,* 1 October 1999, A1, A6.

23. United Nations Security Council, *Security Council Resolution 1333 (2000)*, S/RES/1333, New York, 19 December 2000, par. 8(c).

24. A listing of the officials was published in Pakistani newspapers. See "UN Lists Taliban Officials for Freezing Their Assets," *News* (Islamabad), 1 February 2001. The article noted errors in the list and reported that one of the designated officials was deceased.

25. R. Richard Newcomb, "Targeted Financial Sanctions: The U.S. Model," paper presented at the Second Expert Seminar on Targeting UN Financial Sanctions, Interlaken, Switzerland, 29–31 March 1999; Swiss Federal Office for Foreign Economic Affairs, "Smart Sanctions Conference: Interlaken II Papers," <www.smartsanctions.ch/int2_papers.htm> (26 July 2001).

26. The papers and report from the Interlaken seminars are available at the Swiss Federal Office for Foreign Economic Affairs, <www.smartsanctions.ch/> (26 July 2001).

27. See Naval War College, *A Report of the Proceedings of the Targeted Financial Sanctions Simulation*, Newport, R.I., 11–13 May 2000, sponsored by the Watson Institute for International Studies at Brown University and the Decision Strategies Department of the Center for Naval Warfare Studies of the U.S. Naval War College, DSD Report, 01-2.

28. Swiss Confederation, United Nations Secretariat, and Watson Institute for International Studies at Brown University, *Targeted Financial Sanctions: A Manual for Design and Implementation—Contributions from the Interlaken Process* (Providence, R.I.: Thomas J. Watson Jr. Institute for International Studies, 2001).

29. Stephen Kobrin, "Electronic Cash and the End of National Markets," *Foreign Policy* (Summer 1997): 75.

30. Naval War College, *Report of the Proceedings of the Targeted Financial Sanctions Simulation*, 01-2, 16.

31. Remarks of Jeremy P. Carver, meeting of the Security Council Working Group on Sanctions, United Nations, New York, 17–18 August 2000.

32. Beth Simmons, "International Efforts Against Money Laundering," in Dinah Shelton, ed., *Commitment and Compliance: The Role of Nonbinding Norms*

*in the International Legal System* (Oxford: Oxford University Press, 2000), 245, 247.

33. Natalie Reid et al., "Targeted Financial Sanctions: Harmonizing National Legislation and Regulatory Practices," in Cortright and Lopez, *Smart Sanctions: Targeting Economic Statecraft.*

34. Newcomb, "Targeted Financial Sanctions: The U.S. Model."

35. R. Richard Newcomb, "Targeting Financial Sanctions," paper presented at the First Expert Seminar on Targeting UN Financial Sanctions, Interlaken, Switzerland, 17–19 March 1998; Swiss Federal Office for Foreign Economic Affairs, "Smart Sanctions Conference: Interlaken I Papers," <http://www.smart-sanctions.ch/int1_papers.htm> (26 July 2001).

36. Naval War College, *Report of the Proceedings of the Targeted Financial Sanctions Simulation,* 01-2, 23.

37. Reid et al., "Targeted Financial Sanctions."

38. William F. Wechsler, "Follow the Money," *Foreign Affairs* 80, no. 4 (July–August 2001): 45.

39. Simmons, "International Efforts Against Money Laundering," 249.

40. Ibid., 255–257.

41. Wechsler, "Follow the Money," 50–51.

42. U.S. General Accounting Office, *Money-laundering: FinCEN's Law Enforcement, Support, Regulatory and International Roles,* T-GGD-98-83 (Washington, D.C.: U.S. Government Printing Office, 1 April 1998).

43. Remarks of Stanley E. Morris, former director of FinCEN, at the symposium "Teamwork in Conflict Prevention: Implementing Preventive Strategies," sponsored by the Carnegie Commission for Preventing Deadly Conflict, Washington, D.C., 22–24 November 1998.

44. Simmons, "International Efforts Against Money Laundering," 259.

45. Ibid., 260.

46. U.S. Department of State, Bureau for International Narcotics and Law Enforcement Affairs, *International Narcotics Control Strategy Report, 1996* (Washington, D.C.: U.S. Government Printing Office, March 1997), 17.

47. Ibid.; see also Robert M. Morganthau, "On the Trail of Global Capital," *New York Times,* 9 November 1998, A29.

48. Wechsler, "Follow the Money," 42.

49. Ibid., 48.

50. Naval War College, *Report of the Proceedings of the Targeted Financial Sanctions Simulation,* 01-2, 27.

51. Wechsler, "Follow the Money," 50.

52. Ibid., 51.

53. U.S. Department of State, Bureau for International Narcotics and Law Enforcement Affairs, *International Narcotics Control Strategy Report, 1997* (Washington, D.C.: U.S. Government Printing Office, March 1998), 15.

54. *G-7 Statement,* G-7 Summit, Okinawa, Japan, 21 July 2000, available at University of Toronto Library, "G-8 Information Center," <www.g7.utoronto.ca/g7/summit/2000okinawa/statement.htm> (2 July 2001).

55. Swiss Confederation, United Nations Secretariat, and Watson Institute, *Targeted Financial Sanctions.*

# 7

## Carrots and Sticks for Controlling Terrorism

In the unfolding campaign against international terrorism, economic sanctions and incentives are playing a significant, perhaps decisive, role. Economic statecraft was mobilized quickly as an important part of the U.S. and international response to the 11 September 2001 attacks against the World Trade Center and the Pentagon.[1] The United States and the United Nations have employed both carrots and sticks, lifting sanctions and offering economic assistance to certain nations to encourage their cooperation in counterterrorism efforts while applying targeted financial sanctions against individuals and organizations associated with terrorist activities.

Immediately after the attacks, the United States lifted sanctions on Pakistan that had been imposed in response to that country's testing of nuclear weapons in 1998. The easing of sanctions was designed to encourage Islamabad's cooperation in pressuring the Taliban in neighboring Afghanistan. To keep a balance in its South Asia policy, the White House ended similar sanctions on India. At the United Nations, diplomatic sanctions that had been in place against Sudan since 1996 were lifted in response to Khartoum's sharing of intelligence information with the United States and its reported arrest of thirty people suspected of being associates of Usama bin Laden.

While offering carrots, the United States and the United Nations also applied sticks. In Security Council Resolution (SCR) 1373 (2001), the UN Security Council adopted a groundbreaking resolution ordering countries to impose financial sanctions against persons and entities that commit or abet terrorist acts. As part of the resolution, the Council created the Counter-Terrorism Committee and vested it with authority and resources to carry out broad new antiterrorism mandates. The United States and other countries also acted individually to impose financial sanctions on dozens of individuals and organizations believed to be associated with bin Laden and his al-Qaida network. More than 100 countries reportedly agreed to cooperate in an unprecedented global effort to cut off and trace the financing of bin Laden's terrorist activities.[2] The USA Patriot Act, approved by the U.S. Congress in the wake of 11 September, included sweeping new measures to curtail bank secrecy, regulate money-changing operations, and prohibit U.S. financial institutions from doing business with foreign banks that lack proper regulation and legal supervision. These developments produced an extraordinary upsurge of activity on the sanctions front and reflected the importance decisionmakers have attached to economic sanctions as means of countering terrorism.

In this chapter, we review past uses of sanctions for counterterrorism purposes, analyzing both U.S. unilateral and UN multilateral cases. We complement the analysis in Chapter 6, where we examined the increased use of targeted sanctions to suppress the financing of terrorism, by reviewing the unilateral initiatives of the U.S. government and the multilateral efforts of the Security Council. We conclude that sanctions and incentives can indeed help to tame terrorism but that much greater international cooperation and compliance will be needed to realize this objective.

## Lessons from Recent Cases: Sudan and Libya

The United States has employed economic sanctions and incentives frequently in dealing with nations that harbor, aid, or directly sponsor international terrorism. One of the most important sanctions tools available to the U.S. government is the State Department's list of states sponsoring terrorism. Nations placed on the terrorism list are subjected to harsh sanctions. They are denied economic assistance, dual-use technologies, and military-related exports. The United States is required to oppose loans to these countries from the World Bank and other international financial institutions. The designated states are essentially excluded from access to the U.S. economy. The desire to avoid being placed on the list or to be removed once there is a powerful motivator for states to reduce their support for terrorism and to cooperate in international counterterrorism efforts. This list provides important carrot-and-stick leverage for U.S. policymakers.

Nations most recently on the list include Iran, Iraq, Syria, Libya, Cuba, North Korea, and Sudan.[3] Iran has been at the top of the State Department list for years. According to the latest State Department report on patterns of global terrorism, Iran remains the most active state sponsor of terrorism.[4] It was placed on the terrorist list because of its assistance to various organizations, including Hezbollah and Hamas (Lebanon), which have carried out terrorist attacks in Israel and engaged in assassination throughout Europe and the Middle East. In recent years, respected analysts have questioned the policy of unrelenting sanctions toward Iran and have called for a partial easing of economic restrictions as a means of inducing Tehran's cooperation on a range of issues, including the struggle against terrorism.[5] Such concerns became particularly acute in the wake of the 11 September attacks.

Sudan has been subject to unilateral sanctions by the United States and multilateral measures by the UN Security Council. Sudan was added to the State Department terrorism list in August 1993 because of its support for a wide range of terrorist groups, including al-Qaida, Islamic Jihad (Egypt), and Hamas. Sudan also allowed terrorist training camps to operate on its soil. An additional concern at the time was the presence in Sudan of the increasingly active but not yet well known wealthy Saudi dissident, Usama bin Laden. In 1997, the Clinton administration issued Executive Order 13067, imposing a general trade embargo and a total freeze on Sudan's assets. The United States objected not only to Khartoum's support for terrorism but its military attacks against rebels in southern Sudan, its human rights violations, and its denial of religious freedom.

The UN Security Council had become involved in 1995, following a failed assassination attempt against Egyptian president Hosni Mubarak during a state visit to Ethiopia in June of that year. The suspects involved were traced to sites in Sudan. In January 1996, the Council adopted SCR 1044, demanding that Khartoum extradite the three suspects and desist from aiding and providing sanctuary for terrorist groups. Three months later, in the face of Sudan's refusal to meet UN demands, the Security Council adopted SCR 1054, imposing diplomatic sanctions. The resolution was adopted on 26 April 1996.[6] Just three weeks later, on 18 May, bin Laden was expelled from the country.[7] Although the UN sanctions were very mild, they seem to have prompted Sudan's request that bin Laden leave the country.

A few months later, in August 1996, the Council approved SCR 1070, establishing a ban on international flights to Sudan. The United States and other Council members were dissatisfied at Sudan's failure to comply fully with UN demands and wanted to increase the pressure on Khartoum. A ninety-day delay in the implementation of the aviation sanctions was approved to permit the sending of a humanitarian study team to assess the potential impact of the flight ban on Sudan's fragile social situation.[8] The delay was also intended to give time for diplomatic maneuvering to gain Sudanese compliance. Although Sudan did not take further steps toward compliance, the Council chose not to implement the threatened travel sanctions, in part for humanitarian reasons and also because of Egypt's unwillingness to support stronger measures. Nonetheless, the U.S. and UN sanctions had some impact on Khartoum's decision to expel bin Laden from the country.

In the late 1990s, the United States entered into a quiet dialogue with Sudan to explore ways of cooperating on counterterrorism efforts. The discussions produced positive results. By the end of 2000, Sudan had signed a number of the UN conventions for combating terrorism and had closed down the Popular Arab and Islamic Conference, a terrorist front organization. A U.S. counterterrorism team visited the country and verified that Sudan had taken concrete measures to reduce its support for terrorist groups. The U.S. dialogue with Sudan intensified after the terrorist attacks on 11 September. Senior Sudanese intelligence officials met in London with State Department representatives to share information on al-Qaida and other terrorist networks.[9] In response to this general pattern of cooperation, the United States encouraged the Security Council to remove diplomatic sanctions. On 28 September 2001, the Council adopted SCR 1372, officially lifting sanctions. After the vote, Secretary of State Colin Powell praised Sudan for arresting extremists linked to terrorist organizations and for cooperating with the investigation of those responsible for the 11 September attacks.[10] In this instance, the United States and the UN used a reward strategy for responding to Sudanese cooperation and encouraging additional support in the future.

As noted in Chapter 8, Libya was subjected to UN travel sanctions because of its support of terrorism. They constituted the first use of Security Council sanctions to combat international terrorism.[11] The Security Council imposed SCR 748 in March 1992, demanding that the two suspects wanted for the bombing of Pan Am flight 103 over Lockerbie, Scotland, and Union des Transports Aériens (UTA) flight 772 over Niger be handed over for trial. The Council also demanded that the Libyan regime end its support for and harboring of international terrorist organizations. To back up its demand, the Council banned all flights to and from Libya. In November 1993, in the face of Libyan defiance of UN demands, the Council broadened UN sanctions to include a ban on oil equipment and all aviation-related services.

The sanctions against Libya did not lock down the entire economy. Selective measures were imposed to isolate Libya from the rest of the world community, reduce its ability to support terrorism, and impose modest but targeted economic hardships on the country. The aviation sanctions were effective in halting nearly all international flights to the country. The sanctions caused some economic losses, but their primary impact was diplomatic and symbolic, isolating Libya from the global community and branding it an international pariah. The sting of the sanctions in this regard proved more painful to Libya than some would have estimated.

When sanctions were initially imposed, the Qaddafi regime offered to turn over the terrorist suspects to an international tribunal, but this offer was unacceptable to the Security Council and was rejected. A diplomatic stalemate ensued, which was not broken until August 1998, when the United States and the United Kingdom responded to demands from Arab and North African states to negotiate a compromise settlement. Washington and London offered to hold the trial of the two Libyan suspects under Scottish law in a court in the Netherlands. Libya accepted the deal, although it took months of additional diplomatic wrangling before the suspects were finally delivered to The Hague for trial in April 1999.

When the Security Council suspended the sanctions against Libya, Secretary-General Kofi Annan was asked if the sanctions regime had been effective. He responded:

> I prefer to think it played a role. . . . No country likes to be treated as an outcast and outside the society of nations. . . . I think Libya wanted to get back to the international community. Libya wanted to get on with its economic and social development. And Libya wanted to be able to deal freely with its neighbors and with the rest of the world.[12]

Although the sanctions had only limited economic impact, they provided bargaining leverage that eventually led to a settlement.

The UN sanctions also had a positive effect in restraining Libyan government support for international terrorism. In the years preceding the imposition of sanctions in 1992, the government of Libya was implicated in attacks against Pan Am flight 103 and UTA flight 772. After sanctions were imposed, Libya ceased its terrorist attacks against international aviation. The U.S. State Department's 1996 report on global terrorism stated flatly, "Terrorism by Libya has been sharply reduced by UN sanctions."[13] This assessment was reaffirmed for us in 1999 in interviews at the Central Intelligence Agency and the State Department. It suggests that the UN sanctions were partly effective in reducing Libyan support for international terrorism. The State Department's 2000 report on terrorism confirmed that "Libya continued efforts to mend its international image."[14] It paid compensation to the families of victims of UTA flight 772 and played a high-profile role in negotiating the release of a group of hostages seized in the Philippines by the Abu Sayyaf group, reportedly in exchange for a ransom.

In the fight against global terrorism, the cooperation of Libya, as with Sudan, could be invaluable in securing intelligence about terrorist networks. As part of a larger carrot-and-stick strategy, the United States might begin to ease sanctions on Libya in return for a specific series of cooperative steps, including the signing of UN antiterrorist conventions and active assistance in the hunt for the perpetrators of the 11 September attacks. A strategy of easing coercive pressure could be an effective means of obtaining such cooperation.

## Targeting the Taliban

In the late 1990s, much of the U.S. response to the Taliban regime in Afghanistan was channeled through the UN Security Council. As noted in Chapter 3, the Council imposed targeted financial sanctions, an aviation ban, and an arms embargo against Afghanistan to pressure the Taliban to end its support for international terrorism and turn over Usama bin Laden for trial.

The UN sanctions halted all international flights by Ariana Afghan Airlines, reducing state revenues and isolating the Taliban. It became more difficult for al-Qaida leaders to move resources to and from Afghanistan. The freeze on financial assets netted considerable resources. According to a September 2001 Library of Congress report, the United States impounded $254 million in Taliban assets.[15] British chancellor of the exchequer Gordon Brown reported the capture of an additional $88 million of Taliban funds in British banks.[16] These were considerable sums for such an impoverished country. The financial sanctions also served as an impediment to the rehabilitation of Afghanistan's decrepit and barely functional banking system. They were an obstacle to the country's ability to attract investment, acquire foreign exchange, and develop its economy.

Following the overthrow of the Taliban and the installation of a new government in Kabul in December 2001, the United States, the United Kingdom, and other governments released Afghan government and Ariana Afghan Airlines funds. The U.S. government released $217 million in gold and assets, and the British government released $79 million in assets.[17] These funds, combined with pledges of more than $5 billion in financial support from various donor countries, were provided in recognition of the overthrow of the Taliban regime and as an essential step toward rebuilding the shattered Afghan economy and infrastructure.

## Carrots as Well as Sticks

The counterterrorism strategy in Afghanistan has included inducements as well as sanctions. Even before the 11 September attacks and subsequent military campaign against the Taliban, international leaders recognized the need for economic inducements to rebuild the country. In an April 2001 report to the Security Council, Secretary-General Annan urged "the development of proposals, including incentives, that will encourage an internal dynamic" toward resolution of the conflict in Afghanistan.[18] In October 2001, U.S. secretary of state Colin Powell testified before the House of Representatives that the strategy for creating a more cooperative regime in Afghanistan should include a smaller version of the post–World War II Marshall Plan.[19] The United Kingdom proposed a five- to ten-year economic reconstruction program for Afghanistan costing $40 billion.[20] U.S. national security adviser Condoleezza Rice pledged a substantial U.S. effort to aid "the reconstruction of Afghanistan."[21] Private research groups made similar recommendations for a large-scale program of institution building, development, and economic aid.[22] Such support would be conditional on the Afghani government's cooperation with U.S. and UN demands to bring terrorist suspects to justice and close terrorist support bases.

Many observers have also urged an economic incentives package for Pakistan, which has incurred major political and economic costs for its cooperation with U.S.-led antiterrorism efforts. In September 2001, the United States encouraged the International Monetary Fund to proceed with a sizable loan package for Islamabad to cushion the impact of severing political and economic links with Afghanistan. The United States adopted measures of its own, including substantial debt relief.[23]

One of the most important incentives initiatives the United States and other nations could take to solidify international cooperation and address the sources of terrorist violence would be an international plan for the development of impoverished Middle Eastern and central Asian nations. In remarks before the U.S. Commission on National Security in the Twenty-First Century, former speaker of the House Newt Gingrich urged a major economic development effort for the entire region. "For Muslims at large," Gingrich declared, "we should aggressively be reaching out economically . . . to create a better future."[24] Just as the United States helped to rebuild Japan and Germany after World War II, Gingrich argued, the United States should seek to work with "non-fanatics" in the Islamic world to overcome the poverty and despair that feed terrorism. A key element of a regional development plan would be debt relief, as the Group of 7 leaders emphasized at the Genoa summit in July 2001. Including debt relief in a development plan for the region would provide significant help for local economies and demonstrate a genuine commitment from the United States and other Western nations to the well-being of Islamic societies.

British chancellor of the exchequer Gordon Brown called for wealthy countries to increase international development funds by $50 billion a year, to fulfill the pledge made by world leaders at the Millennium Summit in 2000 for halving the world's poverty rate over the next fifteen years. Brown argued that "national safety and global reconstruction are inextricably linked" and that advancing social justice is necessary to achieve global security.[25] A large-scale economic development effort by the Security Council, international financial institutions, the United States, and other major financial powers would constitute a powerful inducement for participation in the antiterrorism coalition. Debt relief and other forms of economic development assistance would depend on the recipient states cooperating fully with global antiterrorism efforts, including the enforcement of sanctions and financial restrictions on terrorist networks and states that support them. A multilateral initiative that included carrots as well as sticks would greatly enhance the legitimacy of the antiterrorism cause, especially in Arab and Islamic nations, and strengthen the commitment to prevent terrorist attacks in the future.

## Suppressing Terrorist Finances

Terrorists need money to carry out their murderous business. Such funding pays for weapons, travel, training, housing, and benefits for the families of suicide terrorists. Estimates of the total cost of the 11 September 2001 attacks against New York and Washington, D.C., range from as little as $200,000 to more than $1 million.[26] U.S. officials traced more than $325,000 that was transferred to the 11 September hijackers, mostly from accounts in the United Arab Emirates.[27] This relatively small sum represents only the tip of a larger financial iceberg. According to a September 2001 Library of Congress report, the al-Qaida network consists of some 3,000 militants scattered among more than thirty countries.[28] This suggests an annual budget for the bin Laden network alone of tens of millions of dollars. Add to this the budgets of associated organizations, and the annual cost of global terrorism reaches hundreds of millions of dollars. Eliminating this financial base is crucial to reducing the terrorist capacity and threat. Financial sanctions are a vital tool in this effort.

The United Nations recognized the importance of curtailing the funding of terrorism when it approved the International Convention for the Suppression of the Financing of Terrorism in 1999. Building upon previous UN resolutions and agreements, the convention established a comprehensive set of international obligations to prevent the financing of terror and to prosecute those who commit or abet terrorist acts. As of September 2001, thirty-five nations had signed the convention, although only three completed the ratification process. Since the attacks against New York and Washington, D.C., support for the agreement has increased, and most nations are now expected to sign and ratify the document.

Under the terms of the convention, states are required to establish laws criminalizing all forms of involvement in or support for terrorism. States are directed to identify, detect, and freeze any funds used or allocated for the purpose of committing terrorist acts and are encouraged to use the funds derived from such forfeitures to compensate the victims of terrorist attacks or their families. Governments are also obligated to apprehend terrorist suspects and present them for prosecution and, if appropriate, extradition. They must assist one another in the criminal investigation and prosecution of terrorist acts, and they may not refuse such mutual intelligence and legal assistance on the grounds of financial confidentiality.

The convention effectively bans the practice of bank secrecy. Governments must adopt domestic legislation prohibiting the opening of accounts in which the holders or beneficiaries are unidentified or unidentifiable. Financial institutions must verify the legal existence of customers and maintain records of all transactions.[29] Governments must license money-transmitting agencies and establish measures for monitoring international financial transactions. As of September 2001, thirty-five nations had signed the convention. If implemented, these provisions would strike a powerful blow at the financing of international terror. With the adoption of SCR 1373, many of the provisions of the convention became mandatory for all states, whether or not they had ratified the convention. The operative paragraphs of SCR 1373 were lifted directly from the text of the convention.

## Toward Financial Transparency

In the United States and other major financial centers, including Switzerland, banks are no longer allowed to offer complete anonymity to clients. Government authorities with proper judicial warrants are permitted to scrutinize accounts if criminal activity is suspected. But in many parts of the world, including the Middle East, financial institutions remain closed to regulatory scrutiny and judicial inquiry. A related problem is the presence of unregulated offshore financial centers in places like Nauru in the Pacific or the Cayman Islands in the Caribbean. Terrorists and money launderers use these havens and the secret accounts they offer to hide their criminal activities.

As noted in Chapter 6, major efforts are under way to crack down on offshore financial havens. The Financial Action Task Force (FATF), based at the Organization for Economic Development (OECD) in Paris, has identified more than a dozen jurisdictions that have refused to cooperate with anti-money-laundering efforts.[30] They are referred to as noncooperative countries and territories (NCCTs). As of January 2002, the NCCT list comprised nineteen countries, including Indonesia, Egypt, Israel, Nauru, Russia, and Ukraine.[31] Like the State Department's list of states sponsoring terrorism, the FATF list of noncooperative countries and territories has the potential to serve as an effective tool for influencing the policies of designated jurisdictions. The use of financial carrots and sticks would add weight to the NCCTs list and help to strengthen financial compliance. Jurisdictions that comply with tightened financial controls would receive assistance from international financial institutions and creditor nations; those that refuse to cooperate with disclosure rules would be excluded from these benefits. The FATF has considered the imposition of countermeasures on noncooperative states, including limiting financial transactions with those countries.[32]

The United States is seeking to end the practice of bank secrecy by barring banks that permit anonymous accounts from having access to U.S. financial markets. The U.S. Congress has passed legislation requiring foreign banks that operate in the United States to disclose the identity of each customer and to provide information on the beneficial ownership of every account opened or maintained in the United States.[33] The secretary of the Treasury would have the authority to designate a specific foreign jurisdiction or financial institution as a "primary money-laundering concern" and to bar or limit its access to U.S. markets. Among the criteria the secretary would apply for determining whether a country qualified as a primary money-laundering concern would be the presence of a mutual legal assistance treaty between that jurisdiction and the United States. Countries without such treaties would find it more difficult to operate in U.S. financial markets.

The new U.S. legislation bans so-called shell banks that have no physical presence in any country. It allows the Treasury Department to place limits on correspondent or pay-through accounts.[34] Foreign banks use these accounts for conducting business in the United States. They provide means by which a secret depositor in such banks can gain access to the U.S. market. Under the new legislation, the Treasury Department can prohibit correspondent accounts unless the bank in question complies with disclosure and reporting requirements.

The new U.S. laws also place limits on money-transmitting businesses. The International Convention for the Suppression of the Financing of Terrorism mandates the regulation of these operations as well. Of special concern is the informal *hawala* system widely employed in South Asia.[35] Under this system, cooperating brokers in separate countries transfer money from one currency to another without paying taxes or bribes and without bookkeeping. A broker in Pakistan asked to transfer $100,000 worth of rupees will contact a counterpart in the United States, perhaps through a coded message over the Internet, who will pay the equivalent sum in dollars to the designated recipient. No permanent records are kept. It is estimated that $2–5 billion is transferred through the *hawala* system annually in Pakistan, more than the amount of foreign transfers through the official banking system.[36] Although *hawalas* are illegal in Pakistan, as in most countries, they have eluded law enforcement efforts. New regulations in the United States require the registration of all money services businesses that engage in check cashing and currency exchange or transmittal. Such firms are now required to register in the state in which they operate and to maintain records of all financial transactions. Similar requirements in other countries would begin to place limits on the use of such brokers for the financing of terrorism and other criminal activities.

Because *hawala* brokers often operate informally, innovative efforts in the areas of immigration, commerce, and aviation will be needed to enforce such registration and licensing requirements. Educational efforts will be needed to explain the importance of regulating *hawala* operations as part of international efforts to prevent terrorist attacks and to crack down on money laundering. Incentives might be provided for brokers to register and legalize their operations. Exemptions from registration fees and taxes might be offered for those who come forward during an initial registration period.

## The Counter-Terrorism Committee

The Security Council took strong action to crack down on international terrorism when it approved SCR 1373. Adopted just two weeks after the 11 September attacks, the counterterrorism resolution was the most sweeping sanctions measure ever adopted by the Security Council. It imposed worldwide financial sanctions, travel restrictions, and military sanctions on terrorists and those who support them.[37] It required every country in the world to freeze the financial assets of terrorists and their supporters and ordered states to deny safe haven to terrorists and prevent the use of their territory for terrorist activities. SCR 1373 required countries to prevent the movement of terrorists by means of effective border control and restrictions on the issuance of travel documents. It mandated measures to prevent recruitment by or the supply of weapons to terrorist groups. The terms of the resolution are summarized in Table 7.1.

Recognizing the need for a concerted effort to implement these far-reaching mandates, the Security Council created a special committee to monitor compliance and provide assistance to states in need of technical expertise. The new body, called the Counter-Terrorism Committee, was not just another sanctions committee. It was a special body that received priority attention and resources. It was chaired by Sir Jeremy Greenstock, permanent representative of the United Kingdom to the United Nations, one of the Security Council's most dynamic leaders. Vice chairs of the committee included the Council's senior diplomat, Sergey Lavrov, permanent representative of the Russian Federation to the United Nations, along with Ambassador Alfonso Valdivieso of Colombia and Ambassador Anund Jagdish Koonjul of Mauritius. To demonstrate the importance of the effort, the Counter-Terrorism Committee met initially at the ambassadorial level rather than among lower-level officials. Staff support and technical experts were assigned to the committee to facilitate its work. The committee's initial request for states to report on their efforts to implement SCR 1373 produced an overwhelmingly positive response. As of March 2002, more than 135

**Table 7.1 Counterterrorism Measures Contained in Resolution 1373 (28 September 2001)**

**Mandatory Obligations**

*Financial Sanctions*

Criminalize the willful provision or collection of funds for conducting terrorist acts;

Freeze the funds and other economic resources of persons or entities participating in or facilitating terrorism;

Prohibit persons or entities from making available funds and economic resources for purposes related to the commission of terrorist acts.

*Territorial Control*

Deny safe haven to those who finance, plan, support, or commit terrorist acts;

Prevent those who facilitate or commit terrorist acts from using national territory.

*Travel Sanctions*

Employ effective controls on borders and the issuance of travel documents to prevent the movement of terrorists.

*Cooperative Criminal Prosecution*

Ensure that persons who participate in or support terrorist acts are brought to justice and that terrorist acts are defined as serious criminal offenses in domestic law;

Afford other states the greatest measure of assistance in connection with criminal investigations;

Provide early warning of possible terrorist acts by exchange of information with other states.

*Military Sanctions*

Suppress recruitment by terrorist groups and eliminate the supply of weapons to terrorists.

**Recommended Actions**

Intensify and facilitate the exchange of information on the movement of terrorists, the falsification of travel documents, trafficking in arms and explosives, the use of communications technologies by terrorists, and the threat posed by the possession of weapons of mass destruction;

Become parties to international conventions against terrorism, including the International Convention for the Suppression of the Financing of Terrorism;

Ensure that asylum seekers have not planned, facilitated, or participated in the commission of terrorist acts;

Ensure that refugee status is not abused by those who commit or plan terrorist acts.

**UN Action**

Establish a committee of the Security Council to monitor implementation of the resolution, and call upon all states to report to the committee on the steps taken to implement this resolution.

states had replied to the committee, an unprecedented level of compliance in terms of the number and speed of member state responses.

Not since the adoption of SCR 661 in August 1990 had the United Nations acted so decisively and comprehensively to mobilize international participation. Never before had the Security Council attempted such a massive transformation of the legal capabilities and financial practices of its member states. The success of this groundbreaking effort ultimately depends on the willingness of member states to cooperate. In the early months of 2002, the prospects for compliance seemed favorable.

## Aiding Implementation

As the Security Council Counter-Terrorism Committee began its work, it quickly discovered that many countries lacked the legal or institutional capacity to enforce the measures mandated in SCR 1373. Most nations did not have the legal authority and regulatory means to monitor the transactions of their financial institutions or to freeze financial assets. Even where such capacity did exist, legal and administrative systems varied greatly and impeded coordination.

The Interlaken process sponsored by the government of Switzerland in 1998 and 1999 identified the types of assistance states needed to enhance their capacity for the enforcement of financial sanctions. The Watson Institute for International Studies at Brown University contributed to this effort by convening a series of meetings at the Council on Foreign Relations in New York and at the Naval War College in Rhode Island to explore options for improving the implementation of financial sanctions. The Swiss Confederation, United Nations Secretariat, and the Watson Institute also produced a detailed handbook, *Targeted Financial Sanctions: A Manual for Design and Implementation*, released in October 2001, to assist the Security Council and individual countries in the design and implementation of effective financial sanctions.[38] The manual was published under the aegis of the Swiss government and in cooperation with the UN Secretariat. It contained very detailed guidelines and instructions on the multiple legal and institutional requirements for implementing the financial sanctions mandated in SCR 1373 and other Security Council resolutions. The most helpful instructions provided by the Watson manual were the guidelines for model national legislation. They were relevant to distinct dimensions of sanctions administration, such as assets management and exemptions, and also offered states options for such matters as sharing information and establishing sunset provisions.

## Lessons from the Anti-Money-Laundering Front

Many of the mechanisms needed for the fight against terrorism are the same as those used to prevent money laundering. As documented in Chapter 6, the international community has devoted substantial efforts in recent years to combating illicit financial flows. The FATF has worked among its twenty-nine member countries as well as nonmember countries to strengthen legal authority and administrative capacity for interdicting illegal transactions. The Financial Crimes Enforcement Network, established by the United States, has assisted dozens of countries in strengthening their intelligence-gathering and law enforcement efforts. The mutual legal assistance treaties signed between the United States and dozens of countries have provided a foundation for the exchange of information and criminal evidence in money-laundering and assets forfeiture cases.

At the heart of U.S. efforts to freeze and block illicit financial transactions is the Treasury Department's Office of Foreign Assets Control and its system of interdicting the accounts of specially designated nationals (SDNs). More than 3,000 names were on the SDN list before the 11 September 2001 attacks, including that of Usama bin Laden. Dozens of additional names were added in the weeks following the attacks, including other prominent figures in the al-Qaida network.

As noted in Chapter 6, the SDN operation depends on name recognition software systems. These systems are only as good as the accuracy of the published list upon which they are based. In the case of the 11 September terrorists, there was considerable uncertainty about the reliability of the identities of those involved. The list of nineteen hijackers released by the U.S. Justice Department in September 2001 contained a number of errors and cases of mistaken identity, partly because the terrorists stole identities. In one case, a hijacker used the name of a Saudi citizen living in Riyadh whose passport had been stolen in 1995. Problems also resulted from the proliferation of similar names in Arab countries, where thousands of people may have the same given and family name. A related complication is the varying standard for the English transliteration of Arab names. The same name can be spelled in several different ways. Even the spelling of the bin Laden network varies: al Qaeda in some renderings and al-Qaida in others. Another problem is the use of otherwise legitimate businesses and charitable organizations as fronts for illegal financial transactions. The United States has cast a wide net in its crackdown on the financing of terrorism. Inevitably, some innocent people and organizations have been caught in this process. Inadvertent financial harm to certain individuals and entities may be the unavoidable price of waging an aggressive campaign against the financing of terror. Improved procedures will be needed, however, to provide prompt judicial remedy for individuals and entities mistakenly affected by the freezing of financial assets.

## Conclusion

The UN's fight against terrorism will be long and will require a major commitment of resources by member states. Providing economic assistance and other inducements to enhance international cooperation will cost billions of dollars and will lie outside the direct purview of the Counter-Terrorism Committee. Strengthening the capacity to enforce financial sanctions and other restrictions on terrorists will require vast changes in economic and political practice among many nations. Here the UN can be most helpful. Building sustained political will for the necessary changes in domestic legislation will be difficult. Results will not come quickly, but over time, UN tools of economic statecraft can make a significant contribution to the worldwide campaign against terrorism, much as earlier UN sanctions were vital to dissuading Libya and Sudan from supporting terrorism in the 1990s.

## Notes

1. In this chapter, we depart from the book's exclusive examination of UN sanctions to include U.S. actions as well. As the injured party in the 11 September 2001 attacks, the United States has been a leader in calling for effective financial sanctions in response to these attacks.

2. Joseph Kahn, "Assets Worth $24 Million Frozen as U.S. Goes for More," *New York Times,* 12 October 2001, B5.

3. U.S. Department of State, *Patterns of Global Terrorism—2000* (Washington, D.C.: U.S. Government Printing Office, April 2001).

4. Ibid.

5. Lee H. Hamilton, James Schlesinger, and Brent Scowcroft, *Thinking Beyond the Stalemate in U.S.–Iranian Relations* 1, policy review (Washington, D.C.: Atlantic Council of the United States, May 2001) <www.acus.org/> (9 October 2001).

6. For an account of UN sanctions on Sudan, see David Cortright and George A. Lopez, with Richard W. Conroy, Jaleh Dashti-Gibson, and Julia Wagler, *The Sanctions Decade: Assessing UN Strategies in the 1990s* (Boulder, Colo.: Lynne Rienner Publishers, 2000), 121–126.

7. Barton Gellman, "Sudan's Offer to Arrest Militant Fell Through After Saudis Said No," *Washington Post,* 3 October 2001, A1.

8. The report concluded that the proposed aviation sanctions could exacerbate humanitarian hardships. See United Nations, Department of Humanitarian Affairs, *Note from the Department of Humanitarian Affairs Concerning the Possible Impact of the International Flight Ban Decided in Security Council Resolution 1070 (1996),* New York, 20 February 1997.

9. David Rose, "Spy Blunder: Resentful West Spurned Sudan's Key Terror Files," *The Observer* (London), 30 September 2001, 4.

10. William Douglas, "Weighing the Cost of Coalition: Human Rights Advocates Warn of Concessions," *Newsday,* 30 September 2001, A45.

11. This account draws from Cortright, Lopez, Jaleh Dashti-Gibson, and Richard W. Conroy, "Taming Terrorism: Sanctions Against Libya, Sudan, and Afghanistan," in Cortright and Lopez, *The Sanctions Decade,* 107–121.

12. United Nations, *Transcript of Press Conference by Secretary-General Kofi Annan at Headquarters, 5 April,* SG/SM/6944, New York, 5 April 1999, 3–4.

13. U.S. Department of State, *Patterns of Global Terrorism—1996,* Publication 10535 (Washington, D.C.: U.S. Government Printing Office, 1996).

14. U.S. Department of State, *Patterns of Global Terrorism—2000.*

15. Kenneth Katzman, "Terrorism: Near Eastern Groups and State Sponsors, 2001" (Washington, D.C.: Congressional Research Service report for Congress, 10 September 2001, 12) <www.house.gov/htbin/crsprodget?/rl/RL31119> (9 October 2001).

16. Alan Cowell, "Blair Says He's Seen Proof of bin Laden Role," *New York Times,* 1 October 2001, B4.

17. Joseph Kahn, "Afghanistan Gets Access to Frozen Funds," *New York Times,* 25 January 2002, A10.

18. United Nations General Assembly and Security Council, *The Situation in Afghanistan and Its Implications for International Peace and Security: Report of the Secretary-General,* A/55/907-S/2001/384, New York, 19 April 2001, par. 61.

19. John Diamond, "Powell Sets Terms for a New Regime," *Chicago Tribune,* 26 October 2001, <chicagotribune.com/news/nationworld/chi_0110250279oct25. story> (26 October 2001).

20. Steve Erlanger, "Britain Presses U.S. for 'Nation Building' in Afghanistan," *New York Times,* 12 October 2001, B3.

21. David E. Sanger and Jane Perlez, "Bush Plans to Send $320 Million in Food and Medicine to Afghans," *New York Times,* 5 October 2001, A1.

22. Barnett R. Rubin et al., *Afghanistan: Reconstruction and Peacemaking in a Regional Framework.* KOFF Peacebuilding Reports (Bern, Switzerland: Center for Peacebuilding, June 2001), 33.

23. Joseph Kahn, "U.S. Is Planning an Aid Package for Pakistan Worth Billions," *New York Times,* 27 October 2001, B4.

24. "U.S. Commission on National Security in the Twenty-First Century: After the Attack—A New Urgency" (transcript of the 14 September 2001 General Meeting, Council on Foreign Relations, Washington, D.C., 25 September 2001, 12–13), <www.cfr.org/public/resource.cgi?pub!4049> (9 October 2001).

25. Gordon Brown, "Marshall Plan for the Next 50 Years," *Washington Post,* 17 December 2001, A23.

26. For the lower estimate, see "Banks 'On Notice': President Says Foreign Financial Institutions May Be Punished," *New York Times,* 25 September 2001, A1; for the higher estimate, see U.S. Senate, Committee on Banking, Housing, and Urban Affairs, "Statement of Stuart Eizenstat before the Hearings on the Administration's National Money Laundering Strategy for 2001," 107th Cong., 1st sess., *Congressional Record* (26 September 2001), <banking.senate.gov/01_09hrg/092601/index.htm> (9 October 2001).

27. Dan Eggen and Kathleen Day, "U.S. Probe of Sept. 11 Financing Wraps Up," *Washington Post,* 7 January 2002, A1.

28. Katzman, "Terrorism: Near Eastern Groups and State Sponsors, 2001," 13.

29. United Nations General Assembly, *International Convention for the Suppression of the Financing of Terrorism,* A/RES/54/109, New York, 25 February 2000.

30. William F. Wechsler, "Follow the Money," *Foreign Affairs* 80, no. 4 (July–August 2001): 50.

31. U.S. Department of the Treasury, Financial Crimes Enforcement Network, *SAR Bulletin,* Issue 4, January 2002.

32. James Mackintosh, "Money Laundering Sanctions Plan," *Financial Times,* 2 February 2002, 6.

33. U.S. Senate, Committee on Banking, Housing, and Urban Affairs, "Statement of Stuart Eizenstat."

34. U.S. Senate, Committee on Banking, Housing, and Urban Affairs, "Testimony of the Honorable Carl Levin Before the Hearings on the Administration's National Money Laundering Strategy for 2001," 107th Cong., 1st sess., *Congressional Record* (26 September 2001), <banking.senate.gov/01_09hrg/092601/index.htm> (9 October 2001).

35. Douglas Frantz, "Ancient Secret System Moves Money Globally," *New York Times,* 3 October 2001, B5.

36. Ibid.

37. United Nations Security Council, *Security Council Resolution 1373 (2001),* S/RES/1373, New York, 28 September 2001.

38. Swiss Confederation, United Nations Secretariat, and the Thomas J. Watson Jr. Institute for International Studies at Brown University, *Targeted Financial Sanctions: A Manual for Design and Implementation—Contributions from the Interlaken Process* (Providence, R.I.: Watson Institute, 2001).

# 8

## Beyond Symbolism:
## Travel and Aviation Sanctions

Aviation and travel sanctions have become an increasingly common form of targeted sanctions policy in recent years. Travel and aviation restrictions were first imposed on Iraq in 1990 (Security Council Resolution [SCR] 670) and have since been adopted by the Security Council in numerous cases, as detailed in Table 8.1. Travel sanctions were approved but never enacted against Sudan in SCR 1070 (1996). In addition, the European Union approved travel sanctions against Serbian elites during the Kosovo crisis (1998–2000). In March 2002, UN travel and aviation sanctions were still in place in Angola, Sierra Leone, Iraq, and Liberia, with varying degrees of success in implementation, enforcement, and compliance. Once thought of as only token or symbolic sanctions, travel and aviation sanctions have acquired new relevance and effectiveness.

In this chapter, we examine the implementation and enforcement of current travel and aviation sanctions cases. We highlight the importance of air transportation as a means of supplying weapons to sanctioned rebel movements and emphasize the need for more effective air interdiction efforts to strengthen prohibitions on weapons imports. We review the findings of the various United Nations special investigative panels and summarize the most important recommendations from various sources for the improvement of travel sanctions in the future.

### Travel Bans and Aviation Sanctions

Travel sanctions have become a favored tool of Security Council policy because their scope is much more limited than that of general trade sanctions, with their attendant humanitarian costs. Travel sanctions consist of two distinct types of measures: visa bans, which restrict the travel of designated individuals; and aviation sanctions, which prohibit

Table 8.1    Selected Cases of Travel Sanctions, 1990–2001

| Country | Aviation Sanctions | Travel Bans |
|---|---|---|
| Iraq | Security Council Resolution 670 (S/RES/670) (September 1990) restricted all flights to and from Iraq. | S/RES/1137 (November 1997) denied travel of designated Iraqi officials obstructing UN weapons inspections; never imposed. |
| Libya | S/RES/748 (March 1992) banned all flights to and from Libya and prohibited the supply of aircraft parts and maintenance; S/RES/883 (November 1993) tightened aviation sanctions by prohibiting any commercial transactions with Libyan Arab Airlines. | S/RES/748 also banned travel of designated individuals. |
| Yugoslavia | S/RES/757 (May 1992) banned flights to and from Yugoslavia. | European Union/U.S.–imposed travel ban (1999) on designated individuals, in relation to the Kosovo crisis.[a] |
| Haiti | S/RES/917 (May 1994) banned most flights to and from Haiti, exempting commercial passenger flights. | S/RES/917 also banned the travel of designated members of the military junta and their families and supporters. |
| Sudan | S/RES/1070 (August 1996) denied Sudanese aircraft permission to take off from, land in, or overfly other countries; never implemented. | |
| Angola | S/RES/1127 (August 1997) prohibited all flights by or for UNITA and prohibited landing, takeoff, and overflight rights to any aircraft destined for UNITA-controlled territory. | S/RES/1127 also banned the travel of senior UNITA officials and their families and supporters. |
| Sierra Leone | | S/RES/1132 (October 1997) imposed travel restrictions on members of the military junta and their families; S/RES/1171 (June 1998) maintained the travel ban on the junta and members of the RUF. |

*Table 8.1 continues*

**Table 8.1  Continued**

| Country | Aviation Sanctions | Travel Bans |
|---|---|---|
| Afghanistan | S/RES/1267 (October 1999) denied takeoff and landing rights for any aircraft owned, leased, or operated by the Taliban unless approval was received for humanitarian/ religious purposes; S/RES/ 1333 (December 2000) denied overflight, landing, or takeoff privileges to any aircraft if said aircraft had taken off from or was destined to land at any territory under Taliban control, unless approved in advance. | S/RES/1333 denied travel privileges of all deputy ministers and higher-ranking officials of the Taliban unless travel was for humanitarian, religious, or peacemaking purposes. |
| Liberia | | S/RES/1343 (March 2001) banned the travel of designated individuals associated with armed rebel groups, their family members, and their representatives. |

*Note*: a. All aviation sanctions and travel bans imposed have been through the UN, with the exception of EU/U.S.–imposed travel ban against designated individuals in relation to the Kosovo crisis in 1999.

some or all flights to a targeted regime. The social and economic impact of visa bans is highly concentrated and falls primarily on the targeted decisionmaking elites. The social impact of aviation sanctions is slightly broader but still relatively focused because only a small portion of a population, usually elites, travel abroad. Aviation sanctions result in a loss of revenue for the affected airline company, which is often state-owned, and may cause unemployment and a loss of income for those whose business depends on the targeted airline. Sanctions may cause shortages of certain aviation-dependent supplies, such as cold-storage medicines, and diminish opportunities to travel abroad for medical emergencies or specialized health care. However, the resolutions imposing aviation sanctions usually provide for exemptions in cases of special humanitarian need, religious pilgrimages, and travel to conduct peace negotiations.

Visa bans are frequently imposed in combination with targeted financial sanctions. In the case of Angola, for example, the Security

Council developed a list of targeted officials in the National Union for the Total Independence of Angola (UNITA) and directed that their assets be frozen and their travel prohibited. The European Union applied a similar policy of freezing assets and denying travel for a designated list of Serbian government leaders. This approach allows for the targeting of a specific group of wealthy elites, political officials, military leaders, and their family members. The travel bans, if properly enforced, prohibit the designated individuals from traveling abroad, which in turn limits their ability to conduct business, raise money, and purchase weapons. Visa bans may also deny elites privileges that they covet, such as sending their children abroad to be educated.

Although a highly effective form of targeted pressure in theory, travel sanctions, like other Security Council measures, often suffer from inadequate monitoring and enforcement. The implementation of travel sanctions requires the active participation of member states and depends upon the provision to member states of highly specific information from sanctions committees and the UN Secretariat. A key requirement is an accurate, detailed, and regularly updated list of the targeted individuals, including passport numbers, aliases, and other pertinent information. Only recently has the Secretariat begun to develop the ability to produce such lists. The effectiveness of travel bans also depends on comprehensive international compliance. It takes only one country issuing illegal travel documents to open a huge hole in the sanctions net. Aviation sanctions are much easier to enforce and have generally enjoyed greater compliance. It is relatively easy to monitor a flight ban with proper air surveillance. Moreover, the prohibitions on insurance and support services that usually accompany aviation sanctions raise the costs and risks of unauthorized flights and reduce the likelihood of such violations.

## Haiti: A Limited Test

The travel sanctions in Haiti were imposed relatively late in that crisis, nearly three years after the overthrow of the Aristide government and after more than two years of inconsistent and unevenly applied sanctions by the Organization of American States and the Security Council.[1] SCR 917 (1994) was part of a significant toughening of pressure against Haiti, primarily by the United States, that four months later led to the deployment of U.S. troops and the resignation of the military junta. The travel ban prohibited all Haitian military officers and their families, all current and past coup participants and their families, and all those employed by or acting on behalf of the military junta from traveling to other countries.[2] These measures were intended to restrict the commercial and shopping privileges of political and economic elites while allowing other Haitians to return to the country (primarily from the United States) to help their families.

Although SCR 917 exempted commercial passenger flights, the United States imposed a unilateral ban on such flights, and other air carriers followed suit. The last commercial flight left Haiti on 29 July 1994. The impact of these travel sanctions and of the financial sanctions imposed by the United States at the same time was limited because of their short duration. Although the tougher and more targeted sanctions imposed against Haiti in May and June 1994 had begun to cause real hardships for the military junta and its supporters, these measures were made redundant in September 1994 by the use of military force.

## Libya: A Partial Success

Libya represents the only case in which travel sanctions were the primary form of coercive pressure. It also constitutes a case in which sanctions were at least partially successful in achieving UN objectives, in this case, bringing terrorist suspects to justice. SCR 748 (1992) noted that two indicted Libyans were fugitives from international justice and demanded that they be handed over to international authorities to stand trial for their involvement in the bombing of Pan Am flight 103 over Lockerbie, Scotland, in 1988 and French flight UTA 772 in 1989. These sanctions against the state of Libya were intended as a deterrent against future acts of terrorism and as a means of encouraging the Libyan regime to end its suspected harboring of and support for international terrorist organizations. Both policy objectives were partially achieved, although only after years of often fruitless and frustrating bargaining.

The aviation sanctions against Libya were specifically tailored to the offense: a ban on flights was instituted in response to the bombing of airliners. Adopted in March 1992, SCR 748 imposed aviation sanctions, an arms embargo, diplomatic sanctions, and a ban on the travel of designated Libyans. The resolution called upon Libya to cooperate with criminal investigations, cease all support for international terrorist activities, and compensate the families of the Pan Am and UTA disasters. The sanctions targeted the entire Libyan aviation industry. They banned all flights to and from Libya by requiring that states refuse landing, takeoff, and overflight rights for Libyan-bound aircraft. They required states to close Libyan Arab Airlines offices. They prohibited the supply of aircraft parts, maintenance, engineering, and airworthiness certification for Libyan aircraft. They also banned the payment of insurance claims and the provision of flight insurance for Libyan airlines.

Even before sanctions were adopted, the threat of their imposition had an impact on Libyan authorities, prompting attempts to negotiate a resolution of the dispute. In February 1992, as pressure for sanctions was mounting, Libyan leader Muammar Qaddafi offered to turn over the UTA suspects to a French court and the Lockerbie suspects to an international tribunal. Washington and London insisted that the Lockerbie trials be held in a U.S. or British court. A month later, Qaddafi made another last-minute attempt to stave off sanctions by announcing that the suspects would be turned over to the Arab League. Again the offer was deemed inadequate, and the Security Council proceeded to impose sanctions.

In June 1992, the Libyan government tried to seek a compromise, offering to try the two Lockerbie suspects in a court monitored by either the Arab League or the United Nations. At the same time, the secretary-general of Libya's General People's Congress publicly rejected international terrorism and called for improved relations with Western countries. These initiatives from Libya were indications of the impact of the travel sanctions on the Libyan regime. The United States and the United Kingdom, however, dismissed the Libyan offers and demanded full compliance. The Qaddafi regime refused to make any further concessions.

In November 1993, the Security Council adopted SCR 883, imposing additional sanctions. The resolution tightened the aviation sanctions and banned the import of some oil-transporting equipment. It prohibited the sale or validation by other airlines of Libyan Arab Airlines tickets, banned the sale of equipment and services to maintain or construct aviation infrastructure such as airfields, and proscribed any provision of training services to Libyan aviation personnel. These additional measures made the aviation sanctions against Libya the strongest ever imposed. In terms of operational goals, the travel sanctions sought to isolate Libya from the rest of the international community, reduce its ability to support terrorism, and impose modest economic hardships on the country.[3]

The aviation sanctions against Libya were remarkably effective, virtually eliminating all but a few symbolic flights. The only ways to reach Libya were by flights to neighboring states, followed by overland travel or ferry service from Malta. The only exceptions to the nearly universal flight ban were Muslim pilgrimages to Saudi Arabia. SCR 748 (1992) allowed flights for the hajj, the Muslim pilgrimage to Mecca, on EgyptAir under very restricted conditions. Some limited unauthorized flights for other purposes also took place. The Security Council issued mild verbal reprimands for such flights but otherwise looked the other way so as not to offend Muslim sensibilities.[4]

The economic impact of the aviation sanctions appears to have been modest, although the Libyan government claimed quite the opposite. A 1997 Libyan report to the UN listed more than $2 billion in aviation-related losses allegedly caused by sanctions,[5] but a French news source cited a 1998 Libyan government figure of $378 million lost in Libya's aviation sector.[6] Only one major oil company, Royal Dutch Shell, stopped doing business in Libya because of the travel difficulties. Libya suffered shortages of aviation spare parts because of the sanctions, but they were not sufficiently severe to shut down domestic flights, which the sanctions permitted. Libya continued to operate such domestic flights, although these flew at well below capacity because many Libyans feared that the lack of spare parts had degraded flight safety.[7] The aviation sanctions were clearly an irritant and caused some economic losses to Libya. Their impact appears to have been greater and more significant symbolically and psychologically, isolating Libya from the global community and branding it an international pariah.[8]

The diplomatic stalemate over the accused terrorists and the sanctions continued until 1998, when Arab and North African states began to exert pressure on U.S. and British officials to accept Libyan offers to settle the dispute. In June 1998, the Organization of African Unity (OAU) announced that it would openly defy the aviation sanctions if the dispute was not settled by September of that year.[9] A week before the OAU deadline, the United States and Great Britain unveiled a new proposal that closely resembled Libya's initial plan in 1992, offering to hold the trial of the two Libyan suspects under Scottish law in a court in the Netherlands. Two days later, the Security Council unanimously approved the new plan, as did the Arab League and major African states. Diplomatic wrangling over the fine print in the agreement took several more months, but in April 1999, Libya finally delivered the two suspects to The Hague for trial. The Security Council promptly suspended the sanctions.[10]

As Secretary-General Kofi Annan observed, the sanctions regime "played a role" in convincing Libya to hand over the suspects for trial.[11] As noted in Chapter 7, the UN sanctions also led to reduced Libyan government support for international terrorism. UN sanctions clearly irritated the Libyan government. Although they did not cause major economic disruption, they were a significant inconvenience and embarrassment. They impeded Libya's aspirations to earn a larger international role commensurate with its great oil wealth. The severe isolation Libya endured undoubtedly also had an impact. The combination of these factors caused sufficient pressure to induce the Qaddafi regime to seek a negotiated settlement of the dispute and, demonstrably, to curtail its support for international terrorism. Although the case might well have ended years earlier if the United States and the United Kingdom had been more willing to accept a diplomatic settlement that was just short of full compliance with SCR 748, the entire episode indicates how sanctions can work if they have the continued support of the large powers. Only when Arab and African states began to apply pressure for greater diplomatic flexibility did the United States and the United Kingdom respond with a proposal that satisfied their demands for a trial under French or British law while also meeting Libya's demand for a trial under international auspices. The settlement resulted from a unique form of double pressure: the weight of sanctions on Libya and the threat of noncompliance from Arab and African states.

### Iraq: A Limited Role

Travel sanctions have been a relatively minor part of the draconian trade sanctions and oil embargo that were imposed on Iraq in SCR 661 (1990). Iraqi Airways, which before the Gulf War had been a relatively successful airline, was shut down completely, its fleet of fifteen aircraft parked in foreign countries. SCR 670 (1990) confirmed that the original sanctions resolution banned all travel to Iraq, including by aircraft. It specified that countries were to deny takeoff and landing rights to any plane "if the aircraft would carry any cargo to or from Iraq" other than food.[12] The resolution also required states to "deny permission to any aircraft destined to land in Iraq . . . to overfly their territory," subject to two conditions: if the aircraft landed within their territory to permit inspections to ensure that no cargo was on board and if the flight received approval from the sanctions committee.[13] The initial application of these measures went beyond the specific wording of the resolutions. All civilian passenger and commercial cargo flights to and from Iraq came to a complete stop. Baghdad was totally cut off from the rest of the world, with an arduous overland drive from Jordan the only transportation option.

By 2000, as international opposition to continued trade sanctions mounted, unauthorized flights began to arrive at newly reopened Saddam Hussein International Airport. Most flights were humanitarian or political in nature, with passengers delivering aid supplies and expressing opposition to continued sanctions. In some instances, the states and groups sponsoring these flights justified them by using the loopholes in the original sanctions resolutions. SCR 661 said nothing specific about banning flights, and the wording of SCR 670 was ambiguous. Paragraph 3 of SCR 670 seemed to be aimed only at cargo flights, whereas paragraph 4 referred to "any" aircraft. But nowhere did SCR 670 specifically ban all flights to and from Iraq or specifically shut down passenger flights. It only demanded the inspection of the cargo contents of flights.

The draft UK/U.S. resolution offered in June 2001 as a means of restructuring sanctions in Iraq sought to address these ambiguities. The draft resolution called for a new system for controlling unauthorized cargo shipments to Iraq. All non-Iraqi aircraft would be permitted to travel to Iraq, provided that the aircraft gave advance notification to the Iraq sanctions committee and stopped at designated intermediary airports for cargo inspection.[14] The resolution was designed to apply to passenger and cargo flights and to replace the ambiguous provisions of SCR 670.

One of the anomalies of SCR 661 and subsequent SCRs 678 and 687 was that they did not ban the travel of Iraqi leaders, despite being extremely broad and comprehensive in all other areas. As noted in Chapter 6, these resolutions also did not freeze the personal financial assets of Iraqi leaders. The Iraq sanctions came early in the new era of sanctions diplomacy, before the Security Council began to apply more selective and targeted measures and before officials were willing to cross the personal-political divide. Later, when the Council needed a means of responding to Iraqi defiance of UN weapons inspectors in 1997, it decided to impose targeted travel sanctions against designated Iraqi leaders. SCR 1134 (1997) condemned Iraq's refusal to cooperate with the UN Special Commission (UNSCOM) and warned that travel restrictions would be imposed on designated Iraqi military officials responsible for obstructing weapons inspections. A few weeks later, in the face of continued Iraqi defiance, the Council adopted SCR 1137, imposing the threatened sanctions and directing that a list of designated officials be established.

Oddly, despite the adoption of these measures, no implementation action was taken. Three months after the resolutions were approved and following threats of intensified U.S. bombing raids, Iraq relented and signed an agreement with Secretary-General Annan granting UNSCOM inspectors access to potential weapons-related sites. The immediate purpose of the resolutions had been achieved. When cooperation between Iraqi officials and UNSCOM collapsed a few months later, however, the Security Council again chose not to enact the travel ban authorized in SCR 1137. Why that was the case is unclear, but it appears to have been part of the general malaise associated with Iraq sanctions.

### Sierra Leone: Small Steps

The Security Council sanctions against the Revolutionary United Front (RUF) rebel faction in Sierra Leone were first imposed in SCR 1132 (1997).[15] Included in these measures was a ban on travel by members of the RUF and their adult family members. Exemptions to the sanctions were provided for humanitarian purposes and so that RUF officials could participate in meetings designed to end the conflict. SCR 1132 established a sanctions committee for Sierra Leone and directed it to designate members of the military junta and their families to whom the ban would apply.[16] The committee issued the list and transmitted it to member states in January 1998, marking the first time that the Security Council published a list of designated individuals subject to sanctions.[17] This practice has now become commonplace, with lists of designated names issued for targeted sanctions in Angola, Afghanistan, and Liberia. The Sierra Leone list contained the names of fifty individuals associated with the RUF, pared down from a much larger list submitted by the government of Sierra Leone. However, pertinent information such as passport numbers and birth dates was not included because the Sierra Leone government claimed not to have access to the necessary files.[18]

The travel sanctions in Sierra Leone have had little or no impact. Liberia openly violated the sanctions by allowing members of the RUF to travel freely. Other countries of the region did little to enforce the travel ban.[19] The Sierra Leone panel of experts did not even report on the violations of travel sanctions, focusing their attention instead on diamonds, weapons, and air transportation. The panel of experts found that air transportation was essential to the survival of the RUF, serving as the main avenue of weapons supply. Helicopter shipments from Liberia were a major source of RUF weapons and supplies.[20]

*Angola/UNITA: Increasing the Pressure*

As part of its attempt to strengthen sanctions on UNITA officials, the Security Council passed SCR 1127 in August 1997, denying the entry or transit through member states of senior UNITA officials and their family members.[21] The Council also revoked the travel documents, visas, and residence permits of senior UNITA officials and their family members and imposed an aviation ban on flights by or for UNITA. The UNITA sanctions committee was asked to develop a list of designated individuals whose travel was to be banned. Exemptions were provided for cases of medical emergency and humanitarian need. Although SCR 1127 was initially adopted in August, the Council delayed its implementation for two months in the hope (which proved unfounded) that UNITA would begin to implement the demobilization provisions of the Lusaka Protocol. In February 1998, the sanctions committee published a list of names of eighty designated UNITA officials covered under the travel ban.

The travel ban and aviation sanctions against UNITA initially proved to be porous. UNITA managed to circumvent these travel sanctions, in part because a number of UNITA officials were citizens of European and North American countries and thus were able to travel freely in spite of the sanctions. Côte d'Ivoire, Togo, and Burkina Faso openly violated the sanctions by providing UNITA officials with passports and allowing them to conduct business as usual without restriction.[22] The ban on flights to UNITA-controlled territory also had little impact at first. In fact, in the months after the flight ban took effect, more flights entered UNITA territory than in the period preceding the UN action. Numerous small airstrips in the northern part of South Africa were utilized to smuggle supplies into UNITA-controlled territory. The South African government subsequently closed many of these airstrips, but sanctions violations continued.[23] Enforcement of the travel sanctions was further undermined by the spreading regional war in the Democratic Republic of the Congo and central Africa, with UNITA and the Luanda government on opposite sides of this conflict and neighboring states providing military and political support to one or another faction. The unwillingness or inability of governments in the region to control their airspace or to monitor and enforce border controls greatly undermined compliance with Security Council sanctions.[24]

The Fowler mission recommended UN support for customs monitoring in the region and the interdiction of UNITA supply flights.[25] The panel of experts report urged that countries be reminded to revoke passports of UNITA officials, that the list of banned individuals be updated to include passport numbers, and that the Security Council consider imposing sanctions against countries intentionally violating the sanctions placed on UNITA.

One of the crucial findings of the expert panel was the importance of air transportation in supplying UNITA with weapons. The report described air cargo as an "essential and irreplaceable lifeline" for UNITA.[26] The monitoring mechanism created to follow up on the expert panel report came to similar conclusions. UNITA had always been highly dependent upon air supply, the mechanism report concluded, and was therefore vulnerable to an interruption of such supply. The monitoring mechanism urged the international community to put an end to illegal air transportation by strengthening law enforcement efforts and tightening requirements for valid documentation and licensing.[27] The monitoring mechanism report also recommended that member states tighten controls on flags of convenience (the registering of planes and ships in foreign countries) and revoke the registration of aircraft of sanctions busters, particularly planes registered in Liberia. Other policy suggestions included revoking the licenses of pilots who make sanctions-busting flights and providing assistance to states in the region to improve air-monitoring capabilities.[28]

Attempts to restrict the travel of UNITA officials or members of any other group run counter to the trend in Europe and other parts of the world toward more open borders and fewer international travel restrictions. Under the terms of the 1985 Schengen agreement, European countries are legally bound to allow unimpeded border access to citizens of other signatory nations. This requirement makes it extremely difficult for these countries to enforce the travel restrictions mandated by the Security Council.[29] A related problem is that UNITA officials with dual citizenship have the right to travel freely in their second country, which is usually in Europe or North America. The monitoring mechanism final report recommended that member countries of the Schengen agreement adopt special measures to allow for the enforcement of travel restrictions against UNITA members.[30]

With the general strengthening of sanctions compliance following the Fowler mission, the travel sanctions against UNITA began to have greater success. The addendum report of the monitoring mechanism noted progress in the enforcement of the travel ban and aviation sanctions against UNITA.[31] The supplementary report of the monitoring mechanism observed that the combination of more effectively enforced travel and financial sanctions caused the UNITA network to experience "a decrease in liquidity." According to the report, the travel restrictions "proved particularly important in this regard."[32] By denying and restricting the travel opportunities of senior UNITA officials, the travel sanctions contributed to the political and financial isolation of the rebel movement.

## Afghanistan: Isolating the Taliban

The Security Council sanctions imposed on the Taliban in October 1999 included a ban on Ariana Afghan Airlines. When the Council strengthened the sanctions in December 2000, it added specific travel sanctions prohibiting the entry or transit through member states of senior officials of the Taliban.[33] The sanctions committee subsequently published a list of forty-five Taliban officials to be subjected to the travel ban and accompanying financial assets freeze. The Council also broadened the aviation sanctions to prohibit all flights to and from Afghanistan, not just those operated by the state airline.

The aviation sanctions had a significant impact on air travel in Afghanistan, according to reports by the Secretary-General.[34] International flights of Ariana Afghan Airlines came to a halt, disrupting overseas commercial and business activities.[35] The ban on maintenance services conducted in other countries affected the safety of the airline's domestic flights as well. The insurance provider for Ariana Afghan Airlines revoked coverage in compliance with the sanctions. These measures added to the diplomatic isolation of the Taliban and denied the regime not only revenues but international legitimacy.

## Liberia: Targeting the Taylor Regime

The travel and aviation sanctions imposed against Liberia in March 2001 included the usual ban on the travel of designated military and government elites, their spouses, and all other individuals known to be providing assistance to the rebel RUF.[36] Exemptions to the travel ban were granted for meetings of the Mano River Union, the Economic Community of West African States (ECOWAS), and the OAU and for religious, humanitarian, and peace negotiation purposes.[37]

The Council did not impose mandatory aviation sanctions on Liberia per se, but it demanded that the Monrovia government ground all Liberian-registered aircraft until it updated the register of these planes in compliance with international aviation standards and provided the Council with information on the registration and ownership of the aircraft.[38] This demand was a direct response to the recommendations of the Sierra Leone and Angola investigative panels.

The Liberian government announced that it was taking action to comply with Security Council concerns even before the sanctions were approved. In February 2001, Monrovia ordered air operators in the country to authenticate their registry information in conformity with International Civil Aviation Organization (ICAO) standards. When the air carriers did not comply, the Ministry of Transport issued a press release in March indicating that the government had revoked the registration of all planes in the Liberian civil aircraft registry.[39] In his subsequent report, the Secretary-General could not provide verification that this action had been carried out. To date, no independent reports are available on the status of Liberian-registered aircraft.[40]

In June 2001, the sanctions committee on Liberia published a list of persons covered by the travel ban.[41] The list contained names and titles for those designated, but dates of birth were missing for many, and only nine of the 136 names included passport numbers. The government of Liberia protested that the list exceeded the categories defined in SCR 1343 and urged the Council to suspend the list because it was "fraught with inaccuracies."[42] In May 2001, Liberian president Charles Taylor retaliated against the travel ban by prohibiting UN employees and international officials and employees inside Liberia from traveling more than 27 miles from the capital of Monrovia. These restrictions in turn threatened international relief efforts in the country.[43]

Liberian elites have traditionally enjoyed traveling to the United States, where they take advantage of business and educational opportunities. The sanctions have restricted these options, making it more difficult for the designated elites to conduct business as usual.[44] Travel sanctions have also had psychological effects. In July 2001, Liberian minister of foreign affairs Monie Captan (named on the travel ban list) requested permission from the UN for senior Liberian ministers to travel to Sierra Leone to attend a World Cup soccer qualifying match.[45] When the request was denied, infuriated Liberian officials vowed to attend the match in spite of the sanctions request. In the end, officials did not attend the match, their pride clearly wounded in the episode.[46]

## Conclusion

Assessing the impact of travel bans and aviation sanctions is a daunting enterprise fraught with uncertainty. These sanctions are most often imposed with other measures, thus rendering the assessment task particularly problematic. The cases examined here offer mixed results. Although the measures against Haiti had no demonstrable impact, in part because they were in force for only a few months, the aviation sanctions against Libya seem to have been a partial success. They brought the government of Libya to the bargaining table and ultimately helped produce an agreement leading to the trial of the two terrorism suspects. They also contributed to the goal of reducing state-supported terrorism in Libya.

In Iraq, the general trade embargo cut off all air travel to Baghdad for ten years. It contributed to the country's economic and diplomatic isolation, and also added to the resulting humanitarian crisis. The reopening of Saddam Hussein International Airport in 2000 and the partial resumption of flights at that time were harbingers of a general erosion of sanctions compliance, especially among neighboring states. The partial unraveling of sanctions helped to spark U.S. and UK efforts to restructure the sanctions in ways that would permit commercial flights and greater civilian commerce while retaining the arms embargo.

This pattern of declining compliance in Iraq in some respects paralleled the reverse pressure from Arab and African states that helped to produce greater bargaining flexibility in the Libya sanctions case. A general principle can be derived from these two cases: states neighboring a targeted regime can exert substantial diplomatic leverage on the major powers by withholding compliance. They can use this leverage to encourage a negotiated resolution of conflict and an easing of sanctions pressure.

In Angola, travel sanctions had little impact initially, but they became more effective, in combination with other sanctions measures, as international compliance generally improved. One of the problems of enforcement in Angola, as in West Africa, is the lack of legal and administrative means to control air traffic and monitor borders. The UN could help matters by offering material assistance to neighboring states and former trading partners to strengthen monitoring and enforcement efforts. The Council could mandate the placement of UN inspectors at major airports to assist with the inspection of planes suspected of violations. It could also help with such simple matters as providing more accurate and functional lists of designated persons, including passport numbers and dates of birth, so that customs officials could more effectively implement the travel bans.

One of the most important findings of the UN investigative panels on Angola and Sierra Leone was the central role of air transportation in the circumvention of UN sanctions. Without weapons and other supplies arriving by air, it is doubtful that UNITA and the RUF could sustain military operations. Cutting off illicit air supply was identified as an essential requirement for realizing UN objectives. Among the recommendations for achieving this objective was the imposition of sanctions against countries that knowingly allow the use of their territory for illegal air transportation to sanctioned rebel movements. Some progress in this direction was achieved when the Council approved sanctions against Liberia. As noted in Chapter 9, the Council could also take action against individual companies, such as Air Cess, and demand that countries shut down the operations of companies known to be violating UN sanctions.

The challenge of enforcing travel sanctions, as with all sanctions, is fundamentally a question of political will. The Libyan sanctions were partly successful because the Permanent Five were committed to maintaining and enforcing these measures. The sanctions against UNITA became more successful over time because neighboring states and trading partners were encouraged to comply by a strengthened international campaign against the rebel movement. When the major powers demonstrate a genuine commitment to sanctions enforcement, they are better able to persuade other nations to comply as well. The Security Council can influence whether governments choose to comply with sanctions by altering the structures of reward and benefit. By imposing penalties on those who violate UN sanctions, the Council can increase the costs of noncompliance and create incentives for countries to cooperate. Governments that encourage or permit violations of sanctions or that refuse to take the necessary steps to curb illegal transactions should themselves be subject to sanctions. This approach, combined with substantial rewards and assistance for compliance, can make travel and aviation sanctions more effective tools of UN policy.

## Notes

1. For a thorough discussion of the reasons for and character of the inconsistency of sanctions on Haiti, see David Cortright, George A. Lopez, and Jaleh Dashti-Gibson, "Helping Haiti?" in Cortright and Lopez, with Richard W. Conroy, Jaleh Dashti-Gibson, and Julia Wagler, *The Sanctions Decade: Assessing UN Strategies in the 1990s* (Boulder, Colo.: Lynne Rienner Publishers, 2000), 87–106.

2. The sanctions committee did not produce a list of designated individuals, however, making it difficult to determine exactly who was included in the travel ban.

3. Gideon Rose, "Libya," in Richard Haass, ed., *Economic Sanctions and American Diplomacy* (New York: Council on Foreign Relations, 1998), 136.

4. "UN Unsure How to Respond to Iraqi, Libyan Violations of Flight Ban," *Chicago Tribune*, 11 April 1997, 24.

5. United Nations Security Council, *Letter Dated 27 May 1997 from the Permanent Representative of the Libyan Arab Jamahiriya to the United Nations Addressed to the Secretary-General*, S/1997/404, New York, 27 May 1997, 9.

6. "Libyan Air Sector Says It Has Lost 378 Million Dollars Since Embargo," Agence France Presse, 2 February 1998.

7. Rose, "Libya," 141.

8. The economic impact of the Libyan sanctions cannot be assessed without understanding the effects of a number of mismanaged government programs during the 1990s that generated inflation and a serious downturn in the Libyan economy. One underexplored impact of the sanctions was the large-scale withdrawal of public and private Libyan assets from overseas accounts. Evidently, this occurred in response to Libyan fears that travel sanctions were only the beginning of their encounter with UN sanctions. The anticipation of stricter financial measures prompted Libyans to bring their money home rather than have it frozen overseas. Regarding the negative humanitarian effects of sanctions, the Libyan government maintained that the impacts of the travel sanctions were severe. In 1996, the government claimed that because of the air ban, Libyans were forced to seek health care in Tunisia and Egypt and that the increased road traffic resulted in 10,200 recorded accidents between 1992 and 1995. Libya claimed that these accidents produced 2,560 deaths and at least 12,700 injuries. See Tim Niblock, *Pariah States and Sanctions in the Middle East: Iraq, Libya, Sudan* (Boulder, Colo.: Lynne Rienner Publishers, 2001), 60–93; and United Nations Security Council, *Letter Dated 27 May 1997*, S/1997/404.

9. Organization of African Unity, Assembly of Heads of State and Government, *The Crisis Between the Great Socialist Peoples Libyan Arab Jamahiriya and the United States of America and the United Kingdom*, AHG/DEC.127 XXXIV, Addis Ababa, Ethiopia, 8–10 June 1998.

10. The use of a sanctions "suspension" in this case has potentially important implications for future cases, as discussed in Cortright and Lopez, *The Sanctions Decade*, chap. 11.

11. United Nations, *Transcript of Press Conference by Secretary-General Kofi Annan at Headquarters, 5 April*, SG/SM/6944, New York, 5 April 1999, 3–4.

12. United Nations Security Council, *Security Council Resolution 670 (1990)*, S/RES/670, New York, 25 September 1990, par. 3.

13. Ibid., par. 4.

14. United Nations Security Council, "Iraq: Draft Resolution," nonpaper (United Nations, New York, 8 June 2001).

15. United Nations Security Council, *Security Council Resolution 1132 (1997)*, S/RES/1132, New York, 8 October 1997.

16. Ibid., pars. 10(b), 10(f).

17. United Nations Security Council, *Security Council Committee on Sierra Leone Issues List of Junta Members Affected by Sanctions*, press release SC/6464, New York, 8 January 1998.

18. Richard W. Conroy, "The UN Experience with Travel Sanctions: Selected Cases and Conclusions," in David Cortright and George A. Lopez, eds., *Smart Sanctions: Targeting Economic Statecraft* (Lanham, Md.: Rowman and Littlefield, 2002), 243.

19. Ibid.

20. United Nations Security Council, *Report of the Panel of Experts Appointed Pursuant to Security Council Resolution 1306 (2000), Paragraph 19, in Relation to Sierra Leone,* S/2000/1195, New York, 20 December 2000, pars. 198–201.

21. United Nations Security Council, *Security Council Resolution 1127 (1997),* S/RES/1127, New York, 28 August 1997.

22. Global Witness, *Angola Sanctions: Recent Developments* (London: Global Witness, 22 April 1999).

23. "South Africa Takes Action," *Angola Peace Monitor* 4, 19 December 1997, 3.

24. Conroy, "The UN Experience with Travel Sanctions," 228–230.

25. United Nations Security Council, *Security Council Committee Established Pursuant to Resolution 864 (1993) Concerning the Situation in Angola: Report on the Chairman's Visit to Central and Southern Africa, May 1999,* S/1999/644, New York, 4 June 1999; United Nations Security Council, *Security Council Committee Established Pursuant to Resolution 864 (1993) Concerning the Situation in Angola: Report on the Chairman's Visit to Europe and Participation in the Seventieth Ordinary Session of the Council of Ministers of the Organization of African Unity, July 1999,* S/1999/829, New York, 28 July 1999.

26. United Nations Security Council, *Report of the Panel of Experts on Violations of Security Council Sanctions Against UNITA,* S/2000/203, New York, 10 March 2000, par. 164.

27. United Nations Security Council, *Final Report of the Monitoring Mechanism on Angola Sanctions,* S/2000/1225, New York, 21 December 2000, pars. 111, 113.

28. Yet another suggestion comes from Jeremy Carver of Clifford Chance in London, who has advocated that states legislate to void the insurance policies of any transportation company found to be guilty of sanctions busting.

29. United Nations Security Council, *Final Report of the Monitoring Mechanism on Angola Sanctions,* S/2000/1225, pars. 71, 80.

30. Ibid., pars. 107, 108.

31. United Nations Security Council, *Addendum to the Final Report of the Monitoring Mechanism on Sanctions Against UNITA,* S/2001/363, New York, 11 April 2001, par. 39.

32. United Nations Security Council, *Supplementary Report of the Monitoring Mechanism on Sanctions Against UNITA,* S/2001/966, New York, 12 October 2001, par. 225.

33. United Nations Security Council, *Security Council Resolution 1333 (2000),* S/RES/1333, New York, 19 December 2000, par. 14.

34. The Secretary-General issued two reports on the humanitarian impact of sanctions on Afghanistan: United Nations Security Council, *Report of the Secretary-General on the Humanitarian Implications of the Measures Imposed by the Security Council Resolutions 1267 (1999) and 1333 (2000),* S/2001/241, New York, 20 March 2001; and United Nations Security Council, *Report of the Secretary-General on the Humanitarian Implications of the Measures Imposed by Security Council Resolutions 1267 (1999) and 1333 (2000) on Afghanistan,* S/2001/695, New York, 13 July 2001.

35. United Nations Security Council, *Report of the Secretary-General on the Humanitarian Implications of the Measures Imposed by Security Council*

*Resolutions 1267 (1999) and 1333 (2000) on Afghanistan,* S/2001/695, pars. 33, 37(b).

36. United Nations Security Council, *Security Council Resolution 1343 (2001),* S/RES/1343, New York, 7 March 2001, par. 7(a).

37. Ibid., par. 7(b).

38. Ibid., par. 2(e).

39. Republic of Liberia, Ministry of Transport, "Press Release," Monrovia, 6 March 2001.

40. An email inquiry to ICAO offices in Montreal in July 2001 produced only an acknowledgment that the Liberian government had made such an announcement.

41. United Nations Security Council, *Security Council Committee Issues List of Persons Affected by Resolution 1343 (2001) on Liberia,* press release SC/7068, New York, 4 June 2001.

42. Peter Kahler, "Liberia Protests UN List on Travel Sanctions," Pan African News Agency (Monrovia, Liberia), 14 June 2001, <www.reliefweb.int> (16 July 2001); "UN Travel Ban on Liberia Fraught with Inaccuracies, Says GOL," *Perspective,* 15 June 2001, <www.theperspective.org/list_inaccurate.html> (5 July 2001).

43. "World in Brief," *Atlanta Journal and Constitution,* 12 May 2001, 4A.

44. "The Sanctions and the Future of Liberia," *Perspective,* 21 June 2001, <www.theperspective.org/sanctions_liberia.html> (5 July 2001).

45. "Liberia Slams UN over Football Travel Ban," *Independent Online,* 14 July 2001, <www.iol.co.za> (17 July 2001).

46. "Liberia Backs Down from Threat to Break United Nations Travel Sanctions," theprovince.com (Vancouver), 16 July 2001, <www.vancouver-province.com> (17 July 2001).

# 9

## Sanctions Sans Commitment:
## Arms Embargoes

An impeccable logic makes arms embargoes a potentially powerful instrument in the array of United Nations peace- and security-building mechanisms. By denying aggressors and human rights abusers the implements of war and repression, arms embargoes contribute directly to preventing and reducing the level of armed conflict.[1] There could hardly be a more appropriate tool for international peacemaking. Moreover, in constricting only selected weapons and military-related goods and services and in denying these to ruling elites, their armies, and other violent combatants, arms embargoes constitute the quintessential example of a smart sanction. Not only do arms embargoes avoid doing harm to vulnerable and innocent civilian populations, but if they are effectively enforced, they have the potential to save innocent lives.

This logic may explain why arms embargoes are the most frequently employed form of economic sanction. Since 1990, the UN Security Council has imposed mandatory arms embargoes in twelve of its fourteen sanctions cases. See Table 9.1 for a complete listing of Security Council arms embargoes in the past decade. Only in the cases of Cambodia and Sudan did the Security Council choose not to apply a restriction on arms imports. In most cases, arms embargoes were part of a broader package of sanctions measures. In some cases (Angola, Rwanda since 1995, and Sierra Leone since 1998), arms embargoes have been targeted against rebel movements fighting an established government. In all other cases, arms embargoes were applied against governments deemed to be violating human rights and posing a threat to international peace. Through March 2002, UN arms embargoes remained in place against seven rebel movements or states.

Regional institutions have also employed arms embargoes. The European Union (EU), under its Common Foreign and Security Policy, has applied arms embargoes frequently. As of mid-2001, EU arms embargoes were in place against eleven countries.[2] In addition, the

**Table 9.1    Selected Cases of Arms Embargoes, 1990–2001**

| Country | Arms Embargoes |
| --- | --- |
| Iraq | S/RES/661 (1990) |
| Yugoslavia | S/RES/713 (1991)<br>S/RES/1160 (1998) |
| Somalia | S/RES/733 (1992) |
| Libya | S/RES/748 (1992) |
| Liberia | S/RES/788 (1992)<br>S/RES/1343 (2001) |
| Haiti | S/RES/841 (1993) |
| Angola/UNITA | S/RES/864 (1993) |
| Rwanda | S/RES/918 (1994) |
| Sierra Leone | S/RES/1132 (1997) |
| Ethiopia/Eritrea | S/RES/1298 (2000) |
| Afghanistan | S/RES/1333 (2000) |

Economic Community of West African States (ECOWAS) has imposed a general, albeit ineffectual, moratorium on all arms shipments in the region.

Unilateral arms embargoes have also been utilized intensely. The United States alone has imposed arms restrictions against dozens of countries in recent years. Even when the UN has suspended arms embargoes and other sanctions, for example, in the case of Libya in 1999, U.S. restrictions have often remained firmly in place. Moreover, decisions to discontinue arms restrictions are often met with criticism, as was evident when the new administration of George W. Bush decided to renew training and exchange programs with the Indonesian armed forces.

The task of embargoing arms is a complicated one because it occurs at such different levels in the international community, with distinct challenges in each area. As the experience with sanctions against Iraq indicates, controlling the production of weapons of mass destruction requires not only very tight sanctions on a nation's borders but inspectors within the country itself, especially regarding chemical and biological materials. Transfers of major conventional arms and the spare parts and fuels that support them may be easier to control if the Permanent

Five, who are the principal suppliers of these weapons, are willing to cooperate. Effective participation by suppliers and frontline states (as in the case of the monitoring and control system imposed in 1993 by Europeans against the former Republic of Yugoslavia) can stifle such trade. Trafficking in small arms may be the most difficult to monitor and curtail because of both the wide diversity of suppliers and the ability of gunrunners to evade even serious border controls. The problem, of course, is that most of the people dying in the wars that the UN wants to end are being killed by these small arms.

The control of small weapons has become a high-profile issue at the UN. The UN Conference on the Illicit Trade in Small Arms and Light Weapons in All Its Aspects in July 2001 brought an intense focus to the problem, with a general consensus on the need to control more stringently the lethal trade in these weapons. In the end, however, the United States, despite its frequent reliance on arms embargoes, was unwilling to support strong measures to clamp down on small arms trafficking.

The effectiveness of arms embargoes is hard to measure or to isolate from the impact of other sanctions. In some cases, such as the five cases in which arms embargoes were imposed as stand-alone measures, the impact of UN sanctions in reducing the supply of weapons or ending armed conflict has been minimal.[3] In other cases, however, most notably Iraq, arms embargoes have successfully constrained the military capabilities of the targeted regime. When arms embargoes are combined with other measures, they can help to achieve UN objectives. In some cases, arms embargoes have driven suppliers underground and forced targeted regimes to rely on illicit networks that are inherently more expensive and riskier. Purchasing arms on the black market compels the targeted regime to pay a premium for weapons supplies and is an indicator of the impact of sanctions.[4] The increased cost and difficulty of acquiring military goods may influence a targeted regime's calculus of the costs and benefits associated with an objectionable policy and prompt a greater readiness to seek a resolution of the conflict. In recent years, there has been a marked trend toward enhanced enforcement and a greater willingness by governments around the world to comply with UN arms embargoes. These developments, to be examined below, offer hope that arms embargoes will become more effective instruments of international peacemaking. Part of that effectiveness derives from the reality that an embargo does not need to prohibit or confiscate every weapon but rather be sufficiently strong to raise the cost of arms and their supply to prohibitive levels.

In this chapter, we review UN arms embargoes since 1990 and distill relevant lessons from these experiences. We explore the means used by targeted regimes, arms suppliers, and brokers to circumvent UN sanctions and analyze the problems of inadequate enforcement capacity within the UN and among member states. We conclude with an assessment of the available tools for enhancing compliance and a summary of the most important policy recommendations for improving UN arms embargoes.

## A Systematic Pattern of Neglect

The Security Council imposed stand-alone arms embargoes in Somalia in Security Council Resolution (SCR) 733 (1992), in Liberia in SCR 788 (1992), and in Rwanda in SCR 918 (1994). The embargo against the government of Rwanda was suspended in 1995 with the adoption of SCR 1011, but it was maintained against Hutu rebels operating in eastern Zaire (now the Democratic Republic of the Congo). In none of these cases was any serious effort made to enforce the sanctions. In the case of Somalia, the UN sanctions committee rarely met and took no action to encourage compliance. In the Liberian case, the sanctions committee was created two years after the sanctions were first imposed. The Rwanda sanctions constitute a classic case of too little, too late. The UN arms embargo was not imposed until May 1994, after most of the genocidal killings by Hutu extremists had already occurred. In none of these instances did the Council appear willing to create effective multilateral enforcement mechanisms.

Recent evidence confirms that arms have continued to flow freely into Somalia, Liberia, and the Hutu rebel regions of eastern Congo. In Somalia, warlords and private militias have remained well equipped with Kalishnikovs, which are visibly and readily available in local markets. According to an investigative report in the *Atlanta Constitution,* the average Russian-made Kalishnikov sold for $200 at the Bakhar market in Mogadishu, well below the official price.[5] As we examine below, the flow of arms into Somalia has been partly a spillover effect of the war between neighboring Ethiopia and Eritrea. As noted in Chapter 5, the arms embargo against Liberia was renewed in 2001 with the adoption of SCR 1343. The sanctions were a response to Liberia's continued material support of the Revolutionary United Front (RUF) rebels in neighboring Sierra Leone. The report of the Sierra Leone panel of experts confirmed that weapons continued to flow into Liberia, mainly from Eastern Europe, and that Liberia provided substantial military assistance to the RUF.[6] Notwithstanding these new developments, the long-standing UN arms embargo had virtually no impact on the outcome of the Liberian civil war and only a marginal effect on the conflict in neighboring Sierra Leone.

The sanctions against the Hutu rebels in eastern Congo have remained ineffective. Reports of the UN International Commission of Inquiry (UNICOI) documented vast networks of arms suppliers, brokers, and transportation companies providing a steady flow of weaponry to central Africa.[7] In fact, the Hutu rebels became stronger militarily during the embargo. The flow of arms increased with the rebellion led by Laurent Kabila against Zairian president Mobutu Sese Seko and during the subsequent regional conflict that involved troops from Rwanda, Uganda, Angola, Libya, Zimbabwe, and a variety of rebel movements. To finance their additional weapons and armed militias, some of these governments and rebel movements systematically looted the Congo's natural resources.[8] The war became as much an economic venture as a dispute over security issues.[9]

Under these circumstances, the continuing UN arms embargoes against the Hutu rebels in the region became utterly meaningless. The panel of experts on the Congo recommended that the Security Council consider declaring an arms embargo on all the rebel groups operating in the Congo and the governments supporting them. Yet no action was taken on this recommendation, and none appears likely.[10] Given the obvious ineffectiveness of the existing arms embargo, it would only further discredit the Security Council and its sanctions policies to attempt to impose additional limitations in a setting where such restrictions are impossible to enforce. This raises the question whether the Secretary-General should advise against sanctions that he knows will not be seriously enforced.

## Sanctioning UNITA and the RUF

The arms embargo and other UN sanctions against the National Union for the Total Independence of Angola (UNITA) have attracted substantial international attention in recent years. The 1999 Fowler mission report, the March 2000 report of the panel of experts, and the reports of the Angola monitoring mechanism thoroughly documented the means by which UNITA circumvented the sanctions and acquired supplies for its armed forces. UNITA acquired weapons in two principal ways: capturing them in battle from the Angolan armed forces and purchasing cold war stocks from Eastern Europe. Governments and arms dealers in

Africa also played a crucial role in supplying and transporting weapons to UNITA. The panel of experts report specifically implicated Burkina Faso, Togo, Zaire, Congo-Brazzaville, Rwanda, and South Africa, in some cases naming those responsible for sanctions violations, including the heads of state of Burkina Faso and Togo.

The reports of the monitoring mechanism on Angola sanctions identified private arms brokers as crucial players in violating UN arms embargoes. The role of these brokers, according to the addendum report, is "overwhelming and cannot be over-emphasized."[11] Arms brokers have been responsible for purchasing and supplying the bulk of UNITA's weapons and, in some cases, providing training.

Some modest progress toward better enforcement of the arms embargo has occurred recently. These advances, combined with the success of military offensives by the Luanda government, have dealt a severe blow to UNITA. The rebel movement has lost control of important diamond-producing areas, limiting its revenue and eliminating many of the bases and supply routes previously used to import arms. With diminished territory and fewer resources, UNITA has faced a drop in arms imports. According to the monitoring mechanism final report, the flow of arms to UNITA is "highly reduced. . . . nothing enters in significant amounts."[12] These changes have resulted primarily from reverses on the battlefield, but the persistent UN efforts to monitor and enforce the arms embargo and other sanctions against UNITA have also played a part.

The arms embargo and other sanctions against Liberia and the RUF in Sierra Leone have also become steadily more effective in recent years. The arms embargo, oil embargo, and travel sanctions initially imposed against the military junta in 1997 were reimposed against the RUF in 1998 after troops from the Economic Community of West African States Military Observer Group (ECOMOG) forced the Armed Forces Revolutionary Council from office. ECOWAS strongly encouraged the sanctions against the RUF and in October 1998 instituted a moratorium on all arms shipments to West Africa as part of an attempt to stem the violence, not only in Sierra Leone but throughout the region. The Security Council strengthened the sanctions in July 2000, imposing a diamond embargo and establishing a panel of experts.

The panel's report documented violations of the arms embargo and confirmed that Sierra Leone and all of West Africa are "awash in small arms."[13] The report found a pattern of supply and transshipment similar to that utilized by UNITA. Arms were procured primarily in Eastern Europe, usually with the assistance of private arms brokers, and transshipped to Liberia through Burkina Faso. From Liberia, helicopters shuttled the supplies, primarily small arms, to RUF forces in the field.[14] The report acknowledged that the RUF also obtained many weapons during confrontations with the Sierra Leone army, ECOMOG forces, and UN peacekeepers. The panel found little evidence that the arms embargo or the ECOWAS moratorium on arms imports was having much effect in constraining the military capabilities of the RUF.

The Sierra Leone panel came to many of the same conclusions as the Angola panel and monitoring mechanism. Governments in Eastern Europe needed to exercise greater restraint and due diligence in monitoring and controlling arms dealers operating from their territory.[15] Greater international efforts were needed to license and control private arms brokers. The panel documented the crucial role of air transportation in ferrying weapons to RUF forces from Liberia. It noted the problem of lax procedures for aircraft registered in Liberia and recommended that all aircraft registered there be grounded immediately.

Despite the Security Council's efforts to improve the monitoring and enforcement of the arms and diamond embargoes in Sierra Leone, these sanctions had little impact in pressuring the RUF to end its military rebellion and demobilize its forces. However, the extension of UN sanctions to Liberia had a significant impact in applying pressure on the rebel movement's principal patron. The additional sanctions on Liberia, the presence of British troops in Sierra Leone, and the RUF's battlefield reverses at the hands of the Guinean armed forces combined to change the political dynamics of the struggle in Sierra Leone, resulting in a cease-fire and a greater willingness by the rebels to cooperate with UN peacekeepers. The continuing arms embargo and other sanctions against the RUF and Liberia helped restrain military hostilities.

## Crisis in the Horn

The UN arms embargo imposed against Ethiopia and Eritrea in May 2000 (SCR 1298) paralleled the Rwanda case in its futility. The embargo was not imposed until after the war had already begun and the two countries had spent the previous years arming themselves to the teeth. Between them, Ethiopia and Eritrea squandered a staggering $1 billion on arms in the two years leading up to the war.[16] Military spending in Ethiopia rose sharply in the late 1990s to more than $500 million in 2000.[17] Eritrea spent equivalent amounts. This frenzied spending spree occurred in two deeply impoverished countries whose residents were suffering desperate hunger. The arms spending was so excessive that the International Monetary Fund suspended its program in Ethiopia.[18] While all this was going on, the Security Council did nothing other than to issue a nonbinding resolution in February 1999 (SCR 1227) "strongly" urging countries to ban the sale of arms and munitions to Ethiopia and Eritrea. For a listing of sanctions against Ethiopia and Eritrea, see the box on page 161.

A December 2000 editorial in the *New York Times* criticized the U.S. government for failing to prevent the war between Ethiopia and Eritrea and for resisting calls to impose an arms embargo. The newspaper also took issue with Washington's unwillingness to suspend more than $1 billion in World Bank loans "at a time when the two countries were hemorrhaging cash on weapons."[19] U.S. priorities were focused elsewhere, on neighboring Sudan, and the Ethiopia-Eritrea conflict was seen as a sideshow. The United States seemed to be more interested in supporting the Sudanese rebels fighting against the government in Khartoum than in pressuring Ethiopia and Eritrea to halt their arms buildup. Both Ethiopia and Eritrea were supporting American policy aims in Sudan, and U.S. officials did not want to jeopardize this cooperation by imposing UN sanctions.

The conflict between Ethiopia and Eritrea has been closely linked to disputes in neighboring countries. Former U.S. national security official John Prendergast has described the horn of Africa as "an integrated conflict zone."[20] Ethiopia and Eritrea have supported rival militias in Somalia and have aided the rebels battling the Khartoum government in Sudan. When fighting broke out between Ethiopia and Eritrea in 1998 and then again in 1999 and 2000, the flow of weapons to rival factions in Somalia increased, helping to reignite the civil war there.[21] At the same time, the two countries reduced their support for Sudanese opposition groups.[22] In the end, U.S. policy seems to have failed on all fronts. It stopped neither the outbreak of war between Ethiopia and Eritrea nor renewed fighting in Somalia. Nor did it prevent a reduction of Ethiopian and Eritrean support for the Sudanese rebels. The failures of U.S. policy in the region obviously contributed to the failure of UN policy there.

The arms embargo against Ethiopia and Eritrea marked the debut of a sanctions policy reform advocated by France and Russia: time limits. SCR 1298 (2000) specified that the sanctions would remain in place for only one year or until the Secretary-General reported that a peace settlement had ended the conflict. The demand for time limits was motivated by the desire of some Security Council members, particularly France, to avoid a replay of the Iraq impasse, where sanctions have continued with

**ETHIOPIA AND ERITREA,**
**Security Council Resolutions**

| Resolution Number | Action |
|---|---|
| 1227 | **(10 February 1999)**<br>Strongly urged states to end sales of arms and munitions |
| 1298 | **(17 May 2000)**<br>Imposed binding arms embargo |

no end in sight. Ironically, the demand for time limits has itself become a divisive issue among the Permanent Five, preventing agreement within the Security Council on sanctions reform. Nonetheless, the Council has adopted time limits in all of its recent sanctions resolutions, including the Ethiopia and Eritrea case. When the Council adopted SCR 1298, Russia's permanent representative to the UN, Sergey Lavrov, hailed the provision as a historical first for the Security Council.[23] The wording of the resolution required an affirmative vote of the Security Council to continue the sanctions beyond May 2001.

Despite the tentative nature of the cease-fire and evidence of blatant violations of the arms embargo, the Council duly allowed the embargo to expire in May 2001.[24] A terse announcement from the president of the Council noted that the provisions of SCR 1298 "have not been extended."[25] The statement by James Cunningham, acting permanent representative of the United States, urged Ethiopia and Eritrea "to ensure that efforts are redirected from weapons procurement and other military activities toward the reconstruction and development of both economies and regional reconciliation, with a view to achieving stability in the horn of Africa." The statement also encouraged UN member states "to exercise the highest degree of responsibility in discouraging arms flows to countries and regions emerging from armed conflicts."[26] These were hollow words that masked the Council's inability to agree upon or enact an effective policy to prevent the continued flow of arms to the region.

The United States attempted to lift the arms embargo even earlier, as part of an apparent political bargain with Ethiopia to halt its military advance into Eritrean territory and accept a UN-monitored cease-fire.[27] Following the signing of a peace agreement between the two parties in January 2001, the United States proposed that the Security Council lift the arms embargo. A number of member states objected to the suggestion, particularly Canada and the Netherlands, whose troops were part of the UN peacekeeping force monitoring the cease-fire. Some countries were concerned about the continuing tensions between the combatants and were reluctant to give a green light to additional arms shipments into the region. These same concerns were expressed a few months later when the twelve-month time limit was reached, but the Council could not muster the political support for continuing the arms embargo.

## Flawed Policy in Yugoslavia

A UN arms embargo was in place against Yugoslavia from 1998 through 2001. The Security Council adopted SCR 1160 (1998), which banned military sales or support to Serbia and Montenegro. Few noticed or paid attention to the arms embargo, however, and enforcement efforts were practically nonexistent. The Yugoslavia sanctions committee was among the least active of recent years. Despite a commitment to peacekeeping in the region, the Security Council did not mount a monitoring effort for the arms embargo. NATO and the security institutions in Europe also stood on the sidelines. The European agencies that played a major role in supporting the earlier UN sanctions in Yugoslavia (1992–1995) did not offer the resources for monitoring the arms embargo.[28]

Even with the best of monitoring, an arms embargo against Yugoslavia would face overwhelming obstacles. The region has been overflowing with arms for decades. Serbia drew from the well-stocked arsenal of the Yugoslav army, and the Albanian rebels of the Kosovo Liberation Army (KLA) and the Macedonian National Liberation Army benefited from the looting of Albania's military stockpiles after the meltdown of government authority in 1997. Some of these Albanian arms also flowed into Macedonia to fuel armed rebellion there, and the supply of new weapons from areas of the former Soviet Union has continued unabated. Ironically, the one party that did take steps to enforce the arms embargo was Serbia, which deployed the Yugoslav army on the Kosovo-Macedonia border in 1998. As a result of these efforts, the cost of an AK-47 rifle reportedly increased from 50 deutsche Marks (DM) to DM 1,000.[29] This result provided evidence that the deployment of enforcement units could make a difference, if not in stopping arms flows completely, then at least in raising the price of weapons and possibly limiting some of the supply.

The UN arms embargo in Yugoslavia is another example of a flawed policy in which the Security Council and member states were unwilling to take the steps necessary to implement the measures they adopted. The same pattern that was evident in the cases of Ethiopia and Eritrea, Somalia, Liberia, and the Rwandan Hutu rebels reappeared in the Balkans, despite substantial investments in other dimensions of security building. Stand-alone UN arms embargoes have been utterly feckless. They are commonly referred to as "a joke," although the consequences of failed policy are no laughing matter for the victims of armed conflict. Diplomats go through the motions of responding to a crisis without actually doing anything. The adoption of Security Council resolutions may give the appearance that something is being done and may bring political benefit to the decisionmakers involved, but the impact of these measures on the ground is usually nil. When there is no prospect of an enforcement effort, it might be preferable for the Council to do nothing. It would at least preserve some semblance of credibility for future UN arms embargoes that are seriously implemented and give greater weight and deterrent force to such sanctions.

## Iraq: The Importance of Enforcement

Iraq represents the one case in which an arms embargo has effectively curtailed the military capability of a targeted regime. The combination of comprehensive trade sanctions, intrusive UN weapons inspections, and selective military attacks by the United States and the United Kingdom have significantly degraded Iraq's weapons of mass destruction programs and its overall military capabilities. Even as compliance with the general trade sanctions has eroded, the effective military containment of Iraq has been sustained. As noted in Chapter 2, the Security Council has considered a restructuring of the Iraq sanctions to ease restrictions on civilian trade while maintaining a strict embargo on imports of weapons and military-related goods, but as of March 2002, the Council had not yet agreed on such a plan.

The continuing UN control of Iraqi oil exports has denied the Baghdad regime the ability to use its oil-generated revenues to purchase arms. Rough calculations suggest that since 1990, Iraq has foregone or lost control of over more than $150 billion in oil revenues, which has prevented Iraq from rebuilding and modernizing its armed forces after the Gulf War.[30] The loss of control over revenue has also impeded the regime's efforts to reestablish and develop its weapons of mass destruction. Since the imposition of UN sanctions, Iraqi military spending has plummeted. According to estimates from the U.S. Department of State, Iraqi military expenditures dropped from $22.5 billion in 1990 to $1.25 billion in 1997 (see Figure 9.1).[31]

As a result of sanctions, the huge volume of military goods that flowed into Iraq in the 1980s has slowed to a trickle. The cumulative arms import deficit for the period from 1991 to 1998 has been calculated at $47.7 billion.[32] This figure represents the total shortfall in arms imports compared with the annual average of such imports in the five years preceding the Gulf War. A 1998 report from the Center for

**Figure 9.1    Military Expenditures in Iraq, 1987–1997**

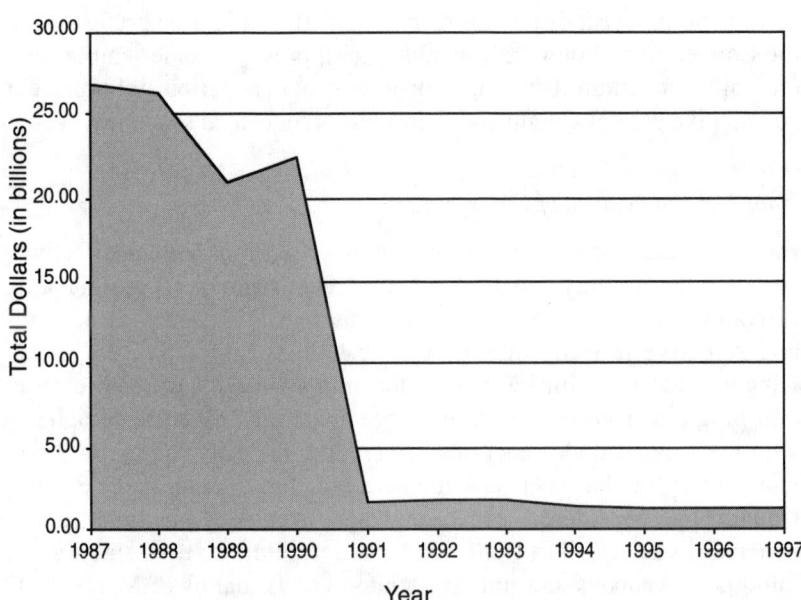

*Source:* U.S. Department of State, *World Military Expenditure and Arms Transfer 1998,* (Washington, D.C.: Government Printing Office, April 2000).

Strategic and International Studies stated that Iraqi armed forces had "decaying, obsolete, or obsolescent major weapons."[33] Although Baghdad has pursued various weapons-smuggling efforts, which have no doubt expanded as cracks in the sanctions regime have widened, these black market operations have been no substitute for the large-scale, diversified weapons supply that equipped the Iraqi armed forces for war with Iran in the 1980s. The sanctions have been highly effective in curtailing Iraq's military capabilities.

There is no mystery about the reasons for the success of the arms embargo in Iraq: the control of oil revenues and effective international enforcement. The first factor is unique to the case of Iraq and stems from the special circumstances of the oil for food program. Revenues from permitted oil sales are deposited in a UN-controlled fund and can be used only for approved humanitarian and civilian infrastructure expenditures. In light of the Security Council's increased emphasis on commodity controls as means of constraining the revenue used for weapons purchases by targeted governments and rebel movements (see Chapter 10), it is conceivable that future arms embargoes might attempt to develop financial capture mechanisms similar to those employed in Iraq.

The second factor, widespread international compliance, is more general and could be replicated in other cases, but only if the major powers consider it to be in their interest. The United States and other countries have made substantial commitments to monitoring and interdicting shipments to Iraq, especially by sea. The most important part of this enforcement effort has been the Maritime Interception Force (MIF), which monitors naval traffic in the northern Gulf. Maritime transport represents the largest threat of smuggling, because one ship can carry the freight equivalent of many truckloads of goods. The MIF began as a bilateral effort of the United States and the United Kingdom in 1990. Although it has received naval support from nearly a dozen Western nations, the MIF has remained primarily a U.S. operation. In ten years of operation, the MIF searched more than 12,000 ships.[34] Until 1994, it also monitored ships entering the Jordanian port of Aqaba, a major transshipment point for goods entering Iraq. In 1994, MIF patrols were replaced by dockside inspections conducted by Lloyd's Register under arrangement with the UN. These inspections came to an end in December 2000 and as of this writing have not been replaced. The weakening of these monitoring efforts and the general erosion of sanctions compliance have increased the likelihood of prohibited weapons imports into Iraq.

*Sanctioning the Taliban*

As noted in Chapter 3, the Security Council strengthened the sanctions imposed against the Taliban in 1999 (SCR 1267) by imposing an arms embargo and other measures in SCR 1333 (2000). The idea of restricting the flow of arms to a country at war appeared to make sense, theoretically, but as a practical matter, the arms embargo faced substantial obstacles. The problems in Afghanistan were similar to those that bedeviled UN arms embargoes in Africa and Yugoslavia. The legacy of the 1980s war against the Soviets and more than a decade of continuous civil conflict left the region brimming with weapons. The supply lines into Afghanistan from unrestricted outside sources, primarily Pakistan, are numerous and virtually impossible to monitor. The North-West Frontier along the Pakistani border with Afghanistan is largely ungovernable and has many links (including shared Pashtun ethnicity) with the Taliban in Afghanistan.

An unofficial study produced by the UN Secretariat acknowledged the many difficulties in attempting to cut off the flow of weapons from Pakistan to Afghanistan. The border between the two countries is more than 1,500 miles long, much of it along sparsely populated mountainous or desert terrain.[35] The two main roads to Kandahar and Jalalabad in Afghanistan can be monitored with relative ease. But there are numerous secondary routes and trails, well worn from the resistance effort against Soviet occupation, that can be used to bring in supplies of arms and ammunition. These secondary routes have been used since time immemorial as pathways for smuggling and the movement of people between the two countries. Many Taliban and al-Qaida fighters who escaped from U.S.-led military attacks in October and November 2001 no doubt fled along these same routes. Over the decades, imperial powers and regional governments have attempted in vain to establish control over these border areas. The prospect that a UN arms embargo could stem the flow of arms in this region is extremely remote.

## The Limitations of Arms Embargoes

From the preceding case analyses, it is obvious that UN arms embargoes suffer from numerous problems. In some cases, there are structural factors over which the Security Council and member states have no influence. When an armed conflict has already broken out and weapons supplies in a region are already abundant, the imposition of even a well-monitored and well-enforced arms embargo will likely have little impact in reducing the violence. Even in such instances, though, early action by the international community to restrict the flow of arms could increase the prospects for preventing deadly conflict. In the case of Ethiopia and Eritrea, the buildup of arms on both sides began before the first armed clashes in 1998 and continued to accelerate into 2000. An earlier and more effective effort to cut off the supply of arms to the two countries might have made a difference in preventing or at least reducing the scale of subsequent military hostilities.

In most cases, the limitations of UN arms embargoes can be traced to specific political factors. One of the greatest problems is the unwillingness of the major powers to create and enforce an effective international arms monitoring and enforcement system, which is linked to efforts by these same countries to promote, or at least not restrain, arms exports by their own producers.

Some of the obstacles are technical and administrative. They include vague wording in Security Council resolutions, inadequate monitoring of air cargo, improper documentation of end-use certificates, and lack of implementation capacity among UN member states and within the UN Secretariat.

## Grounding Arms Smugglers

The means by which arms traffickers violate UN arms embargoes are well documented. The role of air transportation in supplying arms to sanctioned rebel movements is particularly crucial. The panel of experts and the monitoring mechanism reports on sanctions in Angola identified air transportation as "the main avenue" for supplying arms to UNITA.[36] The panel of experts on Sierra Leone came to similar conclusions about the central role of air transportation in providing military supplies to RUF rebels.[37] Air shipments have also been used to violate the sanctions against Ethiopia and Eritrea.

The considerable effort the United States has devoted to preventing the smuggling of drugs via airplane or ship illustrates that, with the investment of sufficient resources, illegal air transport operations can be detected and curtailed. The U.S. antidrug program has required a concentrated air surveillance and interdiction effort. For such a program to be effective for sanctions enforcement, the United States and other major powers would have to provide airborne surveillance and other expensive detection systems, since air-monitoring capabilities in many regions of conflict are very limited. Support would be needed as well in managing interdiction operations to avoid interference with legitimate flights while ensuring effective action against unregistered and illicit missions. International enforcement efforts against drug smuggling in Latin America have had dramatic effects in reducing the volume of unregistered flights in the region and have significantly constrained the efforts of drug exporters.[38] The flow of drugs to the United States has not stopped, but smuggling efforts via aircraft have become more difficult and dangerous.

Improvements are also needed in the present international system for regulating cargo planes. Current procedures are archaic and inconsistent, according to the U.S. International Air Cargo Association.[39] A related problem is the lack of regulation and monitoring for aircraft registered in Liberia. As documented in UN reports, such planes have been used frequently as means of evading international controls and delivering illegal arms shipments. The Sierra Leone panel of experts recommended that all Liberian aircraft be grounded until they were properly registered with the International Civil Aviation Organization in Montreal.[40]

UN reports have repeatedly noted the crucial role of arms brokers in violating UN arms embargoes. Instead of buying arms directly from producers, rebel movements and sanctioned governments often obtain weapons through intermediaries. Utilizing unregulated brokers makes it easier for a sanctioned regime to acquire weapons and complicates the task of monitoring and preventing violations. In many cases, arms brokers not only supply weapons but arrange for transportation, training, maintenance, and spare parts. According to the Angola panel of experts report, a small number of known brokers have accounted for the bulk of weapons imports to UNITA.[41] A concerted international effort to regulate arms brokers and shut down firms that violate UN sanctions could significantly curtail illicit arms trafficking.

One of the frequently used tools of evasion is the falsification of end-user certificates. When brokers arrange arms shipments from suppliers, many of them in Eastern Europe, they often file documents claiming that the weapons are destined for such countries as Burkina Faso and Togo. When the arms arrive at these locations, however, they are forwarded to Liberia, Angola, or other conflict zones. The Angola monitoring mechanism confirmed that the arms shipped to Togo from Bulgaria ended up in the hands of UNITA.

The central figure in the shadowy world of arms brokering, transportation, and falsification has been Victor Bout. UN investigative panels on Angola, Sierra Leone, and the Democratic Republic of the Congo have identified Bout and his company, Air Cess, as the principal suppliers of weapons to rebel groups. Air Cess has been the single carrier of most weapons supplied to UNITA in Angola.[42] The final report of the Angola monitoring mechanism on sanctions provided an extensive profile of Bout and his air transportation operations.[43] Bout was born in Tajikistan; has passports from five countries, including Russia and Ukraine; and is reportedly a former KGB officer. He formed Air Cess in 1996 and built a fleet of approximately fifty Russian-made Antonov transport planes, registered in Liberia.[44] Bout originally headquartered his operations in Ostende, Belgium, but when Belgian officials tightened their monitoring efforts, Bout moved Air Cess to the United Arab Emirates (UAE). Public exposure also prompted Bout to restructure his company and shift his operations to a network of subcontractors and partners while continuing his sanctions-busting activities.[45] The British government has exerted pressure on the UAE to shut down Bout's operations.[46] In response, Air Cess moved its headquarters from Sharjah to Ajman, a smaller emirate 10 miles away, but its sanctions-busting activities have continued. "We know that he is still selling weapons to Liberia and Angola in breach of sanctions," said Peter Hain of the British Foreign Office in July 2001. "Bout is the principal merchant of death in Africa. If you want to stop sanctions-busting, you have to stop Bout."[47]

The case of Bout and Air Cess highlights both the dilemma and the opportunity in enforcing UN arms embargoes. A company that has repeatedly violated UN sanctions should be required to face the consequences of its actions. If the Security Council was serious about enforcing the various arms embargoes in Africa, it would support nationally coordinated efforts to shut down Air Cess's operations. The voluminous evidence of the company's violations should be publicized to the international community and formally presented to the countries directly involved in Bout's operations, including the UAE and Liberia, with the demand that these countries take action against the company. Similar actions could be taken against other known arms traffickers as part of a systematic effort to drive these merchants of death out of business.

## Promoting Arms

Much of the discussion of UN arms embargoes has rightly focused on the huge demand for weapons by rebel movements and governments in

Africa and other conflict zones and the underworld of private brokers and transportation companies that traffic in illegal arms. But the largest producers and promoters of arms exports are the major powers and permanent members of the Security Council. The same governments that have applied pressure on other countries to tighten arms export laws and limit the sales of weapons to areas of conflict are themselves engaged in a feverish competition to produce and sell arms.

After a decade-long decline associated with the end of the cold war, worldwide military spending levels have started to increase again. In 1999, global military spending increased by 2 percent, to approximately $780 billion.[48] Arms transfers, after declining rapidly at the end of the cold war, have remained at constant levels since 1995.[49] In 1999, the volume of negotiated contracts for future arms deliveries increased from the previous year's figure of $23 billion to more than $30 billion, indicating a trend toward rising arms transfers in the years ahead.[50] The United States continues to dominate the world arms market, having delivered more than $18 billion in arms in 1999. The United Kingdom and Russia were second and third, respectively, in the ranking of global arms merchants.[51]

Officials of the major powers make a distinction between these legal arms sales to legitimate governments and illicit arms trafficking to regimes under UN sanctions. They also point to their domestic arms export control laws that provide assurances against illegal shipments and, in the case of the United States, prohibit military sales or support to regimes that violate human rights. Past experience has shown, however, that weapons delivered to an established government may find their way into the hands of rebel movements or regimes that violate international norms. U.S. arms transferred to Pakistan in the 1980s to counter the Soviet invasion of Afghanistan helped to fuel civil war in Afghanistan. Arms supplied to Iraq in the 1980s were used in the invasion of Kuwait and for the development of weapons of mass destruction. The vast arsenals of weapons produced by the Soviet Union and other Eastern European countries during the cold war have been a major source of supply for arms traffickers violating UN arms embargoes. When so much military hardware is produced and promoted in the world marketplace, a percentage of this lethal equipment inevitably falls into the hands of aggressors and human rights abusers. As long as the major powers continue to depend on large-scale arms exports as a means of economic leverage at home and foreign policy influence abroad, arms will continue to flow into conflict zones, and the enforcement of UN arms embargoes will be more difficult.

While promoting tighter arms export controls abroad, the United States has enacted domestic legislation to promote and expedite its own arms export licensing procedures. Under the Defense Trade Security Initiative, announced in May 2000, Washington introduced changes that made it easier for arms exporters to sell their wares abroad.[52] Human Rights Watch and other groups have expressed concern about these changes and have criticized efforts to weaken U.S. arms export controls. At the UN conference on small arms held in July 2001, the United States blocked international efforts to control weapons trafficking. U.S. undersecretary of state John Bolton told delegates that the United States would not support a proposed UN convention on arms transfers because of concerns over the rights of domestic gun owners. The draft convention under consideration at the UN conference would have created tighter controls on automatic weapons and other light arms that account for most of the deaths in military conflicts around the world. Because of U.S. obduracy, the small arms conference failed to reach agreement on binding measures to restrict arms trafficking and had to settle for vaguely worded platitudes. The opportunity for strengthening UN arms embargoes that the conference presented was lost.

### Moral and Political Hazards

One of the strategic dilemmas the Security Council faces when imposing an arms embargo is whether such action will inadvertently benefit one of the parties in a conflict. When the Council imposed an arms embargo on the former Yugoslavia in 1991 (SCR 713), critics observed that it would benefit Serbia by freezing the enormous military advantage of the Yugoslav People's Army (YPA) over its Bosnian and Croatian adversaries. A study from the Stockholm International Peace Research Institute estimated that the YPA enjoyed a 9 to 1 military advantage over the forces of the Bosnian government.[53] As Serbian attacks against Bosnian forces continued and intensified, the United States and several Islamic states quietly decided to ignore the arms embargo and provided military support and equipment to the beleaguered forces of the Bosnian government. In this instance, a comprehensive arms embargo on all parties was widely perceived as morally and politically unsound, conferring unjustified and unintended advantages to the aggressor.

A similar dilemma emerged in the case of Afghanistan. The Council imposed sanctions only on the Taliban, thereby overtly favoring the forces of the Northern Alliance. In adopting such a policy, the Council abandoned the previous position of neutrality implicit in the UN General Assembly's mission in Afghanistan. Human Rights Watch and other groups questioned the wisdom of this approach and urged the Council to impose an arms embargo on the Northern Alliance as well as the Taliban. But an embargo on both parties would have had unequal results, as Human Rights Watch acknowledged. The arms supply routes available to the Northern Alliance were less numerous and more vulnerable to interdiction than those of the Taliban. An evenhanded embargo would have inadvertently benefited the Taliban.[54]

### Toward More Effective Arms Embargo Enforcement

Despite the many problems and limitations of UN arms embargoes, some significant advances have occurred in recent years. A gradual trend toward enhanced monitoring is clearly visible, and the building blocks for strengthening enforcement capacity are being put in place. By reviewing the progress that has been made and assessing the key recommendations of UN expert panels, we can identify the outlines and structure of a more effective policy on international arms embargoes.

One of the most important recent innovations has been the use of investigative panels to expose sanctions violations and recommend steps to strengthen enforcement. As noted in Chapter 11, the Security Council has established a de facto policy of creating special investigative bodies for each sanctions episode. The reports of these panels have uncovered a wealth of information about the means used to circumvent UN sanctions and the options for preventing such violations. These investigative reports have already had an impact, and the tactic of naming and shaming illegal arms suppliers and brokers and their accomplices has proven rather effective. The intense discussion and debate that accompanied the release of the Angola and Sierra Leone reports indicates the impact that merely exposing violations can have.[55]

Partly in response to the violations documented in UN reports, a number of governments, especially those in Eastern Europe, have taken steps to strengthen export control laws and prevent violations of arms embargoes. Significant progress in this direction has occurred in Bulgaria, which was singled out in reports by the Angola panel of experts and the monitoring mechanism. Anxious to gain membership in the North Atlantic Treaty Organization (NATO) and the EU, the government in Sofia has adopted stronger legislative controls and restrictions on arms exports and has taken steps to verify and certify end-user documents.[56] In April 2001, the government listed twenty countries under UN or EU arms embargoes to which it would not sell arms.[57] Bulgaria has made progress, but it has not yet closed loopholes in its arms export regulations or incorporated human rights criteria into these regulations.[58] Other states that have strengthened legal and administrative regulation of arms exports in the 1990s include Austria, Belgium, Bulgaria, the Czech Republic, Estonia, Finland, Germany, Hungary, Latvia, Lithuania, Poland, Romania, Slovakia, Slovenia, Sweden, and Switzerland.[59] The United Kingdom also recently declared its intention to adopt new arms export controls that, among other things, will require the registering and licensing of arms brokers.[60] This pattern in Europe points in one logical direction: the European Union should require future member states from Eastern Europe to adopt adequate legislative control of arms exports as a criterion for membership in the Union.

Regional organizations have also made progress in controlling arms exports and establishing codes of conduct. In June 1998, the EU adopted a Code of Conduct on Arms Exports that bound member states to refrain from shipping military equipment that could be used for internal repression or international aggression.[61] The ECOWAS moratorium on the importation, exportation, and manufacture of light weapons in West Africa, initially approved in October 1998, was extended in July 2001, although it has proven largely ineffective.[62] The Southern African Development Community drafted a protocol on the control of small arms and took special measures to enforce the arms embargo and other sanctions against UNITA. The various specialized multilateral export control regimes—including the Zangger Committee, the Nuclear Suppliers Group, the Australia Group, the Missile Technology Control Regime, and the Wassenaar Arrangement—have become progressively stronger and more effective in recent years. Taken together, these cooperative arms control efforts are signs of progress in stigmatizing and restricting the proliferation of prohibited arms.

As regional organizations and member states enhance their capacity, parallel efforts are needed within the UN system. Some progress has been made, for example, in the use of more precise and comprehensive wording of Security Council resolutions. Since 1993, the language of arms embargo resolutions has become more consistent and has broadened to include bans on multiple forms of military assistance.[63] Further improvements are necessary, however, to help the Security Council and member states develop a common understanding of the specific items covered in an arms embargo.[64] Defining military-related, dual-use items is a particularly challenging task. It has proven to be a major source of friction in the operations of sanctions committees and in the debate over restructuring the Iraq sanctions. Developing lists of common dual-use items, drawn from the Wassenaar Arrangement and other multilateral arms control regimes, may help in standardizing such definitions. These and other steps toward facilitating the implementation of arms embargoes were addressed in the Bonn-Berlin process sponsored by the German government. The concrete recommendations emanating from the German initiative helped to advance the capacity of the UN to implement arms embargoes. The final outcome of the Bonn-Berlin process provided rich detail on implementation and monitoring for use in future embargo environments.[65]

Human Rights Watch and other groups have proposed the creation of a special arms embargo unit within the UN Secretariat.[66] The proposed unit would collect information on violations, conduct site visits, dispatch teams of experts, issue reports to the Secretary-General and the Security Council, and recommend ways to improve sanctions implementation.[67] To some extent, these functions are already being met through the various ad hoc investigative panels established in recent years. But standardizing and coordinating these efforts within a special unit would facilitate the investigative work and allow for comparative analyses that could identify persistent patterns of violations. A coordinated unit would also help to establish a common database and maintain a ready inventory of expert investigators. The creation of such a unit would ensure that the progress achieved to date through the ad hoc panels is sustained and institutionalized as an ongoing feature of UN sanctions enforcement.

The various expert panels have proposed additional steps that deserve priority support. The Fowler mission, the panel of experts, and the monitoring mechanism on Angola recommended that the Security Council apply sanctions against individuals, companies, and governments found to be intentionally violating UN arms embargoes. Taking such action in cases of documented disregard for Security Council sanctions could significantly strengthen enforcement efforts.

The expert panels also recommended greater international efforts to license and regulate arms brokers. Arms brokers and air transportation companies that do not meet international standards for licensing and certification should be subject to fines and lawsuits, thus dramatically increasing the cost of sanctions busting.[68] Concerted UN and international action against sanctions violators would have the benefit of making it easier politically for states in which such violators operate to take national action against them. For a nation worried about the repercussions of constraining private economic interests, the external support and legitimacy conferred by acting in concert with the UN and the international community may be crucial in making such action possible.

The UN, regional organizations, and member states must assume the primary responsibility for monitoring and enforcing arms embargoes, but nongovernmental organizations (NGOs) can also play a critical role. Citizen monitoring and verification efforts have become increasingly important in international arms monitoring and control. Reports by Human Rights Watch, Saferworld, Global Witness, International Alert, and other groups have provided groundbreaking information on arms trafficking and violations of UN arms embargoes. The first UN investigative panel, UNICOI, was the direct result of NGO efforts to examine the flow of arms into the Great Lakes region of Africa.[69] A number of the expert investigators employed in subsequent UN investigative panels have come from the leading independent research groups. Citizen organizations have also played a direct role in monitoring international arms limitation agreements.

The best example of the importance of NGOs for arms control may be the work of the Nobel Prize–winning International Campaign to Ban Landmines, which played a decisive role in persuading governments to adopt the 1997 Convention on the Prohibition of the Use, Stockpiling, Production, and Transfer of Anti-Personnel Mines and on Their Destruction and has since created a monitoring network, with researchers in ninety-five countries, to verify and encourage compliance with the land mine convention.[70] This campaign represents the first time a grassroots citizens movement played a central role in ensuring compliance with an international treaty. This precedent illustrates the potential importance of citizen involvement and indicates the role NGOs might play in strengthening the implementation of UN arms embargoes.

The potential of arms embargoes as tools of international peacemaking has yet to be fully realized, but progress in the form of usable roadmaps for stifling the flow of arms has been achieved in recent years. It is unlikely that the supply of weapons can ever be curtailed completely, but concrete steps to increase the costs and risks associated with illicit arms trafficking can be taken. By steadily improving arms control and strengthening efforts to penalize illegal arms transfers, the UN community can make arms embargoes far more effective means of international peacemaking than they have been to date.

# Notes

1. By an arms embargo, we mean a ban on weapons, materials related to weapons use (e.g., ammunition), and maintenance (e.g., spare parts), as well as a cessation in the training and technical assistance provided to armed services personnel. For an authoritative analysis of the verification side of arms embargoes, see W. Andy Knight, *The United Nations and Arms Embargoes Verification* (Lewiston, N.Y.: Edwin Mellen, 1998).

2. Ian Anthony, "Improving the Cooperation of Major Arms Suppliers," paper presented at the First Expert Seminar on Smart Sanctions, "The Next Step: Arms Embargoes and Travel Sanctions" (Bonn International Center for Conversion, Bonn, Germany, 21–23 November 1999), 3.

3. Somalia, Liberia (until 2001, when other sanctions were added), Rwanda, Yugoslavia (1998), and Ethiopia/Eritrea.

4. Michael Brzoska, "Putting More Teeth in UN Arms Embargoes," in David Cortright and George A. Lopez, eds., *Smart Sanctions: Targeting Economic Statecraft* (Lanham, Md.: Rowman and Littlefield, 2002).

5. Margaret Coker, "Amid War, Famine, Selling Guns 'Guarantees My Family Will Be Fed,'" *Atlanta Constitution,* 9 July 2001, A6.

6. United Nations Security Council, *Report of the Panel of Experts Appointed Pursuant to Security Council Resolution 1306 (2000), Paragraph 19, in Relation to Sierra Leone,* S/2000/1195, New York, 20 December 2000, par. 21–23.

7. See United Nations Security Council, *Final Report of the International Commission of Inquiry (Rwanda),* S/1998/1096, New York, 18 November 1998.

8. United Nations Security Council, *Report of the Panel of Experts on the Illegal Exploitation of Natural Resources and Other Forms of Wealth of the Democratic Republic of the Congo,* S/2001/357, New York, 12 April 2001, pars. 109–125, 173–183.

9. Ibid., par. 175.

10. Ibid., par. 224.

11. United Nations Security Council, *Addendum to the Final Report of the Monitoring Mechanism on Sanctions Against UNITA,* S/2001/363, New York, 11 April 2001, par. 33.

12. United Nations Security Council, *Final Report of the Monitoring Mechanism on Angola Sanctions,* S/2000/1225, New York, 21 December 2000, par. 19.

13. United Nations Security Council, *Report of the Panel of Experts Appointed Pursuant to Security Council Resolution 1306 (2000), Paragraph 19, in Relation to Sierra Leone,* S/2000/1195, par. 19.

14. Ibid., pars. 20–28.

15. Ibid., par. 237.

16. "Peace in the Horn of Africa," editorial, *New York Times,* 12 December 2000, A32.

17. Jane Perlez, "U.S. Did Little to Deter Build-up as Ethiopia and Eritrea Prepared for War," *New York Times,* 22 May 2000, A9.

18. Ibid.

19. "Peace in the Horn of Africa," A32.

20. John Prendergast, *Building for Peace in the Horn of Africa: Diplomacy and Beyond* (Washington, D.C.: United States Institute of Peace, June 1999), 2.

21. Prendergast, *Building for Peace in the Horn of Africa,* 2.

22. U.S. House of Representatives, International Relations Committee, Africa Subcommittee, "Testimony of Susan E. Rice," 106th Cong., 1st sess., *Congressional Record* (25 May 1999).

23. Barbara Crossette, "Arms Embargo Ordered for Eritrea and Ethiopia," *New York Times,* 19 May 2000, A3.

24. A Ukrainian cargo plane carrying 30 tons of weapons to Ethiopia and Eritrea was seized in Bulgaria in April 2001. See Colum Lynch, "Ukraine Firm Denies Seized Arms Were Headed for Eritrea in Violation of Ban," *Washington Post,* 14 May 2001, A16.

25. United Nations Security Council, *Statement by the President of the Security Council,* S/PRST/2001/14, New York, 15 May 2001.

26. Ibid.

27. "Some Leery of Plan to Lift Ban on Arms in Africa Horn," *New York Times,* 8 January 2001, A6.

28. United Nations Security Council, *Letter Dated 26 February 1999 from the Chairman of the Security Council Committee Established Pursuant to Security Council Resolution 1160 (1998) Addressed to the President of the Security Council,* S/1999/216, New York, 4 March 1999, par. 11.

29. Brzoska, "Putting More Teeth in UN Arms Embargoes," 197, citing Chris Smith and Domitilla Sagramoso, "Small Arms Trafficking May Export Albania's Anarchy," *Jane's Intelligence Review* 11, no. 1 (1997): 27.

30. Meghan O'Sullivan, *Iraq, Time for a Modified Approach,* policy brief 71 (Washington, D.C.: Brookings Institution, February 2001), 4.

31. U.S. Department of State, *World Military Expenditure and Arms Transfer 1998* (Washington, D.C.: U.S. Government Printing Office, April 2000), <www. state.gov/www/global/arms/bureau_ac/wmeat98/table1.pdf> (31 July 2001).

32. Anthony H. Cordesman, *Military Expenditures and Arms Transfers in the Middle East* (Washington, D.C.: Center for Strategic and International Studies, July 2001), 79, <www.csis.org/burke/mb/milexpenditurearmstransfer.pdf> (7 August 2001).

33. Anthony Cordesman, "The Iraq Crisis: Background Data" (Washington, D.C.: Center for Strategic and International Studies, 1998), 15.

34. U.S. House of Representatives, Committee on the Armed Services, "Statement of General Anthony C. Zinni," 106th Cong., 2d sess., *Congressional Record* (15 March 2000).

35. Human Rights Watch, *Afghanistan: Crisis of Impunity: The Role of Pakistan, Russia, and Iran in Fueling the Civil War,* paper 13, no. 3 (July 2001), 8, <www.hrw.org> (28 September 2001).

36. United Nations Security Council, *Final Report of the Monitoring Mechanism on Angola Sanctions,* S/2000/1225, par. 112. See also United Nations Security Council, *Report of the Panel of Experts on Violations of Security Council Sanctions Against UNITA,* S/2000/203, New York, 10 March 2000, pars. 163–167.

37. United Nations Security Council, *Report of the Panel of Experts Appointed Pursuant to Security Council Resolution 1306 (2000), Paragraph 19, in Relation to Sierra Leone,* S/2000/1195, par. 22.

38. The success of this program was diminished in the eyes of some observers after civilian missionaries were killed in April 2001 when a Peruvian air force plane mistakenly shot down their plane during a drug interdiction mission. The investigation of the incident revealed that, more than any other factor, language barriers between U.S. and Peruvian pilots were responsible for the missionary plane being wrongly identified and shot down. See "Report Issued in Plane's Downing: Lax

Procedures Are Cited in Peru Shoot-Down," *Washington Post,* 3 August 2001, A2.

39. Cited in Brian Wood and Johan Peleman, "Arms Brokering Emerges from the Cold War," and "Flying the Company 'Flags of Convenience,'" in *The Arms Fixers: Controlling the Brokers and Shipping Agents,* research report 99.3 (London: British American Security Information Council, November 1999), <www.basicint.org> (28 September 2001).

40. United Nations Security Council, *Report of the Panel of Experts Appointed Pursuant to Security Council Resolution 1306 (2000), Paragraph 19, in Relation to Sierra Leone,* S/2000/1195, pars. 255–256.

41. United Nations Security Council, *Report of the Panel of Experts on Violations of Security Council Sanctions Against UNITA,* S/2000/203, par. 15.

42. United Nations Security Council, *Supplementary Report of the Monitoring Mechanism on Sanctions Against UNITA,* S/2001/966, New York, 12 October 2001, par. 97.

43. United Nations Security Council, *Final Report of the Monitoring Mechanism on Angola Sanctions,* S/2000/1225, pars. 120–144.

44. Craig Nelson and Philip Sherwell, "New Address but Business as Usual for Africa's 'Merchant of Death,'" *Sunday Telegraph* (London), 22 July 2001, 29.

45. United Nations Security Council, *Supplementary Report of the Monitoring Mechanism on Sanctions Against UNITA,* S/2001/966, par. 128.

46. Andrew Parker, "Britain Tells UAE to Close Arms Dealer's Freight Business," *Financial Times,* 24 January 2001, 14.

47. Nelson and Sherwell, "New Address but Business as Usual," 29.

48. Stockholm International Peace Research Institute, *SIPRI Yearbook 2000: Armaments, Disarmament, and International Security* (Oxford: Oxford University Press, 2000), 231.

49. *SIPRI Yearbook 2000,* 339.

50. Human Rights Watch, *Human Rights Watch World Report 2001* (New York: 2000), 153.

51. Ibid.

52. Ibid.

53. Reneo Lukic and Allen Lynch, *Europe from the Balkans to the Urals: The Disintegration of Yugoslavia and the Soviet Union* (New York: Stockholm International Peace Research Institute and Oxford University Press, 1996), 246.

54. Human Rights Watch, *Afghanistan: Crisis of Impunity,* 8.

55. Brzoska, "Putting More Teeth in UN Arms Embargoes."

56. Human Rights Watch, *World Report 2001,* 159.

57. Peter Finn, "With Pain and Hope, Bulgaria Curbs Weapons Trade," *Washington Post,* 8 July 2001, A19.

58. Human Rights Watch, *World Report 2001,* 159.

59. Anthony, "Improving the Cooperation of Major Arms Suppliers." See also the Stockholm International Peace Research Institute export control project, Ian Anthony, project leader, <projects.sipri.sc/expcon/expcon.htm> (28 September 2001).

60. "Arms Export Controls," *Times* (London), 25 June 2001.

61. Kathleen Miller and Caroline Brooks, *Export Controls in the Framework Agreement Countries,* BASIC Research Report, 2001.1 (London: British-American Security Information Council, July 2001), 7, <www.basicint.org> (28 September 2001).

62. "ECOWAS Leaders Extend the Moratorium on Light Weapons," press

release no. 63/2001, Lusaka, 6 July 2001, <www.ecowas.int/sitecedeao/english/pub-4-63-2001.htm> (28 September 2001).

63. Edward C. Luck, "Choosing Words Carefully: Arms Embargoes and the UN Security Council" (paper presented at the First Expert Seminar on Smart Sanctions, "The Next Step: Arms Embargoes and Travel Sanctions," Bonn International Center for Conversion, Bonn, Germany, 21–23 November 1999), 4.

64. Brzoska, "Putting More Teeth in UN Arms Embargoes."

65. Michael Brzoska, ed., *Design and Implementation of the Arms Embargoes and Travel and Aviation Related Sanctions: Results of the "Bonn-Berlin Process"* (Bonn, Germany: Bonn International Center for Conversion, 2001).

66. Human Rights Watch, *World Report 2001*, 158.

67. Loretta Bondi, "Arms Embargoes: In Name Only?" in David Cortright and George A. Lopez, eds., *Smart Sanctions: Targeting Economic Statecraft* (Lanham, Md.: Rowman and Littlefield, 2002).

68. We thank Jeremy Carver of Clifford Chance in London for this helpful insight.

69. Interview with Joost Hilterman by David Cortright, George Lopez, and Linda Gerber, Washington, D.C., 11 June 2001.

70. Human Rights Watch, *World Report 2001*, 151–152.

# 10

# The Viability of Commodity Sanctions: The Case of Diamonds

As implied by the term, commodity sanctions are embargoes on specifically named goods or products, most often bans on trade in a valued raw material. Commodity sanctions have been applied with increasing frequency by the United Nations in recent years. The Security Council has imposed commodity sanctions against seven different rebel movements or governments. For a complete listing of these Security Council sanctions, see Table 10.1.

As Table 10.1 indicates, oil and diamonds are the most common goods subject to commodity sanctions. In the case of Haiti, embargoing oil threatened the ability of the country to function, as this import was critical to daily life. In the case of Iraq, the oil embargo shut off more than 90 percent of export earnings. Although oil embargoes are powerful tools of coercion, a new area of commodity sanctions, the embargo on diamonds, has drawn UN attention in recent years and demands considerable discussion. In three recent cases, prohibitions have been imposed against the import of "conflict diamonds," which are defined as "diamonds that originate from areas controlled by forces or factions opposed to legitimate and internationally recognized governments."[1] Scholars, activists, and industry experts agree that trade in conflict diamonds has been used to fund military rebellion and human rights abuse in contravention of the decisions of the Security Council.[2] According to Paul Collier and other analysts, where countries rely on primary commodities like diamonds as income sources, they are also vulnerable to sanctions. As the likelihood and severity of armed conflict increases, the importance of the precious commodity rises for both the conflictual parties and the international community.[3] This reality has led some to use the term *blood diamonds*.[4] As we examine in this chapter, this pattern has been evident in Angola, West Africa, and the Congo.

This chapter was coauthored by Linda Gerber.

181

**Table 10.1   Commodity Sanctions, 1990–2001**

| Cases | Type of Commodity Sanctioned |
|---|---|
| Iraq, 1990– | |
| S/RES/661 (1990) | All |
| | |
| Yugoslavia (Serbia and Montenegro), 1991–1995 | |
| S/RES/757; S/RES/787 (1992) | All |
| | |
| Cambodia, 1992–1994 | |
| S/RES/792 (1992) | Logs, oil |
| | |
| Haiti, 1993–1994 | |
| S/RES/841 (1993) | Oil |
| S/RES/917 (1994) | All |
| | |
| Angola, 1993/1997/1998– | |
| S/RES/864 (1993) | Oil |
| S/RES/1173 (1998) | Diamonds |
| | |
| Sierra Leone, 1997– | |
| S/RES/1132 (1997)[a] | Oil |
| S/RES/1306 (2000)[b] | Diamonds |
| | |
| Liberia, 2001– | |
| S/RES/1343 (2001) | Diamonds |

*Notes:* a. The oil embargo implemented in S/RES/1132 was terminated in 1998 by S/RES/1156.

b. The diamond embargo on government exports was lifted in 2000 when the certification system was implemented. It is still in place for RUF diamond exports.

Conflict diamonds and other forms of smuggled diamonds account for between 20 and 30 percent of the trade in diamonds.[5] These diamonds originate primarily from rebel-controlled territory in Angola, the Democratic Republic of the Congo (DRC), and Sierra Leone, as well as from Liberia. By contrast, legitimate diamond exports, often an essential part of a country's economy, come from Australia, Botswana, Brazil, Canada, the Central African Republic, China, Ghana, Namibia, Russia, South Africa, Venezuela, and Zimbabwe.[6] Legal diamond exports also come from the government-controlled territory of Angola, the DRC, and Sierra Leone. As international attention has focused on conflict diamonds, care has been taken to protect the legitimate diamond business.

In this chapter, we examine current UN diamond sanctions in Angola, Sierra Leone, and Liberia. We also explore the questions of possible commodity sanctions in the DRC. We review the requirements for effective monitoring and enforcement and focus on the unique role of nongovernmental organizations (NGOs) and private industry in implementing multilateral diamond sanctions.

## Angola

Until the late 1990s, the international community was largely unaware of the integral role played by diamonds in the ongoing war in Angola between the rebel movement of the National Union for the Total Independence of Angola (UNITA), led by Jonas Savimbi, and the government of Angola. For much of Angola's history, diamond-mining companies were able to operate with little or no regulation. Thus it was relatively easy for the UNITA faction to control mines in the territory it held at various points in Angola's multidecade civil war. In 1998, the London-based NGO Global Witness published *A Rough Trade: The Role of Companies and Government in the Angolan Conflict,* a report documenting the direct link between UNITA's diamond trading and its flourishing arms imports.[7] According to the report, UNITA diamond sales helped provide the large cash reserve used by Savimbi to countervail the arms embargo imposed in 1993 in Security Council Resolution (SCR) 864.[8] In fact, in 1992, two years before the Lusaka Protocol, UNITA controlled nearly 70 percent of Angola's diamond production.[9] South African industry giant De Beers Corporation admitted to purchasing a significant portion of Angolan rough diamonds sold by UNITA agents during the 1990s.[10]

In 1998, the Security Council responded to the agenda created by the Global Witness report by imposing financial sanctions, additional diplomatic sanctions, and an embargo on diamonds not controlled by the Angolan government (SCR 1173).[11] SCR 1173 required the government of Angola to employ a certificate of origin system for diamonds produced in non-UNITA-controlled areas. The Security Council took this action to strengthen the sanctions because UNITA refused to abide by the 1994 Lusaka Protocol and was continuing to wage war for control of the country's vast natural resources.[12] The specifics of UNITA's violations were detailed in the 1999 Human Rights Watch report, *Angola Unravels*. The report stated that in the five years following the 1994 Lusaka agreement, UNITA illegally exported diamonds worth $1.72 billion.[13] During this time, it was able to amass a huge volume of weapons, oil, and diamonds for future use in military operations.[14]

In addition to imposing stronger sanctions on Angola, the Security

Council took steps to ensure tighter implementation of these measures. The 1999 mission of Ambassador Robert Fowler of Canada began the process. Fowler's report contained numerous recommendations on how to improve the implementation of sanctions. Among Fowler's suggestions was providing support for the government of Angola to develop a system for certifying diamond exports.[15]

The subsequent panel of experts and monitoring mechanism reports provided further evidence of how diamonds were smuggled out of Angola and documented the lack of transparency and internal control within the diamond industry. The panel observed that smuggling routes passed through Burkina Faso, Zaire (now the DRC), Namibia, South Africa, Zambia, and the major diamond exchanges at Antwerp and Tel Aviv.[16] The reports also contained additional recommendations for improving the effectiveness of the sanctions against UNITA. The addendum report of the monitoring mechanism credited the sanctions with encouraging industry efforts to create a worldwide diamond certificate plan, although it noted that the system was not yet in place.[17]

The certification system for the government of Angola mandated by SCR 1173 was announced in February 2000. It established a marketing and certification program to guarantee the origin of diamonds from non-UNITA sources.[18] Most governments, as well as the diamond industry, endorsed the program and pledged their cooperation. Industry interest reflected the desire to avoid a consumer backlash against diamonds.

Despite the certification system and industry efforts to participate in it, illegal diamond exports from Angola continued. The Belgian Secret Service reported in April 2001 on the continued purchase of UNITA diamonds in Antwerp.[19] Implementation of the certification system has also lagged in Tel Aviv, London, and Bombay. Industry and government officials have been reluctant to enforce certification standards because of the costs and effort involved and for fear that tighter controls will send business elsewhere.[20] The reports of the panel of experts and the monitoring mechanism have recommended inducements for compliance and penalties for violations to encourage major trading centers to implement certificate of origin systems.[21]

### Sierra Leone

Diamonds were discovered in Sierra Leone in the 1930s, and the production and trade of those diamonds has been fraught with corruption and mismanagement ever since. During the 1960s and 1970s, then-president Siaka Stevens allowed criminal elements to gain a foothold in the diamond trade, and during the following decades, the official export of government-controlled diamonds from Sierra Leone steadily decreased. According to a report by Partnership Africa Canada, illegal operators have controlled 85 percent of Sierra Leone's diamond production in recent years.[22] Diamond smuggling has funded one of the most horrific and gruesome conflicts in recent history. Sierra Leone's diamonds provided the primary source of funding for the Revolutionary United Front's (RUF) war against the government of Sierra Leone. This conflict was based less on ideology or political differences than on a drive to gain control of natural resources. The conflict has been described by John Hirsch and others as a means for the RUF to engage in profitable crime through war.[23]

As awareness of RUF atrocities increased internationally in the late 1990s, attention focused on the connection between the diamond trade and the financing of the war. NGOs launched a consumer awareness campaign to educate the public about the problem of conflict diamonds. They also pressured industry and governments to take action to boycott RUF-controlled diamonds. Following the Partnership Africa Canada report in January 2000 and with pressure mounting from concerned groups and governments, the Security Council passed SCR 1306 (2000), which placed an embargo on the import of diamonds from Sierra Leone.[24] The resolution expressed concern at the role of the diamond trade in the ongoing conflict in Sierra Leone and directed all states to prohibit the direct or indirect import of rough diamonds from Sierra Leone. The Council also recommended that the government of Sierra Leone institute a certificate of origin system that, when in place, would permit the resumption of legal diamond exports.

The panel of experts created for Sierra Leone worked concurrently with the monitoring mechanism group established for Angola. The panel attempted to collect detailed information on the diamond trade but had mixed results. Some countries, such as Belgium, readily provided the requested statistics, whereas others, notably Gambia, Côte d'Ivoire, and the United Arab Emirates, refused to cooperate.[25] The panel found that diamonds represented the primary source of income for the RUF. Official diamond exports from the government of Sierra Leone declined from more than 2 million carats per year in the 1960s to a total of 36,384 carats exported from 1997 through 1999. This was due in part to decreased diamond production but was also the result of RUF control over the major diamond fields in the eastern part of the country. The panel estimated that the RUF was exporting $25 million to $125 million in carats per year, and it confirmed that the RUF was illegally mining and exporting diamonds in order to finance the war.[26]

A key finding of the panel report was that RUF diamonds were exiting Sierra Leone through Liberia and to a lesser extent through Guinea. The panel made numerous recommendations, most notably that there should be an immediate embargo on diamond exports from Liberia. The panel also recommended that a global certificate of origin system be created or, at a minimum, that such a system be established for all West African countries.[27]

The government of Sierra Leone announced the creation of a national certificate of origin system in October 2000. The plan established an elaborate system of licensing and required officials from the Government Gold and Diamond Office (GGDO) to verify the origin of stones. Each stone was examined by an independent, skilled valuator with many years of experience dealing with stones from Sierra Leone. The stones were then photographed and integrated into an electronic tracking system.[28] These multiple safeguards made the smuggling of conflict stones more difficult. An April 2001 report from Global Witness found the system to be working well, with few problems of misidentification of stones. Global Witness concluded that the staff of the GGDO was committed to working with the Diamond High Council in Antwerp to develop an effective system.[29] As a result of these changes and the improved security situation following a RUF cease-fire in November 2000, official diamond revenues to the government of Sierra Leone increased significantly, from approximately $325,000 for the period from January to June 1999 to almost $6.6 million for the period from January to March 2001.[30] For the first time in its recent history, the government of Sierra Leone was deriving substantial income from the country's natural resources.

Notwithstanding these improvements, the certificate of origin system has not prevented continued illegal diamond exports from Sierra Leone. The United States Agency for International Development (USAID) found that, although the system created by the government has worked efficiently, smuggling outside the system has continued on a large scale.[31] The government of Charles Taylor has allowed and facilitated the illegal diamond trade.

## Liberia

Despite minimal indigenous diamond resources, Liberia exported millions of dollars' worth of diamonds in the 1990s. In 1988, before the wars in Liberia and Sierra Leone erupted, Liberia officially exported $8.4 million in diamonds. In 1995, it exported $500 million in diamonds.[32] According to the Sierra Leone panel of experts report, Liberia's domestic production capacity is approximately 150,000 carats per year. In 1999, however, Liberian diamond exports to Belgium totaled 1.75 million carats.[33] The obvious disparity was the result of Liberia's export of RUF diamonds. Revenues from these exports were used by the Taylor government to finance the RUF rebel movement in Sierra Leone and to purchase weapons from various Eastern European countries.[34] In response to these findings, the Security Council passed SCR 1343 on 7 March 2001, imposing a diamond embargo and other sanctions on Liberia.[35] The Council demanded that Liberia cease the direct or indirect export of uncertified diamonds from Sierra Leone. The Council called upon Liberia to institute a certificate of origin system for rough diamonds and encouraged all diamond-exporting states in West Africa to do the same. The Council also directed that the Secretary-General establish a panel of experts to investigate alleged violations of the sanctions and explore the link between natural resources and conflict in the region.[36]

Notably missing from SCR 1343 was any mention of the role played by timber in the conflict. Several NGOs had recommended an embargo on Liberia's timber exports in addition to the embargo on diamonds as a further means of raising the costs of Liberia's defiance of UN demands. In a January 2001 briefing to the Security Council and subsequent report, Global Witness noted: "It is likely that the timber trade is more financially valuable to [Charles Taylor] and his security forces than is the trade in diamonds and that a significant portion of this revenue is also used by President Charles Taylor to train, arm and supply the RUF."[37] Global Witness also reported that Liberian forestry operations were causing severe environmental damage because of clear-cutting and a lack of replanting. The Sierra Leone panel of experts report identified two members of the board of directors of the Forestry Development Authority in Liberia as weapons dealers to the RUF.[38] The panel's report also suggested a temporary embargo on timber exports as a way of reducing revenues for the acquisition of weapons.[39] Joseph Melrose, U.S. ambassador to Sierra Leone, stated, "As far as sanctions go, timber is crucial."[40]

The Security Council did not approve a ban on timber sales, in part because France and other importing countries depend on Liberian timber.[41] According to data from the Liberian Forestry Development Authority, 37 percent of Liberian timber exports in 1999 were shipped to France.[42] China also imports considerable amounts of Liberian timber. France and China were willing to support diamond sanctions but were not prepared to accept restrictions on timber exports. Alex Yearsley of Global Witness commented, "We are concerned over the possibility that the French government is putting commercial interests before the urgency of putting an end to this brutal conflict."[43] In addition, states from the European Union and the Economic Community of West African States (ECOWAS) that would be charged with monitoring restrictions on timber indicated that they were neither willing nor able to do so.[44] An additional concern mitigating against timber sanctions was the possible humanitarian impact of such action. As indicated in the October 2001 assessment by the UN Office for the Coordination of Humanitarian Affairs, an embargo on Liberian timber exports could result in substantial losses of jobs and income in Liberia.[45] Even though the Security Council did not take action, the mere threat of a timber embargo prompted greater dialogue with Liberia regarding UN concerns.

## The DRC

The DRC (formerly Zaire) has witnessed a series of complicated internal conflicts in recent years. Many Hutu rebels responsible for the Rwandan genocide of 1994 took refuge in the Congo. In 1995, the Security Council adopted SCR 997, applying the arms embargo previously imposed against Rwanda on rebel groups operating in other countries, primarily Zaire. In 1996, Laurent Kabila led the Alliance of Democratic Forces in rebellion against the dictatorship of Zairian president Mobutu Sese Seko, successfully overthrowing the regime in 1997 and renaming the country the Democratic Republic of the Congo. In 1997, forces of the Tutsi-controlled government of Rwanda entered the Congo seeking to weaken the Hutu rebels based there and to support the overthrow of Mobutu.[46] Uganda joined the conflict to help Rwanda and to fight against Ugandan rebels based in the Congo. Burundi sent forces to fight Burundian Hutu rebels in the Congo.[47] In 1998, as the Congo plunged deeper into chaos, Kabila himself faced armed rebellion. With multiple players involved in spreading armed conflict within the Congo and beyond, the crisis in the region was aptly dubbed Africa's First World War.[48]

The armed conflicts in the Congo have been driven in large part by greed and the desire to exploit the region's vast mineral wealth and natural resources. The plunder resulting from military violence has itself led to deeper levels of commodity and environmental devastation. As in West Africa, the presence of particular primary commodity exports has helped to cause and prolong war. Through their military intervention, Rwanda and Uganda took control of over half the country's territory, which enabled their forces to plunder much of the region's riches.

In 2000, the Security Council convened a panel of experts to investigate the illegal exploitation of Congo's natural resources. The panel presented its report in April 2001, establishing a clear link between the ongoing intervention of Rwanda, Uganda, and Burundi and the illegal exploitation of natural resources.[49] It also confirmed that these operations provided funding for illegal arms imports and continued war.[50] The panel reported that Uganda, a country with no previously reported gold production, exported almost 11 tons of gold in 2000.[51] Both Uganda and Rwanda exported large volumes of diamonds starting in 1997, although neither had previously produced diamonds.[52] The panel of experts also presented evidence of illegal timber exports, wildlife depletion, and illegal taxes and price fixing.

The Congo panel developed a series of innovative recommendations for Security Council action, among them:

- placing immediate sanctions on the import or export of coltan, niobium, pyrochlore, cassiterite, timber, gold, and diamonds from Burundi, Rwanda, and Uganda;
- freezing the assets of various rebel leaders and movements;
- imposing a comprehensive arms embargo on all the rebel groups;
- creating a diamond certification system for the region similar to that adopted in Sierra Leone;
- imposing sanctions against governments involved in the mass killing of endangered species;
- establishing a definition and new criteria for "conflict timber"; and
- creating information-gathering and certification systems for temporary bans on timber exports that fuel armed conflict.[53]

The Security Council did not take action, although it extended the panel's mandate through August 2002.[54]

The political climate in the DRC improved slightly following the assassination of Laurent Kabila in January 2001 and the selection of his son Joseph as president. Hopes were raised that the Inter-Congolese Dialogue peace process might yield results, although conflict among Congolese factions and neighboring governments continued.

## Private and Public Sector
## Responses to Conflict Diamonds

Attempts to deal with conflict diamonds have produced a surprising coalition: human rights NGOs, members of the diamond industry, and national governments. These seemingly disparate groups have coalesced around the common goal of eliminating trade in conflict diamonds. Although their methods and motives vary, the groups have been able to work together to achieve their shared objective. In the following section, we examine the steps taken by these actors and identify the remaining challenges to control of this illicit trade.

### NGOs Lead the Way

NGOs have played an important role in documenting the extent of the illegal trade in conflict diamonds. By conducting investigations, issuing reports, and raising global awareness, groups like Global Witness, Human Rights Watch, Partnership Africa Canada, and Physicians for Human Rights have paved the way for significant changes within the diamond industry and among national governments. Five international NGOs—Global Witness, Intermon (Spain), Medico International (Germany), NiZA (Netherlands Institute for Southern Africa), and Novib (Oxfam Netherlands)—have formed the Fatal Transactions Campaign, a consumer awareness coalition with the goal of encouraging the diamond industry to end the trade in conflict diamonds.[55] One hundred U.S. groups have joined the Campaign to Eliminate Conflict Diamonds, created by Physicians for Human Rights to press for legislation regulating diamond imports.[56] The efforts of independent research centers such as Global Witness and Partnership Africa Canada have facilitated the work of the UN expert panels in documenting the role of diamonds and other commodities and in recommending measures to improve sanctions monitoring and enforcement.

Beyond exposing conflict diamond beneficiaries and victims, NGOs and other activists can threaten the diamond industry with a consumer boycott. Slogans and visual images linking the horrors of war with the luxury symbol of love could be extremely effective. Industry leaders know this and have sought to avoid the possibility of a consumer backlash by taking steps to address the conflict diamond issue. NGO activists recognize that the vast majority of diamonds are "clean" and that developing countries such as South Africa, Botswana, and Namibia depend heavily on the legitimate diamond trade. For this reason, NGOs have refrained from advocating boycotts and have encouraged the diamond industry to screen out conflict diamonds. If the diamond industry fails to implement promised reforms, the spirit of cooperation could fade. The threat of consumer awareness campaigns or even a selective boycott remains. NGO coalitions have continued their efforts to educate the public and have encouraged consumers to demand that jewelers guarantee conflict-free diamond sales. Until national jewelers can make such guarantees, the NGO movement will remain engaged and vigilant on this issue.

## Conflict Diamonds and the Diamond Industry

Until the late 1990s, when conflict diamonds entered public consciousness, the diamond industry was a rather opaque, largely unknown entity. International business was dominated by one company, De Beers, which sold approximately 70 percent of the world's uncut diamonds.[57] Known for maintaining huge stockpiles of diamonds, the De Beers oligopoly produced about half the world's supply itself and bought up large supplies of diamonds from other producers. The practice of hoarding diamonds and manipulating the market was a hallmark of De Beers from the 1920s, when its chairman of the board, Sir Ernest Oppenheimer, realized that diamonds were plentiful and that their value could be maintained only by imposing controlled scarcity.[58] The decision to hoard diamonds was also a way of combating the effects of the Great Depression. The company essentially set the price of world diamonds through its Central Selling Organization (CSO), located in London.[59]

This strategy worked fairly well until the late 1990s, when the volatility of world markets made it much more difficult and expensive to maintain huge stockpiles. The corporation realized that consumers were becoming aware of the concept of conflict diamonds and that the De Beers image could very easily become associated with the atrocities in Africa. As a result, De Beers issued a report in March 2000 declaring that its diamonds were "rebel free." CSO director Mike Farmilow stated, "We have to continue to give consumers the confidence that the diamonds they are buying are not funding conflict."[60] There was no way of verifying these claims, however, because very little action had been taken at that time to develop diamond certification controls at trading and cutting centers. In fact, De Beers admitted that it had purchased diamonds from UNITA just the year before.[61]

In 1999, De Beers commissioned the U.S.-based Bain and Company to conduct a study and report on how to adapt to changing market conditions, including the influx of diamonds from new Canadian mines, a trend that threatened De Beers's traditional control of the market.[62] Bain recommended that De Beers make the radical switch from being the "buyer of last resort" to being the "supplier of choice." Essentially, this meant that the industry giant would no longer maintain massive stockpiles of diamonds but rather would brand its diamonds as luxury designer items and sell to the high end of the market.[63] As part of this strategy, the company would also guarantee to the consumer that its expensive diamonds were conflict-free.[64] The new strategy, adopted by De Beers in July 2000, attempted to place the company "above" the conflict diamond issue and to create demand for its "rebel-free" diamonds.[65]

To combat the problem of conflict diamonds, industry executives launched a series of meetings in May 2000 in Kimberley, South Africa, birthplace of the diamond industry. This initiative, known as the Kimberley process, brought together representatives from the diamond industry, research groups, human rights organizations, and governments to develop ways of ending the trade in conflict diamonds. The coalition of groups involved in the Kimberley process proposed that:

- a worldwide system for certificates of origin be required to document the source and progress of each diamond from country of origin to trading and cutting centers;
- diamond-exporting countries be required to regulate and license both producers and traders; and
- diamond-importing countries be required to reject diamonds that are not accompanied by proper documentation.

At a September 2001 meeting in London, the groups reached agreement on the draft of key elements that would form the basis of an international certification system, including the need for effective controls and procedures, information gathering, and credible oversight and monitoring.[66]

Different proposals have been offered on the means of implementing such a global certification system, but all agree on the need for strict controls on both exporting and importing countries. In July 2000, the World Federation of Diamond Bourses and the International Diamond Manufacturing Association founded the World Diamond Council to develop and implement a plan to achieve this objective.[67] The Monitoring Mechanism on Sanctions Against UNITA identified the following key requirements for an effective certification system:

- bringing illicit miners into the system, improving their social conditions, and controlling their activities;
- licensing and controlling diamond intermediaries; and
- developing the capacity to investigate and arrest illicit dealers.[68]

Industry representatives have asserted that research and development currently under way on systems of diamond tracking, marking, and identification will take a long time to develop and will be very expensive, especially for developing countries. Global Witness reported, however, that the requisite technology for diamond tracking already exists for other applications and could be applied to an industrywide certification system.[69] These technologies include using laser refraction to determine an exact fingerprint, or "gemprint," of each stone and imprinting laser-created barcodes or logos on individual diamonds.[70] This practice is already employed by the Ekati mine in Canada, which imprints a polar bear on every gem.[71]

Another option would be microtomography, a technique similar to computed tomography (CT), which is used in the medical field. Microtomography could help to create external profiles that would accompany the diamonds through the production, processing, and marketing pipelines.[72] The development of comprehensive databases maintained by independent, trained professionals would also be essential to a workable certificate of origin system. Without strictly maintained databases to record and track the movement of diamonds, it would be impossible to verify the legitimacy of individual stones or to monitor, interdict, and prosecute illicit transactions.

## Government Responses

The most important requirement for diamond regulation is the adoption of common standards for identifying the country of origin of all rough diamonds.[73] The terms *country of origin* (the country from which the diamond was extracted) and *country of provenance* (the country from which the diamond arrived) are often used interchangeably. Currently, countries have very different diamond import procedures. The Diamond High Council in Antwerp lists the latest country through which the diamond has passed as the country of origin, thus complicating and confusing this identification process.[74] Another difficulty is the problem of regulating diamonds produced through alluvial mining, which involves large numbers of individual workers who can and often do sell stones to unlicensed dealers. Gaining control over these operations is an enormous challenge.[75]

In January 2001, the UN General Assembly formally addressed the issue of conflict diamonds with a resolution urging that member states adhere to the Kimberley process. The resolution called for a "simple and workable" certificate system for rough diamonds. In the resolution, the General Assembly emphasized the necessity of international participation in the certificate system and called for measures to include all concerned parties.[76] The certification systems that have been developed to date have been limited and are insufficient to stem the continued flow of conflict diamonds. Belgium is the only importing country that has officially adopted a certificate of origin system. Under the terms of Security Council resolutions, this means that diamond exports from Angola and Sierra Leone to anywhere other than Antwerp are illegal, although such exports nonetheless continue.[77]

Canada, the United Kingdom, and the United States have been leaders in exposing the problem of conflict diamonds. Developing strict "national" standards on certificates of origin has been more challenging. Both the United Kingdom and the United States have developed but not fully adopted legislation to end the trade in conflict diamonds. Legislation in the United States has been spearheaded by U.S. representative Tony Hall (D–OH), who visited Sierra Leone and witnessed firsthand the role of conflict diamonds in supporting rebel groups that commit atrocities. Representatives Hall and Frank Wolf (R–VA) introduced a bill titled Consumer Access to a Responsible Accounting of Trade (CARAT) in November 1999, noting that the United States imports more than half of the world's gem-quality diamonds. The bill required that certificates of origin accompany diamonds imported into the United States and would impose stiff fines on those who knowingly attempt to violate this requirement.[78]

The introduction of the CARAT bill paved the way for the subsequent Clean Diamonds Act, a bill presented to the U.S. House of Representatives in March 2001 by Representative Hall and seventy-nine other members of the House of Representatives. If enacted, this act would prohibit diamond imports from countries that do not have approved systems of diamond certification and control.[79] The Clean Diamonds Act would also require the freezing of assets of people known to export diamonds from countries violating the provisions of the act.[80] An identical bill was introduced in the U.S. Senate in June 2001 by Senator Richard Durbin (D–IL) and Senator Mike DeWine (R–OH).[81] Passage of these bills would signal a strong commitment to ending the trade in conflict diamonds.[82] Adoption of similar legislation in other countries will be necessary to create an effective worldwide system for enforcing UN commodity sanctions.

## Commodity Sanctions: A Partial Success?

There is little question that sanctions on conflict diamonds, if properly enforced, could effectively reduce funding for war and human rights abuse throughout sub-Saharan Africa. The ultimate success of diamond sanctions will depend on implementation of the Kimberley process and the creation of enforceable industrywide standards for certification. The very fact that the diamond industry and governments have taken steps to restrict conflict diamonds is a positive sign. Industry-government cooperation is a relatively new development in the field of sanctions enforcement, and it contrasts with the usual pattern, in which private industry groups have little incentive to cooperate with UN sanctions. In this instance, the desire of industry groups to preserve the legitimate diamond business has coincided with the UN agenda to curb the trade in conflict diamonds. Much greater cooperation will be needed, though, to implement the various reform measures that have been agreed upon and to achieve genuine progress in eliminating the illicit trade in diamonds. Only if there is a workable system for certification and enforcement will diamond commodity sanctions fulfill their potential as a valuable tool for controlling violence, protecting human rights, and ensuring security and peace in Africa.

## Notes

1. United Nations Department of Public Information, *Conflict Diamonds: Sanctions and War* (report in cooperation with the Sanctions Branch, Security Council Affairs Division, Department of Political Affairs, New York, 21 March 2001) <www.un.org/peace/africa/Diamond.html> (29 June 2001).
2. Ibid.
3. Paul Collier, "Doing Well out of War: An Economic Perspective," in Mats

Berdal and David M. Malone, eds., *Greed and Grievance: Economic Agendas in Civil Wars* (Boulder, Colo.: Lynne Rienner Publishers, 2000), 97.

4. We will use the term *conflict diamonds* throughout this chapter, but we note at the outset that a number of respectable analysts and many in the NGO community prefer the term *blood diamonds*.

5. The Sierra Leone panel of experts estimated the amount of illegal smuggling at 20 percent of total trade, whereas the U.S. Agency for International Development estimated it to be near 30 percent. The diamond industry estimated the amount to be 4 percent. United Nations Security Council, *Report of the Panel of Experts Appointed Pursuant to Security Council Resolution 1306 (2000), Paragraph 19, in Relation to Sierra Leone*, S/2000/1195, New York, 20 December 2000, par. 148; U.S. Agency for International Development, Office of Transition Initiatives, *Sierra Leone: "Conflict" Diamonds: Progress Report on Diamond Policy and Development Program* (New York: USAID, 30 March 2001), 1; "Progress Report," Diamond High Council, Antwerp, 1 November 2000, <www.conflictdiamonds.com/pages/Interface/reportframe.html> (13 July 2001).

6. Diamond production information by country taken from Ian Smillie, Lansana Gberie, and Ralph Hazleton, *The Heart of the Matter: Sierra Leone, Diamonds and Human Security* (Ottawa, Ontario, Canada: Partnership Africa Canada, January 2000), 16, Table 1.

7. Global Witness, *A Rough Trade: The Role of Companies and Government in the Angolan Conflict* (London: Global Witness, December 1998), 2.

8. United Nations Security Council, *Security Council Resolution 864 (1993)*, S/RES/864, New York, 15 September 1993. For an assessment of the efficacy of oil and diamond sanctions in Angola before 2000, see David Cortright, George A. Lopez, and Richard W. Conroy, "Angola's Agony," in Cortright and Lopez, with Richard W. Conroy, Jaleh Dashti-Gibson, and Julia Wagler, *The Sanctions Decade: Assessing UN Strategies in the 1990s* (Boulder, Colo.: Lynne Rienner Publishers, 2000), 147–165.

9. Mats Berdal and David M. Malone, eds., "Introduction," in *Greed and Grievance: Economic Agendas in Civil Wars* (Boulder, Colo.: Lynne Rienner Publishers, 2000), 1–11.

10. According to the company's annual reports, De Beers bought a significant portion of its gem-quality diamonds from Angola. Global Witness, *A Rough Trade*, 4.

11. United Nations Security Council, *Security Council Resolution 1127 (1997)*, S/RES/1127, New York, 28 August 1997; United Nations Security Council, *Security Council Resolution 1173 (1998)*, S/RES/1173, New York, 12 June 1998.

12. Cortright, Lopez, and Conroy, "Angola's Agony," 155–156.

13. Human Rights Watch, *Angola Unravels: The Rise and Fall of the Lusaka Peace Process* (New York: Human Rights Watch, September 1999), 5.

14. Ibid., 136.

15. United Nations Security Council, *Letter Dated 12 February 1999 from the Chairman of the Security Council Committee Established Pursuant to Security Council Resolution 864 (1993) Concerning the Situation in Angola Addressed to the President of the Security Council*, S/1999/147, New York, 12 February 1999.

16. United Nations Security Council, *Report of the Panel of Experts on Violations of Security Council Sanctions Against UNITA*, S/2000/203, New York, 10 March 2000, pars. 92, 94.

17. United Nations Security Council, *Addendum to the Final Report of the*

*Monitoring Mechanism on Sanctions Against UNITA,* S/2001/363, New York, 11 April 2001, par. 107(e).

18. Judy Dempsey, "Upstart Dealer Muscles into Market," *Financial Times,* 11 July 2000, <www.ft.com/diamonds/Tuesday2.htm> (6 July 2001).

19. "Belgium Accuses Continuing Sale of UNITA Diamonds," *Panafrican News Agency,* 24 April 2001, <www.allafrica.com/stories/200104240445.html> (27 June 2001).

20. Andrew Parker, Sathnam Sanghera, and Francesco Guerrera, "Between a Rock and a Hard Place," *Financial Times,* 12 July 2000, <www.ft.com/diamonds/Wednesday1.htm> (6 July 2001).

21. It is not surprising in the case of Angola and also in Sierra Leone that as the government became more effective in its certification system, the issue of counterfeit certification arose. Particularly difficult as well has been collusion between holders of real certificates and rebels for purposes of negating the system. Based on written correspondence with William Reno, 16 October 2001.

22. Smillie, Gberie, and Hazleton, *The Heart of the Matter,* 17–18.

23. John L. Hirsch, *Sierra Leone: Diamonds and the Struggle for Democracy* (Boulder, Colo.: Lynne Rienner Publishers, 2001), 15, 25–28; see also Smillie, Gberie, and Hazleton, *The Heart of the Matter,* 2.

24. United Nations Security Council, *Security Council Resolution 1306 (2000),* S/RES/1306, New York, 5 July 2000.

25. United Nations Security Council, *Report of the Panel of Experts Appointed Pursuant to Security Council Resolution 1306 (2000), Paragraph 19, in Relation to Sierra Leone,* S/2000/1195.

26. Ibid., par. 1.

27. Ibid., pars. 8, 9.

28. U.S. Agency for International Development, *Sierra Leone: "Conflict" Diamonds,* 12.

29. Global Witness, *Review of the Sierra Leone Diamond Certification System and Proposals and Recommendations for the Kimberley Process for a Fully Integrated Certification System (FICS),* London, 25 April 2001, 6.

30. U.S. Agency for International Development, *Sierra Leone: "Conflict" Diamonds,* Table 3.

31. Ibid., 17–18.

32. Smillie, Gberie, and Hazleton, *The Heart of the Matter,* 47.

33. United Nations Security Council, *Report of the Panel of Experts Appointed Pursuant to Security Council Resolution 1306 (2000), Paragraph 19, in Relation to Sierra Leone,* S/2000/1195, pars. 123, 124.

34. "Sierra Leone: The Forgotten Crisis," *Report to the Minister of Foreign Affairs, The Honourable Lloyd Axworthy, P.C., M.P. from David Pratt, M.P., Nepean-Carleton, Special Envoy to Sierra Leone,* 23 April 1999, <www.sierraleone.org/pratt0423399.html> (20 July 1999).

35. United Nations Security Council, *Security Council Resolution 1343 (2001),* S/RES/1343, New York, 7 March 2001.

36. Ibid.

37. United Nations Office for the Coordination of Humanitarian Affairs, Integrated Regional Information Network, "The Role of Liberia's Logging Industry on National and Regional Insecurity" (briefing to the UN Security Council by Global Witness, New York, 24 January 2001), 1.

38. The named arms dealers are Gus Kouwenhoven and Talal El-Ndine.

United Nations Office for the Coordination of Humanitarian Affairs, Integrated Regional Information Network, "The Role of Liberia's Logging Industry," 4; United Nations Security Council, *Report of the Panel of Experts Appointed Pursuant to UN Security Council Resolution 1306 (2000), Paragraph 19, in Relation to Sierra Leone*, S/2000/1195, par. 49.

39. United Nations, *Report of the Panel of Experts Appointed Pursuant to Security Council Resolution 1306 (2000), Paragraph 19, in Relation to Sierra Leone*, S/2000/1195, par. 49.

40. James Astill, "Liberian Regime Under Threat," *Guardian* (London), 28 May 2001, 12.

41. Anthony Lewis, "France and Taylor's 'Presidential Pepperbush,'" *Global Policy Forum,* 5 June 2001, <www.globalpolicy.org/security/issues/liberia/2001/0605timb.htm> (11 September 2001).

42. Global Witness, "The Role of Liberia and Its Logging Industry on National and Regional Insecurity," *Global Witness,* May 2001, <www.oneworld.org/globalwitness> (11 September 2001).

43. "Liberian Timber Profits Finance Regional Conflict," *Africa Online,* 8 May 2001, <www.africaonline.com/> (4 July 2001).

44. Carola Hoyos, "Liberian Timber in UN spotlight," *Financial Times,* 27 January 2001, 8; "Liberia Moves to Ward Off U.N. Embargo," *New York Times,* 24 January 2001, A8; Christopher S. Wren, "New Sanctions Likely to Fall on Liberians," *New York Times,* 26 January 2001, A9; Barbara Crossette, "Behave or Face a Diamond Ban, Security Council Tells Liberians," *New York Times,* 8 March 2001, A6.

45. United Nations Security Council, *Report of the Secretary-General in Pursuance of Paragraph 13(a) of Resolution 1343 (2001) Concerning Liberia,* S/2001/939, New York, 5 October 2001, pars. 34–38.

46. David Cortright, George A. Lopez, and Richard W. Conroy, "Flawed UN Arms Embargoes in Somalia, Liberia, and Rwanda," in Cortright and Lopez, *The Sanctions Decade: Assessing UN Strategies in the 1990s* (Boulder, Colo.: Lynne Rienner Publishers, 2000), 198.

47. "Peace Here Means War Elsewhere," *The Economist,* 23 June 2001, 44.

48. Ian Fisher and Norimitsu Onishi, "Chaos in Congo: Armies Ravage a Rich Land, Creating Africa's 'First World War,'" *New York Times,* 6 February 2000, <www.nytimes.com> (28 June 2001).

49. United Nations Security Council, *Report of the Panel of Experts on the Illegal Exploitation of Natural Resources and Other Forms of Wealth of the Democratic Republic of the Congo,* S/2001/357, New York, 12 April 2001.

50. "Congo's Hidden War," *The Economist,* 17 June 2000, 45–46.

51. Uganda exported 10.83 tons of gold in 2000 and produced only 0.0044 ton. In 1994, Uganda exported only 0.22 ton of gold, producing 0.0016 ton. United Nations Security Council, *Report of the Panel of Experts on the Illegal Exploitation of Natural Resources and Other Forms of Wealth of the Democratic Republic of the Congo,* S/2001/357, Table 1.

52. Ibid., Tables 2 and 5, par. 107.

53. Ibid., pars. 232–235.

54. United Nations Office for the Coordination of Humanitarian Affairs, Integrated Regional Information Network, "DRC: Natural Resources Exploitation Panel Resumes Work," New York, 28 February 2002, <www.reliefweb.int/IRIN/cea/countrystories/drc/20010504.phtml> (11 March 2002).

55. Fatal Transactions Campaign, "Diamond, a *Merciless* Beauty," <www.niza.nl/uk/campaigns/diamonds/index.html> (28 June 2001).

56. Holly Burkhalter, "Getting to Yes," monthly update, *Physicians for Human Rights,* <www.phrusa.org/campaigns/beltway_entries/beltway2.html> (28 June 2001).

57. Global Witness, *Possibilities for the Identification, Certification and Control of Diamonds* (London: Global Witness, June 2000), 7.

58. Blaine Harden, "Africa's Diamond Wars—Africa's Gems: Warfare's Best Friend," *New York Times,* 6 April 2000, A1; Smillie, Gberie, and Hazleton, *The Heart of the Matter,* 20.

59. Smillie, Gberie, and Hazleton, *The Heart of the Matter,* 21.

60. Shaun Gatter, "De Beers Guarantees Rebel Free Diamond Sales," *Rapaport News,* 29 March 2000, <www.diamonds.net> (20 June 2001).

61. Global Witness concluded: "Given that De Beers were, according to their own reports, buying a substantial proportion of Angolan rough diamonds, at a time when a large section of the country's diamond mines were under UNITA's control, one could conclude that the drive to keep the lucrative outside market buoyant was a primary concern—despite the consequences this might have for the people of Angola during this period." Global Witness, *A Rough Trade,* 4.

62. Canada plans to have three diamond mines operational by the year 2005, and if production estimates are accurate, Canada could produce up to 15 percent of the world's diamonds. James Brooke, "Canada Tries to Make Clear Its Diamonds Are Different," *New York Times,* 12 August 2000, A1.

63. Francesco Guerrera and Andrew Parker, "De Beers: All That Glitters Is Not Sold," *The Economist,* 11 July 2000, 12.

64. Francesco Guerrera et al., "The Changing Face of the Diamond Industry," *Financial Times,* 11 July 2000, 16.

65. Lurking behind NGO publicity concerns and whatever civic consciousness it created was a reasonable business assumption by De Beers that the certification system was likely to help its own competitive position in the medium to long term, as it would drive up the cost of local diamonds to its junior competitors, who could no longer rely on a large supply of rebel-based, uncertified diamonds.

66. United Nations Security Council, *Supplementary Report of the Monitoring Mechanism on Sanctions Against UNITA,* S/2001/966, New York, 12 October 2001, par. 152.

67. World Diamond Council, "WDC Calls for International Action on Conflict Diamonds," *Rapaport News,* 7 September 2000, <www.diamonds.net> (21 May 2001).

68. United Nations Security Council, *Supplementary Report of the Monitoring Mechanism on Sanctions Against UNITA,* S/2001/966, par. 167.

69. Global Witness, *Possibilities for the Identification, Certification and Control of Diamonds,* 31.

70. Ibid., 32–33.

71. The Ekati mine in Canada's Northwest Territories has created a chain of custody, from the mine to the consumer, which involves an elaborate database tracking system into which individual stones are checked and monitored throughout the process. Brooke, "Canada Tries to Make Clear."

72. Global Witness, *Possibilities for the Identification, Certification and Control of Diamonds,* 21.

73. Ibid., 49.

74. Smillie, Gberie, and Hazleton, *The Heart of the Matter,* 3.

75. For a more detailed examination of the problems in regulating diamond mining, see United Nations Security Council, *Addendum to the Final Report of the Monitoring Mechanism on Sanctions Against UNITA,* S/2001/363, pars. 52–73.

76. United Nations General Assembly, *The Role of Diamonds in Fuelling Conflict: Breaking the Link Between the Illicit Transaction of Rough Diamonds and Armed Conflict as a Contribution to Prevention and Settlement of Conflicts,* A/RES/55/56, New York, 29 January 2001.

77. U.S. Agency for International Development, *Sierra Leone: "Conflict" Diamonds,* 10.

78. Representative Tony Hall, *Consumer Access to a Responsible Accounting of Trade Act of 2000,* bill introduced in the House of Representatives, 106th Cong., 1st sess., H.R. 3188, Washington, D.C., 1 November 1999.

79. This momentum in the United States toward certification was not just in response to the NGO concerns, of course. In recent years, the U.S. Justice Department has taken legal action against De Beers for antitrust violations.

80. Representative Tony Hall et al., *To Prohibit the Importation of Diamonds Unless the Countries Exporting the Diamonds into the United States Have in Place a System of Controls on Rough Diamonds, and for Other Purposes,* bill introduced in the House of Representatives, 107th Cong., 1st sess., H.R. 918, Washington, D.C., 7 March 2001.

81. Senators Richard Durbin and Mike DeWine, *To Prohibit the Importation of Diamonds Unless the Countries Exporting the Diamonds into the United States Have in Place a System of Controls on Rough Diamonds, and for Other Purposes,* bill introduced in the Senate, 107th Cong., 1st sess., S. 1084, Washington, D.C., 21 June 2001.

82. "Hall Praises Compromise on Conflict Diamonds" (remarks of Representative Tony Hall at a press conference, 21 June 2001, Washington, D.C.), U.S. House of Representatives, <www.house.gov/tonyhall/pr226.html> (12 July 2001).

# 11

## Reform or Retreat?
## The Future of UN Sanctions Policy

As 2001 drew to a close, the United Nations Security Council faced a crossroads in sanctions policy. In a number of cases of threats to peace and deteriorating regional security, the Council responded creatively and appropriately at the design stage of sanctions, only to experience a lack of sanctions effectiveness because of inadequacies in implementation and monitoring on the ground. In some settings, such as Angola and West Africa, the partial security advances that occurred were the result primarily of changes on the battlefield. Sanctions made some contribution to limiting access to wealth and weapons, but UN measures generally underperformed because of inadequate enforcement. In other cases, such as the continuing differences over sanctions policy regarding Iraq and the inability of sanctions to change regime behavior in Afghanistan, the security issues at stake were framed and dealt with by members of the Permanent Five working for the most part outside the aegis of the UN. In similar fashion, divided positions within the Chowdhury working group could not be bridged on singular issues like time limits, thus holding in abeyance a series of reforms on which there was broad consensus.

As we noted in Chapter 1 and documented throughout this volume, the Security Council has adopted significant refinements in sanctions policy in recent years. Most notable have been steps toward improving sanctions design, applying more targeted measures, strengthening monitoring and enforcement, and prioritizing humanitarian concerns. Yet these advances have been compromised by competing political agendas among the Permanent Five, inadequate compliance by member states, and a lack of institutionalized UN monitoring and enforcement capacity. Although the Security Council has made some progress in advancing the art and science of economic statecraft, comprehensive sanctions reform has been elusive.

In this final chapter, we review the many innovations that have

201

been introduced in UN sanctions policy and summarize the most important recommendations for improvement in the future. In so doing, we
hope to highlight the positive developments that have been achieved
and point toward the additional steps needed to enhance sanctions
effectiveness.

## Improving Targeted Sanctions

The dominant trend in UN policymaking has been the shift away from
general trade sanctions toward more targeted and selective measures.
Since 1994, all UN sanctions have been targeted. Financial sanctions,
travel bans, arms embargoes, and commodity boycotts have replaced
general trade embargoes as the preferred instruments of UN policy. The
sweeping counterterrorism measures adopted in SCR 1373 (2001) continued this trend, imposing targeted financial, travel, and other restrictions on terrorists and those who support them. In each of the categories
of selective sanctions—finance, travel, arms, and commodities—the
Security Council has introduced important innovations.

In the area of financial sanctions, the Council has moved beyond
freezing the assets of governments to locking down the accounts of designated entities and individuals as well. In the cases of Iraq, Libya, and
Yugoslavia, financial sanctions were imposed only on government
assets. Beginning with the sanctions against the military junta in Haiti
in 1994 and continuing through the cases of the National Union for the
Total Independence of Angola (UNITA) in Angola and the Taliban
regime in Afghanistan, the Council also applied targeted financial sanctions against designated entities and individuals. The counterterrorism
measures mandated in SCR 1373 were also directed against entities and
individuals. Unlike earlier times, the UN Secretariat now has developed
the capacity, in cooperation with member states, to develop and publish
lists of designated sanctions targets.

Innovations have also occurred in UN arms embargoes. The language and technical terms employed in Security Council arms embargoes have become more precise. Arms embargo resolutions now include
prohibitions not only against the supply of arms and ammunition but
also against training, cooperation, and various support services, including air transportation. This refinement of terms and broadening of
items covered has helped to close loopholes and avoid ambiguities that
impede enforcement.

Another new development was the creation of a special UN arms embargo monitoring and support team to enforce the sanctions against the Taliban regime in Afghanistan. Recognizing the general problem of inadequate implementation of UN arms embargoes and the special problems of attempting to stem the flow of weapons into Afghanistan, the Security Council created a special unit to monitor and enforce the arms embargo against the Taliban regime. SCR 1363 (2001) authorized a five-person monitoring group at UN headquarters in New York and a fifteen-person sanctions enforcement support team to be deployed in countries neighboring Afghanistan, primarily Pakistan. Although a tiny and thus inadequate force, considering the enormity of the challenge, it represented an initial attempt at independent monitoring support. Deployment of the monitors was interrupted by the political turmoil and military action in the region that followed the terrorist attacks on 11 September 2001. In January 2002, as part of SCR 1390, the Council directed the group to monitor the ongoing financial, travel, and arms-related sanctions on targeted Taliban and al-Qaida leaders.

Commodity-specific boycotts have become an important new feature of UN sanctions policy. Oil embargoes were previously imposed against Iraq, Yugoslavia, Khmer Rouge–controlled areas of Cambodia, Haiti, UNITA in Angola, and the military junta in Sierra Leone. An embargo on log exports from Khmer Rouge territory was also imposed in Cambodia and threatened for Liberia. Diamond embargoes are a more recent development. The Council imposed diamond embargoes against UNITA in Angola (SCR 1173, 1998), Revolutionary United Front (RUF) areas of Sierra Leone (SCR 1306, 2000), and the government of Liberia (SCR 1343, 2001). These targeted diamond sanctions have given the Security Council a new means of applying focused pressure on specific rebel groups and curtailing the lucrative funding base that has sustained armed conflict.

## Broadening the Reach of Sanctions

As the threats to global peace and security have changed, the purposes for which sanctions are imposed have steadily widened.[1] During the 1990s, sanctions were imposed to reverse aggression, restore democratically elected governments, protect human rights, end wars, and bring suspected terrorists to justice. Now two additional functions have been added—sanctioning a country for violating UN-mandated sanctions and imposing worldwide financial and other sanctions against terrorism. With the imposition of sanctions against Liberia (SCR 1343, 2001), the

Council for the first time imposed mandatory measures against one country because of its defiance of sanctions against another. Recognizing Liberia's role as the primary supply base for the RUF, the Council imposed a diamond embargo, travel sanctions, and an arms embargo against the Monrovia government. The purpose of the Liberia sanctions was to exert full pressure on a state secondarily involved in norm violation. It was an important step toward broadening the scope of sanctions and strengthening their enforcement.

More sweeping in its implications was the adoption of the counterterrorism resolution (SCR 1373, 2001). As noted in Chapter 7, it was the most far-reaching sanctions measure ever adopted by the Council, effectively mandating that all 189 UN member states impose financial sanctions and travel restrictions against entities and individuals associated with terrorist acts. The resolution demanded that member states take action within their borders to criminalize the financing of terror and adopt other law enforcement and intelligence-sharing measures. It was an unprecedented attempt to mandate changes in the internal law enforcement and legal procedures of UN member states. It established worldwide financial sanctions against terrorists and their supporters. The multiple mandates contained in SCR 1373 would, if effectively implemented and enforced, mobilize the entire international community into a sustained criminal prosecution against the financing and support of terrorist networks.

## Investigative Panels

Analysts have long emphasized that effective monitoring is key to the success of sanctions. In many cases, however, member states have lacked the capacity for effective monitoring and have been unwilling or unable to make the necessary commitment of resources to identify and report sanctions violations. The United Nations has lacked an independent monitoring capacity of its own. But in recent years, the picture has begun to change. The appointment of independent expert panels and monitoring mechanisms has now become a regular feature of sanctions policy making. The first panel was established in conjunction with the arms embargo against Rwandan Hutu rebels (SCR 1013, 1995). The United Nations Independent Commission of Inquiry (UNICOI) issued six reports from 1996 through 1998 thoroughly documenting the supply routes and underground networks used to arm the rebels in eastern Zaire. Some member states were uncomfortable with UNICOI's hard-hitting reports, however, and little was done to follow up on its voluminous evidence of violations or to implement its recommendations.

The breakthrough toward a more integral role for investigative panels came in the case of Angola. As noted in Chapter 4, the 1999 mission of Canadian ambassador Robert Fowler proved decisive in ratcheting up the importance of investigative panels. Fowler's mission both added the diplomatic weight of a sanctions committee chair to the investigative effort and changed the style of panel operation. Fowler not only reported on violations but met with government and private industry representatives to encourage active compliance. His mission led to the appointment of the Angola panel of experts, which issued a groundbreaking report in March 2000. The Angola panel of experts was followed by a similar panel for Sierra Leone, a committee of experts for Afghanistan, and a panel of experts for Liberia. An investigative panel was also created to examine the exploitation of mineral and natural resources in the Congo. These myriad panel reports produced a wealth of data on sanctions violations and illicit transactions in the areas of finance, arms, travel, and commodities. They also contained a series of detailed recommendations for improving sanctions enforcement.[2]

## Name and Shame

The panels of experts and their investigative reports have proved to be an effective means of applying pressure on sanctions violators and encouraging governments to strengthen enforcement. The reports have adopted a name and shame approach specifically identifying the governments, companies, and individuals responsible for sanctions violations. The Angola panel of experts report was particularly hard-hitting, implicating two sitting heads of state in blatant violations of UN sanctions. Because of objections from the countries named, subsequent panel reports were not as direct in naming specific government leaders, but they continued the practice of identifying those involved in circumventing sanctions. The Sierra Leone panel of experts was particularly forthright in documenting the role of the government of Liberia in providing continued support to the RUF in contravention of Security Council sanctions.

The name and shame function of the special investigative panels has stirred debate and controversy. Developed countries have tended to favor the tactic, but many developing nations have been skeptical. The Secretary-General spoke positively of the name and shame process in his millennium report on conflict prevention to the General Assembly: "The best preventive strategy . . . is transparency: 'naming and shaming.'"[3] Many members of the Security Council have similarly viewed the technique of exposure as an important means of mobilizing public opinion and political support for greater sanctions compliance.

The UN's *Human Development Report*, however, expressed concern about this strategy. The annual development report for 2000, published soon after the Secretary-General's millennium report, took a more critical view. "A global change in attitude is needed, moving to a positive approach of support for human rights in place of punitive approaches that emphasize 'naming and shaming' and conditions for aid." The report called for a shift "from reliance on naming and shaming to positive support."[4] This negative assessment reflected the widespread concern among developing nations over the conditions and limitations that international financial institutions and donor nations have placed on development assistance. The *Human Development Report* did not object to exposing malfeasance per se but to the conditioning of aid. When governments or international institutions threaten to withhold assistance because of sanctions violations, developing nations naturally become concerned.

Ironically, this very concern about the conditioning of aid indicates the potential leverage that naming and shaming can provide. As noted in Chapter 1, the mere threat of sanctions can be powerful and may motivate a targeted regime to take conciliatory steps. In a similar way, the naming of a government or private actor as a violator of sanctions can arouse concern about the potential consequences of this exposure. It is the very prospect of a withdrawal of support, or worse, the imposition of secondary pressures, that may be effective at inducing greater cooperation.

The Security Council has attempted to navigate between these differing perspectives by establishing its investigative panels as independent bodies. As noted in Chapter 4, the creation of separate expert panels has allowed members of the Council to distance themselves from the resulting reports and the identification of sanctions violators. This separation provides the necessary leverage of public exposure while allowing UN officials to pursue diplomatic solutions beyond the glare of adverse publicity. There are some indications that the Security Council may move away from naming and shaming techniques toward a more traditional emphasis on quiet diplomacy. This reluctance partly reflects a belief on the part of some states that the methods of public exposure bring diminishing returns over time and may interfere with the delicate diplomatic maneuvering that is often necessary to achieve cooperation. This perspective, together with the stated concerns of developing nations, may lead to diminishing use of this approach in the future. We believe that would be a mistake. Public investigation and exposure have proved to be effective means of generating cooperation with UN sanctions. It is the combination of both approaches—public exposure and quiet diplomacy—that offers the best chance of encouraging compliance.

## Nongovernmental Monitoring

Private industry and nongovernmental organizations have assumed an increasingly important role in evaluating and helping to implement sanctions policies. The role of private industry has been most evident in the enforcement of the diamond embargoes against UNITA in Angola, the RUF rebels in Sierra Leone, and the government of Liberia. As noted in Chapter 10, the De Beers Corporation and the major diamond exchanges have sought to avoid being tarnished with the image of conflict diamonds. They have worked with the United Nations and member states to create certification systems designed to prevent conflict diamonds from entering the market. Industry representatives established the World Diamond Council for the specific purpose of ensuring a conflict-free diamond market. Similar, though less extensive, cooperation in sanctions enforcement has come from the banking industry, especially in the United States. Banking industry representatives participated in the Interlaken seminars sponsored by the government of Switzerland, and they have cooperated with governments, albeit reluctantly at times, in developing software and administrative systems for enforcing financial sanctions.

This novel participation of the private sector suggests new possibilities for strengthening the monitoring and enforcement of sanctions. Some sanctions experts have urged greater efforts to enlist private industry in sanctions enforcement. One means of addressing the problem of illegal air transportation, for example, would be to work with the insurance industry to deny coverage for companies and individual pilots identified as violating UN sanctions.[5]

A related innovation was the decision of the Security Council in 2001 to hire a private security firm to trace the financial assets of UNITA. Individual member states have used private investigative firms in the past, but UN officials have been reluctant to consider this approach. The decision to employ such a firm in the case of Angola indicated the Council's determination to tighten the financial squeeze on UNITA.

As noted in several chapters, the role of nongovernmental organizations has become increasingly prominent in all phases of United Nations sanctions. Groups such as Global Witness, Human Rights Watch, Saferworld, and the International Peace Academy have become major players in documenting the humanitarian and human rights conditions and developing innovative approaches to the improvement of sanctions. Human rights groups and other research organizations played the key role in documenting the problem of conflict diamonds and in tracking the flow of small arms to Africa and other war zones. Human Rights Watch, the Brookings Institution, and the Kroc Institute/Fourth Freedom Forum research project contributed policy proposals for the restructuring of sanctions in Iraq. The Watson Institute and the International Peace Academy played seminal roles in working with UN missions in New York to facilitate continued assessment of the Interlaken and Bonn-Berlin reform processes.

## Prioritizing Humanitarian Concerns

The desire to avoid humanitarian suffering among vulnerable and innocent populations has become a dominant feature of Security Council policymaking. As we have noted, the concern for humanitarian consequences has been the principal factor motivating the trend toward the use of more targeted and selective sanctions. The Security Council has sought to reduce unintended impacts within targeted regimes and among third parties in neighboring states. As sanctions analysts have noted, the effect of sanctions on neighboring states and trading partners of the targeted regime can be severe.[6] The motivation to minimize adverse impacts has prompted a number of innovations in Security Council policymaking.

Humanitarian assessments and impact missions have now become a regular feature of UN sanctions. It was a reform long sought by humanitarian agencies and independent researchers, ourselves included.[7] Assessment reports conducted prior to sanctions imposition or during the early stages of a sanctions regime offer a means for the Security Council to anticipate and prevent potential humanitarian problems and to arrest unanticipated adverse impacts in a timely manner.

The first humanitarian assessment report came in conjunction with the Security Council's consideration of aviation sanctions against Sudan. The February 1997 report from the UN Department of Humanitarian Affairs provided a gloomy assessment of the likely adverse impacts of the proposed flight ban.[8] Partly as a result, the Council did not implement the sanctions. The next assessment report came in the case of Sierra Leone, soon after sanctions were imposed against the military junta in Freetown. The interagency assessment was highly critical of the trade embargo imposed by the Economic Community of West African States (ECOWAS) but found no evidence of major humanitarian consequences from the more limited UN sanctions.[9]

Humanitarian assessment reports have also been ordered in the cases of Afghanistan and Liberia. The Afghanistan report, released in December 2000, evaluated the impact of the financial sanctions and aviation ban against the Taliban regime. The study recounted the horrendous humanitarian conditions in Afghanistan, among the worst in the world, but it found few adverse social consequences that could be attributed to the targeted UN sanctions.[10] The Liberia report, released in October 2001, came to similar conclusions about conditions in Liberia. The diamond embargo and other selective sanctions against the Monrovia government had only limited humanitarian impacts. The Liberia assessment cautioned, however, that timber sanctions, which had been proposed by some member states but not yet implemented by the Council, could result in the loss of thousands of jobs and have significant adverse economic and social impacts on that devastated country.[11]

The methodology for humanitarian assessment developed by the UN Office for the Coordination of Humanitarian Affairs (OCHA) employs recommendations proposed by humanitarian agencies and independent researchers. The 1997 study for the Department of Humanitarian Affairs[12] in which the authors participated recommended a multistep methodology and a series of specific indicators for assessing humanitarian impacts.[13] Many of the indicators suggested in such categories as public health and population displacement have been adopted in the OCHA studies of Afghanistan and Liberia. The development of a standardized methodology permits comparative analysis across cases and makes it easier for policymakers to evaluate humanitarian impacts.

Another recommendation of the 1997 report called for the granting of blanket exemptions for designated humanitarian agencies. Navigating the often tangled administrative procedures of UN sanctions committees has placed substantial burdens on relief organizations. If aviation sanctions are imposed against a country, for example, relief agencies must apply for exemptions to import needed food and medicine. For several years, these agencies have recommended that the Security Council provide blanket exemptions for designated relief groups, so that humanitarian supplies can be delivered expeditiously without the excruciating delays and difficulties involved in seeking approval for each flight or delivery. This proposal was integrated into the sanctions applied in Afghanistan. In paragraph 12 of SCR 1333 (2000), the Security Council authorized the sanctions committee to exempt a preapproved list of relief agencies. Whether it was a one-time decision or the beginning of a trend is uncertain. Humanitarian officials welcomed the Council's action and expressed the hope that the granting of blanket exemptions to designated agencies would become standard policy in future sanctions episodes.

## Time Limits

France and other members of the Security Council have strongly encouraged the policy of establishing time limits as a way of avoiding the open-ended, seemingly endless sanctions that have remained in place against Iraq. The concern with time limits has been not only humanitarian but political, to prevent permanent members of the Council from blocking a consensus for the lifting of sanctions. The United States and the United Kingdom opposed the idea of time limits when it was raised within the Security Council working group as a matter of general principle. In specific cases, however, the two countries have gone along with the establishment of time limits. The first use of time limits occurred in the arms embargo against Ethiopia and Eritrea (SCR 1298, 2000), when the Council set a twelve-month period for the embargo. As noted in Chapter 9, the sanctions were not renewed at the end of that period. Twelve-month time limits were also established for the arms embargo and additional sanctions imposed against the Taliban regime in Afghanistan in December 2000 (SCR 1333) and for the diamond embargo and travel sanctions enacted against Liberia in May 2001 (SCR 1343).

Debate abounds whether time limits will be a positive or a negative feature of UN policymaking. U.S. and UK officials argue that time limits will weaken the coercive impact of sanctions because targeted regimes will take advantage of such limits to delay compliance and block the possible renewal of sanctions. French and Russian representatives counter that pressure on the target to comply will remain. They note that time limits will give the Security Council a guaranteed way of responding to humanitarian hardships that may arise and will force Council members to take more direct responsibility for each sanctions case on a renewable basis. The debate over these issues and the differences within the Security Council are likely to continue.

A summary listing of the many recent innovations in UN sanctions policy is presented in Table 11.1, "Innovations in UN Sanctions Policy." Taken together, these developments represent a significant evolution of UN policymaking.

## The Unfinished Agenda of Reform

The continuing relevance of sanctions—whether to suppress terrorist networks in the wake of the 11 September attacks, to bring closure to the UN mission in Iraq, or to end the scourge of war in sub-Saharan Africa—highlights the importance of the Permanent Five developing consensus on needed policy improvements. In the innovations noted above that developed through practice and the recommendations identified below that appeared in various UN reports, new opportunities have emerged for the Security Council to institutionalize the process of sanctions reform. The task before the Council is to set in place a series of strictures and automatic mechanisms that will sharpen the bite of sanctions and enhance their effectiveness as tools for fostering international security.

The lessons of history may be relevant here. In the early 1930s, the League of Nations, faced with Japanese aggression in Manchuria and Italian aggression in Ethiopia, chose not to employ the power it possessed to impose sanctions against these blatant violations of the league's charter. This decision emasculated the league and led to increasing cynicism and declining participation by member states. It was the beginning of the end of the league as a force for ensuring peace and security.[14] Without being overly dramatic about the tenor of our times, an analogy may be appropriate for the United Nations: the very fate of the UN as an effective global organization may hinge on its ability to use sanctions as instruments for peace and security. This challenge is especially evident in the case of Iraq, where the organization has invested so much time and effort and where its reputation is so much at stake. It also applies to the global campaign against terrorism, where the United Nations stands as the indispensable agency for mobilizing

**Table 11.1   Innovations in UN Sanctions Policy, 1994–2001**

- A general shift toward targeted and selected measures. No general sanctions after 1994.
- Worldwide financial sanctions and other targeted measures imposed in response to terror attacks against the United States.
- Financial sanctions targeted against individuals and entities as well as governments.
- Lists issued from the UN Secretariat of designated individuals subjected to financial sanctions and travel bans.
- Arms embargoes targeted against technical assistance and support services as well as weapons.
- UN enforcement support team created for sanctions against Taliban regime.
- Diamond embargoes imposed against rebel movements in Angola and Sierra Leone and against the government of Liberia.
- Sanctions imposed against Liberia for its violation of sanctions against RUF rebels in Sierra Leone.
- Investigative panels and monitoring mechanisms established as regular features of sanctions policy.
- A name and shame approach employed by investigative panels, identifying specific countries, companies, and individuals responsible for sanctions violations.
- Private industry associations and companies involved in the enforcement of diamond embargoes and financial sanctions.
- Private security firm hired to trace the finances of the UNITA rebel movement targeted by UN sanctions.
- Nongovernmental organizations and private research groups actively involved in analyzing, monitoring, and evaluating UN sanctions policies.
- Minimizing humanitarian hardships a priority concern among UN policymakers.
- Assessments of humanitarian impact established as a regular feature of sanctions cases.
- Standardized methodology developed for assessing humanitarian impacts.
- Blanket exemptions granted for designated humanitarian agencies in the case of Afghanistan.
- Time limits established in sanctions cases.

worldwide participation in the struggle to suppress the financing and organization of terrorist networks. We believe that the challenges of the present and the lessons of history lend urgency to the task of reforming UN sanctions policy.

In the pages that follow, we review and comment on the most frequently recommended and widely supported proposals for sanctions reform. We summarize the most important recommendations to emerge from the report of the Chowdhury working group. We also review the most important recommendations from the eighteen reports issued by expert panels in recent years, to distill the most frequently mentioned policy proposals. The combined recommendations of these two sources offer a blueprint for more effective UN sanctions in the future.

## Advancing the Chowdhury Working Group Proposals

Although the Security Council working group on sanctions was hampered by internal differences among the members, consensus was reached on a broad range of suggestions for improving the administration, design, and implementation of sanctions. The working group went through six drafts of a report and in the process produced dozens of specific policy recommendations. Few of the proposed policies were new. Many had appeared previously in the January 1999 note by the president of the Security Council, and a number were already being implemented.[15] Because of the nature of the consensus process employed, radical and far-reaching proposals were not included. Nonetheless, many of the recommendations outlined by the working group merit detailed consideration and support. We recommend that the Chowdhury report, the "Chairman's Proposed Outcome," dated 14 February 2001, be submitted as a nonpaper in order to give it more status in the record of the Security Council. Below we summarize the proposals that in our judgment would make the greatest difference in advancing UN policymaking.[16] The Chowdhury working group divided its task into three clusters: sanctions administration, sanctions design, and sanctions implementation. We comment on each below and then list the recommendations that we believe are most salient for advancing the reform agenda.

*Administration.* Probably the most important recommendation of the Chowdhury working group was the call for an organizational assessment of the specific staffing and resource needs for upgrading the capacity of the Secretariat. Such an assessment is long overdue and should be followed by effective action to provide the necessary staffing and resources. The minuscule Secretariat staff of less than a dozen professionals cannot possibly cope with the myriad political and administrative tasks associated with the implementation of diverse, simultaneous sanctions regimes.

The working group's specific recommendations were as follows:

- strengthen the implementation capacity of the sanctions branch of the UN Secretariat by providing additional staff, expertise, and resources;
- commission an institutional appraisal of the work of the sanctions branch in the Secretariat to develop recommendations on how to improve its effectiveness;
- prepare a database of outside experts to advise sanctions committees on technical issues related to finance, customs control, border control, immigration, aviation, arms trafficking, raw materials and minerals, and humanitarian impacts;
- promote greater transparency, openness, and efficiency in the work of sanctions committees;
- develop guidelines to assist member states in the implementation of targeted financial sanctions;
- establish a website on the various sanctions regimes to provide greater documentation and implementation information to the public;
- develop a standard template requesting information from member states on the implementation of sanctions; and
- work with relevant international, regional, and subregional organizations to facilitate the flow of information on the implementation of sanctions.

*Design.*  The working group emphasized the importance of defining the objectives of UN policy and establishing criteria that must be met for sanctions to be suspended or lifted. Among the group's specific recommendations were the following:

- specify clearly the conditions that must be fulfilled for sanctions to be lifted;
- consider actions to ease sanctions, short of suspension or lifting, in response to partial compliance by targeted entities;
- use standardized language developed in the Interlaken and Bonn-Berlin processes in drafting sanctions resolutions;
- prepare preassessment or early assessment reports;
- allow exemptions for specific items and designated institutions providing humanitarian assistance; and
- prepare standardized and simplified applications for humanitarian and other exemptions.

*Implementation.*   Monitoring and enforcement are essential to the effectiveness of sanctions. Although these responsibilities rest primarily with member states, the United Nations can assist by investigating and identifying sanctions violations. The working group did not specifically mention the use of expert panels, referring instead to "mechanisms," but it clearly had such panels in mind when it emphasized the value of UN investigative efforts. Among the specific recommendations of the working group were the following:

- appoint appropriate mechanisms for the investigation and identification of sanctions violations;
- give states alleged to be responsible for violations the opportunity to respond to allegations and to take corrective action;
- give sanctions committees explicit guidelines on actions to be taken when violations are identified;
- facilitate the provision of technical assistance to states;
- urge states with relevant expertise to offer technical, legal, and other forms of assistance to other states who request it;
- prepare periodic assessment reports on the implementation of sanctions, with recommendations for improving effectiveness and mitigating unintended impacts;
- include an analysis of third-party effects in assessment reports of sanctions impacts; and
- consider appointing a special representative and fact-finding mission when sanctions cause severe effects on third-party states to identify possible means of assistance.

As this book goes to press, another nationally sponsored process, drawing from the example and contribution of the Interlaken and Bonn-Berlin processes, has emerged that may advance further some of the Chowdhury recommendations. Undertaken by Sweden, this research and policy dialogue is aimed at improving the administrative effectiveness and monitoring of sanctions, especially in the area of refined and targeted measures.

## Institutionalizing the Recommendations of Expert Panels

Many of the expert panels and monitoring committees established by the Security Council produced recommendations for enhancing effectiveness. Because these investigative panels were ad hoc and independent and staffed with experts rather than diplomats, their reports were often hard-hitting and critical. Unimpeded by political and diplomatic constraints, the expert panels were willing and able to "name names" of those responsible for violations. They were free to recommend the kind of tough enforcement actions that some member states may find objectionable but that are needed to enhance sanctions compliance.

We have examined all the reports of the various investigative panels. In the process, we conducted a comparative analysis of their most important recommendations. The results are presented in the "Comparative Summary of Recommendations of UN Security Council Expert Panels" at the end of this chapter. The methodology for this analysis consisted of grouping all the recommendations by theme and identifying how many times and in which reports particular recommendations appeared. Our analysis examined only those recommendations that apply generally to sanctions implementation. We did not include suggestions that were relevant to only one case. Our purpose was to distill the many recommendations in the various reports into a coherent set of most frequently mentioned and widely supported proposals, which may be grouped into four areas: sanctions violators, arms trafficking, commodity sanctions, and investigative panels.

The primary recommendation of the Angola and Sierra Leone investigative committees was that sanctions be imposed against those who violate sanctions. Countries, companies, and individuals proven to be violating sanctions should be held responsible for their actions. As noted in earlier chapters, this concept is controversial among many UN member states. The sanctions imposed against Liberia for its violations of sanctions against the RUF in Sierra Leone may set a precedent, however, and could indicate a greater readiness by the Council to consider such strategies in the future.

Secondary pressures provide a way to encourage member states to take their enforcement obligations more seriously. Inducement policies and offers of support for compliance are the preferred means of encouraging compliance, but if persuasive methods are not effective, the imposition of secondary sanctions may be necessary. In most cases, the secondary pressures need not be as sweeping as those applied to Liberia, which was the prime mover behind the RUF. Usually more limited measures, such as diplomatic sanctions or travel restrictions on designated elites, would be sufficient to express the Council's impatience with inadequate compliance and to warn of sterner measures if enforcement is not strengthened. This principle of applying pressures to encourage member state compliance is crucial to the potential effectiveness of UN sanctions.

Second, because many of the expert panels were commissioned to examine arms embargo violations, they produced particularly viable proposals for strengthening the enforcement of these sanctions. As noted in Chapter 9, the expert panels discovered that air transportation is vital to the supply of arms to sanctioned rebel groups. A group of clearly identifiable arms brokers and transit companies, often registered in Liberia, have been responsible for most of the violations of UN arms embargoes in Africa. The expert panels recommended that all arms brokers and intermediaries, including transit companies, be subjected to registration and licensing requirements. They also called for mandatory procedures for the authentication and reconciliation of end-use certificates related to the delivery of arms and military equipment. Their sharpest recommendations aimed at shutting down the illegal air transportation operations that sustain the armed rebel movements in Angola, Sierra Leone, and the Congo. They proposed UN-supported air traffic surveillance and interdiction in zones of conflict and called for revoking the registration of aircraft and the licenses of pilots responsible for circumventing UN arms embargoes.

Third, the investigative panels focused on the diamond embargoes in Africa and produced a series of pointed recommendations for strengthening these measures. The most important, echoed by many member states and the diamond industry, was the proposal to create a standardized and credible system for certificates of origin for all diamond exports. As noted in Chapter 10, progress in creating such a certification system has been slow. The expert panels recommended additional steps to improve the transparency, accountability, and monitoring of diamond trading in order to strengthen the effectiveness of diamond embargoes. The expert panels also examined options for other forms of commodity sanctions and recommended the establishment of criteria for conflict timber and a system for timber certification.

Not surprisingly, the fourth and most frequent recommendation from the expert panels was that the Security Council continue to commission independent investigative panels. In part, this was a natural expression of the panel members' sense of their own worth in uncovering sanctions violations and recommending steps toward enhanced enforcement. As noted in Chapter 4, the monitoring panels have had the additional benefit of engaging relevant countries in diplomatic dialogue that in a number of cases has led to improved compliance.

The reports produced to date by the various investigative panels are a treasure trove of primary research information on the implementation of UN sanctions. They have been of enormous value to the Security Council in critical situations and to our own research. They stand as essential documents for all analysts and practitioners who wish to understand more thoroughly the workings of sanctions and their potential. Maintaining and building on this base of knowledge and implementing these recommendations are crucial to the future of UN policy.

A summary of the main recommendations of the expert panels is presented in the following chapter appendix. The letter coding after each recommendation refers to the specific report in which that recommendation was presented.

## Appendix: Comparative Summary of Recommendations of UN Security Council Expert Panelsa

### Coding of Reportsb

A     UNICOI reports: March 1996, S/1996/195; December 1997, S/1997/1010; and November 1998, S/1998/1096

B     Fowler mission: June/July 1999, S/1999/644 and S/1999/829

C     Angola Panel of Experts: March 2000, S/2000/203

D     Angola Monitoring Mechanism: Final Report, December 2000, S/2000/1225

---

a. See page 222 for full listing of all Security Council Expert Panels.

b. Listing here does not include the following UNICOI documents that contained no recommendations: the *Interim Report* of January 1996, S/1996/67; the *Addendum to the Third Report* of January 1998, S/1998/63; and the *Interim Report* of August 1998, S/1998/777. The list also does not include the Angola Monitoring Mechanism Addendum Report, United Nations Security Council, *Addendum to the Final Report of the Monitoring Mechanism on Sanctions Against UNITA*, S/2001/363, New York, 11 April 2001, or the Supplementary Report, United Nations Security Council, *Supplementary Report of the Monitoring Mechanism on Sanctions Against UNITA*, S/2001/966, New York, 12 October 2001, which contained no recommendations. Also not listed are the Iraq Panel Reports, United Nations Security Council, *Letters Dated 27 and 30 March 1999, Respectively, from the Chairman of the Panels Established Pursuant to the Note by the President of the Security Council of 30 January 1999 (S/1999/100) Addressed to the President of the Security Council*, S/1999/356, New York, 30 March 1999, which contained only a few recommendations specific to the Iraq case.

E  Sierra Leone Panel of Experts: December 2000, S/2000/1195
F  Panel of Experts on Exploitation of Congo Resources: April 2001, S/2001/357
G  Committee of Experts on Afghanistan: May 2001, S/2001/511
H  Liberia Panel of Experts: October 2001, S/2001/1015

## Major Recommendations

### Apply Sanctions Against Sanctions Violators

- Impose sanctions against leaders and governments found to be deliberately breaking sanctions (C, D, E)
- Place traders and companies violating sanctions on a blacklist (C)
- Urge governments to issue arrest warrants for individuals guilty of sanctions violations (C)

### Strengthen Member State Enforcement Capacity

- Encourage member states to enact legislation criminalizing violations of UN sanctions (A, B, C)
- Provide support for member state enforcement efforts (A)
- Encourage intelligence sharing among nations (B, C)
- Urge private industry associations to sensitize their members to their obligation to respect Security Council sanctions (B)

### Tighten the Enforcement of Arms Embargoes

- Register, license, and monitor the activities of arms brokers and intermediaries and establish a database of these companies and individuals (A, C, D, E)
- Mandate standardized procedures for the authentication and reconciliation of all end-use certificates for arms and military equipment (C, D, H)
- Urge governments to refrain from harboring groups of armed rebels (A)
- Consider a ban on weapons exports from certain countries (E)
- Broaden arms embargoes to include aircraft turbine fuel and special fluids and lubricants needed for armored vehicles (G)
- Support the Economic Community of West African States (ECOWAS) moratorium on arms imports and the Southern

African Development Community (SADC) plan of action to control light arms (D, E, H)

## Shut Down Illegal Air Transportation

- Provide UN support and assistance for air traffic control and interdiction in zones of conflict (B, C, D, E)
- Deploy mobile radar systems and utilize global positioning satellites to assist with air monitoring (C, E)
- Revoke the registration of aircraft that are used to violate sanctions (D)
- Revoke the license of pilots known to be violating sanctions (C, D)
- Develop special training programs for airport and customs officials (E)
- Encourage the International Civil Aviation Organization (ICAO) to assist in air management services (E)
- Ground all aircraft registered in Liberia, including those based outside the country, until operating and insurance documents are filed with international aviation authorities (E, H)

## Certify and Regulate Diamonds and Other Commodities

- Introduce a standardized and credible system requiring certificates of origin for all diamond exports (B, D, F, H)
- Require the forfeiture of diamonds that are traded without proper certificates of origin (B, C)
- Convene experts to develop a system for increased transparency and accountability in the control of diamonds from source to bourse (C)
- Profile the characteristics of diamonds from every mine and establish a comprehensive database of this information (D, H)
- Harmonize procedures and documentation for import and export of rough diamonds (B)
- License and monitor diamond buyers (D)
- Consider placing UN diamond monitors at major diamond exchanges (B, C)
- Develop a uniform system for timber certification and consider establishing criteria for conflict timber (F)
- Establish mechanisms with oil companies and governments to

monitor fuel stocks and movements in areas adjacent to zones of conflict (C)
- Conduct DNA-type analysis of fuel samples to monitor violations of oil embargoes (C)

## Improve Financial and Travel Sanctions

- Update, correct, and improve lists of individuals subject to travel bans and financial sanctions (C, D, H)
- Offer a finder's fee for the identification of sanctioned financial assets (C)
- Urge all countries that have not yet done so to sign the International Convention for the Suppression of the Financing of Terrorism (G)
- Encourage countries to expel individuals subject to UN travel bans (C)

## Enhance UN and International Enforcement Capacity

- Utilize and extend the mandate of expert panels and enhance their monitoring capacity (A, B, D, E, F, H)
- Develop an "information package," including website, to inform the public of sanctions requirements and purposes (C, H)
- Deploy UN customs monitors in key countries and airfields (A, B, E)
- Invite INTERPOL to assist with sanctions enforcement (B, C, E)
- Invite the World Customs Organization to share views on better means of monitoring (E)
- Include compliance with UN sanctions in the criteria for membership in the European Union and North Atlantic Treaty Organization (B, C)
- Create an Office for Sanctions Monitoring and Coordination (Afghanistan) as a nucleus for future sanctions monitoring requirements (G)

**Expert Panels: UN Security Council Sanctions**

| Authorizing Action and Date | Reports, UN Documents |
| --- | --- |

**Rwanda**

United Nations Commission of Inquiry (UNICOI)

S/RES/1013, 7 September 1995
- S/1996/67, *Interim Report,* 29 January 1996
- S/1996/195, *Report of the International Commission of Inquiry,* 14 March 1996
- S/1997/1010, *Third Report of the International Commission of Inquiry,* 24 December 1997
- S/1998/63, *Addendum to the Third Report of the International Commission of Inquiry,* 26 January 1998
- S/1998/777, *Interim Report,* 19 August 1998
- S/1998/1096, *Final Report of the International Commission of Inquiry,* 18 November 1998

**Iraq**

Panels Established Pursuant to the Note by the President of the Security Council of 30 January 1999

S/1999/100, 30 January 1999
- S/1999/356, *Letters Dated 27 and 30 March, Respectively, from the Chairman of the Panels Established Pursuant to the Note by the President of the Security Council of 30 January 1999 (S/1999/100) Addressed to the President of the Security Council,* 30 March 1999.

**Angola**

Angola Sanctions Committee (the Fowler Panel)

S/RES/864, 15 September 1993
- S/1999/644, *Letter Dated 4 June 1999 from the Chairman of the Security Council Committee Established Pursuant to Resolution 864 (1993) Concerning the Situation in Angola Addressed to the President of the Security Council.* S/1999/644, New York, 4 June 1999
- S/1999/829, *Security Council Committee Established Pursuant to Resolution 864 (1993) Concerning the Situation in Angola Report on the Chairman's Visit to Europe and Participation in the Seventieth Ordinary Session of the Council of Ministers of the Organization of African Unity, July 1999,* 28 July 1999

Panel of Experts on Sanctions Against UNITA

S/RES/1237, 7 May 1999
- S/2000/203, *Report of the Panel of Experts on Violations of Security Council Sanctions Against UNITA,* 10 March 2000

Monitoring Mechanism on Sanctions Against UNITA

S/RES/1295, 18 April 2000
- S/2000/1026, *Interim Report of the Monitoring Mechanism on Angola Sanctions Established by the Security Council in Resolution 1295 (2000) of 18 April 2000,* 25 October 2000
- S/2000/1225, *Final Report of the Monitoring Mechanism on Angola Sanctions,* 21 December 2000

- S/2001/363, *Addendum to the Final Report of the Monitoring Mechanism on Sanctions Against UNITA,* 18 April 2001
- S/2001/966, *Supplementary Report of the Monitoring Mechanism on Sanctions Against UNITA,* 12 October 2001

**Sierra Leone**

Panel of Experts on Sanctions in Sierra Leone

S/RES/1306, 5 July 2000 • S/2000/1195, *Report of the Panel of Experts Appointed Pursuant to Security Council Resolution 1306 (2000), Paragraph 19, in Relation to Sierra Leone,* 20 December 2000

Panel of Experts on Exploitation of Congo Resources

S/PRST/2000/20, 2 June 2000 • S/2001/357, *Report of the Panel of Experts on the Illegal Exploitation of Natural Resources and Other Forms of Wealth of the Democratic Republic of the Congo,* 12 April 2001

**Afghanistan**

Committee of Experts Monitoring the Taliban Arms Embargo

S/RES/1333, 19 December 2000 • S/2001/511, *Report of the Committee of Experts Appointed Pursuant to Security Council Resolution 1333 (2000), Paragraph 15(a), Regarding Monitoring of the Arms Embargo Against the Taliban and the Closure of Terrorist Training Camps in the Taliban-held Areas of Afghanistan,* 22 May 2001

**Liberia**

Panel of Experts on Sanctions in Liberia

S/RES/1343, 7 March 2001 • S/2001/1015, *Report of the Panel of Experts Pursuant to Security Council Resolution 1343 (2001), Paragraph 19, Concerning Liberia,* 26 October 2001

# Notes

1. See John Stremlau, *Sharpening International Sanctions: Toward a Stronger Role for the United Nations* (report to the Carnegie Commission for Preventing Deadly Conflict) (New York: Carnegie Corporation of New York, November 1996); see also David Cortright and George A. Lopez, eds., *Economic Sanctions: Panacea or Peacebuilding in a Post–Cold War World?* (Boulder, Colo.: Westview Press, 1995), 6–8.

2. A full listing of all the Security Council investigative panels is presented at the end of this chapter.

3. United Nations General Assembly, *We the Peoples: The Role of the United Nations in the Twenty-First Century: Report of the Secretary-General,* A/54/2000, New York, 27 March 2000, par. 206.

4. United Nations Development Programme, *Human Development Report 2000* (New York: Oxford University Press, 2000), 12–13.

5. This strategy was suggested by Jeremy P. Carver of Clifford Chance, London, at a meeting of the Security Council working group on sanctions, UN headquarters, New York, 17–18 August 2000.

6. See Margaret Doxey, "United Nations Economic Sanctions: Minimizing Adverse Effects on Nontarget States," in David Cortright and George A. Lopez, eds., *Smart Sanctions: Targeting Economic Statecraft* (Lanham, Md.: Rowman and Littlefield, 2002).

7. See, for example, Larry Minear et al., *Toward More Humane and Effective Sanctions Management: Enhancing the Capacity of the United Nations System*, occasional paper 31 (Providence, R.I.: Thomas J. Watson Jr. Institute for International Studies, Brown University, 1998). This report was based on a 1997 study of the same title commissioned by the Inter-agency Standing Committee of the UN Department of Humanitarian Affairs.

8. United Nations Department of Humanitarian Affairs, *Note from the Department of Humanitarian Affairs Concerning the Possible Humanitarian Impact of the International Flight Ban Decided in Security Council Resolution 1070 (1996)*, New York, 20 February 1997.

9. United Nations Office for the Coordination of Humanitarian Affairs, *Interagency Assessment Mission to Sierra Leone: Interim Report*, New York, 17 February 1998.

10. United Nations, Office for the Coordination of Humanitarian Affairs, *Vulnerability and Humanitarian Implications of UN Security Council Sanctions in Afghanistan*, Islamabad, December 2000.

11. United Nations Security Council, *Report of the Secretary-General in Pursuance of Paragraph 13(a) of Resolution 1343 (2001) Concerning Liberia*, S/2001/939, New York, 5 October 2001.

12. The Department of Humanitarian Affairs was the predecessor of the Office for the Coordination of Humanitarian Affairs.

13. Minear et al., *Toward More Humane and Effective Sanctions Management*.

14. For a convincing discussion of the importance of the league's inability to mount credible sanctions in the Abyssinian crisis, see Erica J. Cosgrove, "The Theory and Practice of Multilateral Economic Sanctions: A Reassessment in Light of Iraq," Ph.D. diss., University of Cambridge, 2000, 56–63.

15. United Nations Security Council, *Note by the President of the Security Council: Work of the Sanctions Committee*, S/1999/92, New York, 29 January 1999.

16. The recommendations presented here are drawn from the unpublished "Chairman's Proposed Outcome," a report of the Chowdhury working group on sanctions, New York, 14 February 2001, provided to the authors by staff of the UN Secretariat.

# Acronyms

| | |
|---|---|
| AFRC | Armed Forces Revolutionary Council |
| ANC | African National Congress |
| BICC | Bonn International Center for Conversion |
| CARAT | Consumer Access to a Responsible Accounting of Trade |
| CSO | Central Selling Organization |
| CT | computed tomography |
| DRC | Democratic Republic of the Congo |
| ECOMOG | Economic Community of West African States Military Observer Group |
| ECOWAS | Economic Community of West African States |
| EU | European Union |
| FATF | Financial Action Task Force |
| FinCEN | Financial Crimes Enforcement Network |
| GDP | gross domestic product |
| GGDO | Government Gold and Diamond Office |
| IAEA | International Atomic Energy Agency |
| ICAO | International Civil Aviation Organization |
| ICG | International Crisis Group |
| IPA | International Peace Academy |
| KGB | Komitet Gosudarstvennoi Bezopasnosti (Russian intelligence agency) |
| KLA | Kosovo Liberation Army |
| LURD | Liberians United for Reconciliation and Democracy |
| MIF | Maritime Interception Force |
| NATO | North Atlantic Treaty Organization |
| NCCTs | noncooperative countries and territories |
| NGOs | nongovernmental organizations |
| NiZA | Netherlands Institute for Southern Africa |
| Novib | Oxfam Netherlands |
| NPFL | National Patriotic Front of Liberia |

| | |
|---|---|
| OAU | Organization of African Unity |
| OCHA | UN Office for the Coordination of Humanitarian Affairs |
| OECD | Organization for Economic Cooperation and Development |
| OFAC | Office of Foreign Assets Control |
| RUF | Revolutionary United Front |
| SADC | Southern African Development Community |
| SAMs | sanctions assistance missions |
| SCR | Security Council resolution |
| SDN | specially designated national |
| UAE | United Arab Emirates |
| UN | United Nations |
| UNAMSIL | UN Mission in Sierra Leone |
| UNICOI | United Nations International Commission of Inquiry |
| UNITA | National Union for the Total Independence of Angola |
| UNMOVIC | UN Monitoring, Verification and Inspection Commission |
| UNSCOM | United Nations Special Commission |
| USAID | United States Agency for International Development |
| UTA | Union des Transports Aériens (French airline) |
| YPA | Yugoslav People's Army |

# Bibliography

Ali, Mohamed M., and Iqbal H. Shah. "Sanctions and Childhood Mortality in Iraq." *Lancet* 355 (May 2000).

Andelman, David A. "The Drug Money Maze." *Foreign Affairs* 73, no. 46 (July–August 1994).

Anthony, Ian. "Improving the Cooperation of Major Arms Suppliers." Paper presented to the First Expert Seminar on Smart Sanctions, "The Next Step: Arms Embargoes and Travel Sanctions," Bonn International Center for Conversion, Bonn, Germany, 21–23 November 1999.

Bayart, Jean-Francois, Stephen Ellis, and Béatrice Hibou. *The Criminalization of the State in Africa.* Bloomington: Indiana University Press, 1999.

Berdal, Mats, and David M. Malone, eds. *Greed and Grievance: Economic Agendas in Civil Wars.* Boulder, Colo.: Lynne Rienner Publishers, 2001.

Blanchard, Jean-Marc F., Edward D. Mansfield, and Norrin M. Ripsman, eds. *Power and the Purse: Economic Statecraft, Interdependence, and National Security.* London: Frank Cass, 2000.

Brzoska, Michael, ed. *Design and Implementation of the Arms Embargoes and Travel and Aviation Related Sanctions: Results of the "Bonn-Berlin Process."* Bonn, Germany: Bonn International Center for Conversion, 2001.

Burgerman, Susan. *Moral Victories: How Activists Provoke Multilateral Action.* Ithaca, N.Y.: Cornell University Press, 2001.

Butler, Richard. *The Greatest Threat: Iraq, Weapons of Mass Destruction, and the Crisis of Global Security.* New York: Public Affairs, 2000.

Cordesman, Anthony H. "The Iraq Crisis: Background Data." Washington, D.C.: Center for Strategic and International Studies, 1998.

———. *Military Expenditures and Arms Transfers in the Middle East.* Washington, D.C.: Center for Strategic and International Studies, July 2001.

Cortright, David, and George A. Lopez. "Are Sanctions Just? The Problematic Case of Iraq." *Journal of International Affairs* 52, no. 2 (Spring 1999).

Cortright, David, and George A. Lopez, with Richard W. Conroy, Jaleh Dashti-Gibson, and Julia Wagler. *The Sanctions Decade: Assessing UN Strategies in the 1990s.* Boulder, Colo.: Lynne Rienner Publishers, 2000.

Cortright, David, and George A. Lopez, eds. *Economic Sanctions: Panacea or Peacebuilding in a Post–Cold War World?* Boulder, Colo.: Westview Press, 1995.

———. *Smart Sanctions: Targeting Economic Statecraft.* Lanham, Md.: Rowman and Littlefield, 2002.

Cortright, David, Alistair Millar, and George A. Lopez. *Smart Sanctions:*

*Restructuring UN Policy in Iraq.* Policy brief. Goshen and Notre Dame, Ind.: Fourth Freedom Forum and Joan B. Kroc Institute for International Peace Studies, April 2001.

Cosgrove, Erica J. "The Theory and Practice of Multilateral Economic Sanctions: A Reassessment in Light of Iraq." Ph.D. diss., University of Cambridge, 2000.

Cousens, Elizabeth M., and Chetan Kumar, eds. *Peacebuilding as Politics: Cultivating Peace in Fragile Societies.* Boulder, Colo.: Lynne Rienner Publishers, 2001.

European Union. *Council Directive of 10 June 1991 on Prevention of the Use of the Financial System for the Purpose of Money Laundering.* 91/308/EEC, London, 10 June 1991.

Garfield, Richard. *Morbidity and Mortality Among Iraqi Children from 1990 to 1998: Assessing the Impact of Economic Sanctions.* Occasional Paper Series 16:OP:3. Paper commissioned by the Joan B. Kroc Institute for International Peace Studies at the University of Notre Dame and the Fourth Freedom Forum, March 1999.

Global Witness. *Angola Sanctions: Recent Developments.* London: Global Witness, 22 April 1999.

———. *Possibilities for the Identification, Certification and Control of Diamonds.* London: Global Witness, June 2000.

———. "The Real Price of Sanctions on Timber." 17 October 2001. Supplement to the report, *Taylor-Made: The Pivotal Role of Liberia's Forests and Flag of Convenience in Regional Conflict.* London: Global Witness, September 2001.

———. *Review of the Sierra Leone Diamond Certification System and Proposals and Recommendations for the Kimberley Process for a Fully Integrated Certification System (FICS).* London: Global Witness, 25 April 2001.

———. "The Role of Liberia and Its Logging Industry on National and Regional Insecurity." London: Global Witness, May 2001.

———. *A Rough Trade: The Role of Companies and Government in the Angolan Conflict.* London: Global Witness, December 1998.

Graham-Brown, Sarah. *Sanctioning Saddam: The Politics of Intervention in Iraq.* London: I. B. Taurus, 1999.

Haass, Richard N., and Meghan L. O'Sullivan, eds. *Honey and Vinegar: Incentives, Sanctions, and Foreign Policy.* Washington, D.C.: Brookings Institution, 2000.

Hamilton, Lee H., James Schlesinger, and Brent Scowcroft. *Thinking Beyond the Stalemate in U.S.–Iranian Relations.* Policy review. Washington, D.C.: Atlantic Council of the United States, May 2001.

Hesseldahl, Arik. "How Dictators Manage Their Billions." *Forbes Magazine* (22 June 2000).

Hirsch, John L. *Sierra Leone: Diamonds and the Struggle for Democracy.* Boulder, Colo.: Lynne Rienner Publishers, 2001.

———. "War in Sierra Leone." *Survival* 43, no. 3 (Autumn 2001).

Hope, Kempe Ronald, Sr., and Bornwell C. Chikulo, eds. *Corruption and Development in Africa.* New York: St. Martin's Press, 2000.

Hufbauer, Gary C., Jeffrey S. Schott, and Kimberly Ann Elliott. *Economic Sanctions Reconsidered: History and Current Policy.* 2d ed. Washington, D.C.: Institute for International Economics, 1990.

Human Rights Watch. *Afghanistan: Crisis of Impunity: The Role of Pakistan, Russia, and Iran in Fueling the Civil War,* paper 13, no. 3, July 2001.

———. *Angola Unravels: The Rise and Fall of the Lusaka Peace Process.* New York: Human Rights Watch, September 1999.

———. "Fueling Afghanistan's War." Washington, D.C.: Human Rights Watch, 15 December 2000.

———. *Getting Away with Murder, Mutilation and Rape: New Testimony from Sierra Leone.* New York: Human Rights Watch, June 1999.

———. *Human Rights Watch World Report 2001.* New York: Human Rights Watch, 2000.

International Crisis Group. *Sierra Leone: Time for a New Military and Political Strategy.* Freetown/London/Brussels, 11 April 2001.

Jackson, Robert. *Quasi-States: Sovereignty, International Relations and the Third World.* Cambridge: Cambridge University Press, 1990.

Johansen, Robert C. "Building World Security: The Need for Strengthened International Institutions." In Michael T. Klare and Yogesh Chandrani, eds., *World Security: Challenges for a New Century.* New York: St. Martin's Press, 1998.

Katzman, Kenneth. "Terrorism: Near Eastern Groups and State Sponsors, 2001." Washington, D.C.: Congressional Research Service report for Congress, 10 September 2001.

Knight, W. Andy. *The United Nations and Arms Embargoes Verification.* Lewiston, N.Y.: Edwin Mellen, 1998.

Kobrin, Stephen. "Electronic Cash and the End of National Markets." *Foreign Policy* (Summer 1997).

Krause, Keith, and W. Andy Knight, eds. *State, Society, and the UN System: Changing Perspectives on Multilateralism.* Tokyo: United Nations University Press, 1995.

Love, Janice. *The U.S. Anti-Apartheid Movement: Local Activism in Global Politics.* New York: Praeger, 1985.

Luck, Edward C. "Choosing Words Carefully: Arms Embargoes and the UN Security Council." Paper presented at the First Expert Seminar on Smart Sanctions, "The Next Step: Arms Embargoes and Travel Sanctions," Bonn International Center for Conversion, Bonn, Germany, 21–23 November 1999.

Lukic, Reneo, and Allen Lynch. *Europe from the Balkans to the Urals: The Disintegration of Yugoslavia and the Soviet Union.* New York: Stockholm International Peace Research Institute and Oxford University Press, 1996.

Martin, Lisa. *Coercive Cooperation: Explaining Multilateral Economic Sanctions.* Princeton, N.J.: Princeton University Press, 1992.

Miller, Kathleen, and Caroline Brooks. *Export Controls in the Framework Agreement Countries*, BASIC Research Report, 2001.1. London: British-American Security Information Council, July 2001.

Minear, Larry, David Cortright, Julia Wagler, George A. Lopez, and Thomas G. Weiss. *Toward More Humane and Effective Sanctions Management: Enhancing the Capacity of the United Nations System.* Occasional Paper No. 31. Providence, R.I.: Thomas J. Watson Jr. Institute for International Studies, 1998.

Mingst, Karen A., and Margaret P. Karns. *The United Nations in the Post–Cold War Era.* Boulder, Colo.: Westview Press, 2000.

Naval War College, *Report of the Proceedings of the Targeted Financial Sanctions Simulation.* Newport, R.I., 11–13 May 2000, sponsored by the Thomas J. Watson Jr. Institute for International Studies at Brown University and the Decision Strategies Department of the Center for Naval Warfare Studies of the U.S. Naval War College, DSD Report, 01-2.

Newcomb, R. Richard. "Targeted Financial Sanctions: The U.S. Model." Paper presented at the Second Expert Seminar on Targeting UN Financial Sanctions, Interlaken, Switzerland, 29–31 March 1999.

Niblock, Tim. *Pariah States and Sanctions in the Middle East: Iraq, Libya, Sudan.* Boulder, Colo.: Lynne Rienner Publishers, 2001.

Nordstrom, Carolyn. *A Different Kind of War Story (Ethnography of Political Violence).* Philadelphia: University of Pennsylvania Press, 1997.

O'Sullivan, Meghan. *Iraq: Time for a Modified Approach.* Policy brief 71. Washington, D.C.: Brookings Institution, February 2001.

Organization of African Unity, Assembly of Heads of State and Government. *The Crisis Between the Great Socialist Peoples Libyan Arab Jamahiriya and the United States of America and the United Kingdom.* AHG/DEC.127 XXXIV, Addis Ababa, Ethiopia, 8–10 June 1998.

Pratt, David. "Sierra Leone: The Forgotten Crisis." Report to the Minister of Foreign Affairs, the Honourable Lloyd Axworthy, P.C., M.P., 23 April 1999.

Prendergast, John. "Angola's Deadly War: Dealing with Savimbi's Hell on Earth." Special report. Washington, D.C.: United States Institute of Peace, 12 October 1999.

———. *Building for Peace in the Horn of Africa: Diplomacy and Beyond.* Washington, D.C.: United States Institute of Peace, June 1999.

Reno, William. *Warlord Politics and African States.* Boulder, Colo.: Lynne Rienner Publishers, 1998.

Reychler, Luc, and Thania Paffenholz, eds. *Peace-building: A Field Guide.* Boulder, Colo.: Lynne Rienner Publishing, 2001.

Risse-Kappen, Thomas, ed. *Bringing Transnational Relations Back In.* Cambridge: Cambridge University Press, 1995.

Ritter, Scott. "The Case for Iraq's Qualitative Disarmament." *Arms Control Today* 30, no. 5 (June 2000).

Rose, Gideon. "Libya." In Richard Haass, ed., *Economic Sanctions and American Diplomacy.* New York: Council on Foreign Relations, 1998.

Rubin, Barnett R., Ashraf Ghani, William Maley, Ahmed Rashid, and Olivier Roy. *Afghanistan: Reconstruction and Peacemaking in a Regional Framework.* KOFF Peacebuilding Reports. Bern, Switzerland: Center for Peacebuilding, June 2001.

Ruggie, John Gerard. *Constructing the World Policy: Essays on International Institutionalization.* New York: Routledge, 1998.

Simmons, Beth. "International Efforts Against Money Laundering." In Dinah Shelton, ed., *Commitment and Compliance: The Role of Nonbinding Norms in the International Legal System.* Oxford: Oxford University Press, 2000.

Smillie, Ian, Lansana Gberie, and Ralph Hazleton. *The Heart of the Matter: Sierra Leone, Diamonds and Human Security.* Ottawa, Ontario, Canada: Partnership Africa Canada, January 2000.

Stockholm International Peace Research Institute. *SIPRI Yearbook 2000: Armaments, Disarmament, and International Security.* Oxford: Oxford University Press, 2000.

Stremlau, John. *Sharpening International Sanctions: Toward a Stronger Role for the United Nations.* Report to the Carnegie Commission for Preventing Deadly Conflict. New York: Carnegie Corporation of New York, November 1996.

Swiss Confederation, United Nations Secretariat, and the Thomas J. Watson Jr. Institute for International Studies at Brown University. *Targeted Financial Sanctions: A Manual for Design and Implementation—Contributions from the Interlaken Process.* Providence, R.I.: Watson Institute, 2001.

United Nations. *Transcript of Press Conference by Secretary-General Kofi Annan at Headquarters, 5 April.* SG/SM/6944, New York, 5 April 1999.

———. *Transcript of Press Conference by Secretary-General Kofi Annan at Headquarters, 19 December 2000.* SG/SM/7668, New York, 20 December 2000.

United Nations Department of Humanitarian Affairs. *Note from the Department of Humanitarian Affairs Concerning the Possible Humanitarian Impact of the International Flight Ban Decided in Security Council Resolution 1070 (1996).* New York, 20 February 1997.

United Nations Department of Public Information. *Conflict Diamonds: Sanctions and War.* Report in cooperation with the Sanctions Branch, Security Council Affairs Division, Department of Political Affairs. New York, 21 March 2001.

United Nations Development Programme. *Human Development Report 2000.* New York: Oxford University Press, 2000.

United Nations General Assembly. *A/RES/50/88 A-B: 95th Plenary Meeting 19 December 1995.* A/RES/50/88, New York, 19 December 1995.

———. *Annual Report of the Secretary-General on the Work of the Organization.* A/53/1, New York, 27 August 1998.

———. *International Convention for the Suppression of the Financing of Terrorism.* A/RES/54/109, New York, 25 February 2000.

———. *Report of the Panel on United Nations Peace Operations.* A/55/305-S/2000/809, New York, 21 August 2000.

———. *The Role of Diamonds in Fuelling Conflict: Breaking the Link Between the Illicit Transaction of Rough Diamonds and Armed Conflict as a Contribution to Prevention and Settlement of Conflicts.* A/RES/55/56, New York, 29 January 2001.

———. *We the Peoples: The Role of the United Nations in the Twenty-First Century: Report of the Secretary-General.* A/54/2000, New York, 27 March 2000.

United Nations General Assembly and Security Council. *The Situation in Afghanistan and Its Implications for International Peace and Security: Report of the Secretary-General.* A/55/907-S/2001/384, New York, 19 April 2001.

United Nations. Integrated Regional Information Network. "The Role of Liberia's Logging Industry on National and Regional Insecurity." Briefing to the UN Security Council by Global Witness, New York, 24 January 2001.

United Nations Office for the Coordination of Humanitarian Affairs. *Inter-agency Assessment Mission to Sierra Leone: Interim Report.* New York, 17 February 1998.

———. *Sierra Leone Humanitarian Situation Report, 21 January–12 February 1998.* 98/0016, New York, 17 February 1998.

———. *Vulnerability and Humanitarian Impact of UN Security Council Sanctions in Afghanistan.* New York, 17 August 2000.

———. *Vulnerability and Humanitarian Implications of UN Security Council Sanctions in Afghanistan.* Islamabad, December 2000.

United Nations Office of the Iraq Programme. *Weekly Update, 20 October 2001.* New York, 4 October 2001.

United Nations Security Council. *Addendum to the Final Report of the Monitoring Mechanism on Sanctions Against UNITA.* S/2001/363, New York, 11 April 2001.

———. *Chairs of the Sanctions Committee, Issue Paper Concerning the Sanctions Imposed by the Security Council.* New York, 30 October 1998.

————. *Eighth Report of the Secretary-General on the United Nations Mission in Sierra Leone.* S/2000/1199, New York, 15 December 2000.

————. *Final Report of the International Commission of Inquiry (Rwanda).* S/1998/1096, New York, 18 November 1998.

————. *Final Report of the Monitoring Mechanism on Angola Sanctions.* S/2000/1225, New York, 21 December 2000.

————. *First Report of the Secretary-General Pursuant to Security Council Resolution 1343 (2001) Regarding Liberia.* S/2001/424, New York, 30 April 2001.

————. *Interim Report of the Monitoring Mechanism on Angola Sanctions Established by the Security Council in Resolution 1295 (2000) of April 2000.* S/2000/1026, New York, 25 October 2000.

————. "Iraq: Draft Resolution." Nonpaper. United Nations, New York, 8 June 2001.

————. *Letter Dated 27 May 1997 from the Permanent Representative of the Libyan Arab Jamahiriya to the United Nations Addressed to the Secretary-General.* S/1997/404, New York, 27 May 1997.

————. *Letter Dated 22 November 1997 from the Executive Chairman of the Special Commission Established by the Secretary-General Pursuant to Paragraph 9(b)(i) of Security Council Resolution 687 (1991) Addressed to the President of the Security Council.* S/1997/922, New York, 24 November 1997.

————. *Letter Dated 9 April 1998 from the Secretary-General Addressed to the President of the Security Council, Appendix: Fifth Consolidated Report of the Director General of the International Atomic Energy Agency Under Paragraph 16 of Security Council Resolution 1051 (1996).* S/1998/312, New York, 9 April 1998.

————. *Letter Dated 12 February 1999 from the Chairman of the Security Council Committee Established Pursuant to Security Council Resolution 864 (1993) Concerning the Situation in Angola Addressed to the President of the Security Council.* S/1999/147, New York, 12 February 1999.

————. *Letter Dated 26 February 1999 from the Chairman of the Security Council Committee Established Pursuant to Security Council Resolution 1160 (1998) Addressed to the President of the Security Council.* S/1999/216, New York, 4 March 1999.

————. *Letter Dated 4 June 1999 from the Chairman of the Security Council Committee Established Pursuant to Resolution 864 (1993) Concerning the Situation in Angola Addressed to the President of the Security Council.* S/1999/644, New York, 4 June 1999.

————. *Letter Dated 28 July 1999 from the Chairman of the Security Council Committee Established Pursuant to Resolution 864 (1993) Concerning the Situation in Angola Addressed to the President of the Security Council.* S/1999/829, New York, 28 July 1999.

————. *Letter Dated 6 June 2001 from the Secretary-General Addressed to the President of the Security Council, Annex, Report of the Team of Experts Established Pursuant to Paragraph 15 of Security Council Resolution 1330 (2000).* S/2001/566, New York, 6 June 2001.

————. *Letters Dated 27 and 30 March 1999, Respectively, from the Chairman of the Panels Established Pursuant to the Note by the President of the Security Council of 30 January 1999 (S/1999/100) Addressed to the President of the Security Council.* S/1999/356, New York, 30 March 1999.

————. *Note by the President of the Security Council: Work of the Sanctions Committee.* S/1999/92, New York, 29 January 1999.

————. *Report of the Committee of Experts Appointed Pursuant to Security Council Resolution 1333 (2000), Paragraph 15(a), Regarding Monitoring of the Arms Embargo Against the Taliban and the Closure of Terrorist Training Camps in the Taliban-held Areas of Afghanistan.* S/2001/511, New York, 22 May 2001.

————. *Report of the Executive Chairman on the Activities of the Special Commission Established by the Secretary-General Pursuant to Paragraph 9 (b)(i) of Resolution 687 (1991).* S/1998/332, New York, 16 April 1998.

————. *Report of the Panel of Experts Appointed Pursuant to Security Council Resolution 1306 (2000), Paragraph 19, in Relation to Sierra Leone.* S/2000/1195, New York, 20 December 2000.

————. *Report of the Panel of Experts on the Illegal Exploitation of Natural Resources and Other Forms of Wealth of the Democratic Republic of the Congo.* S/2001/357, New York, 12 April 2001.

————. *Report of the Panel of Experts on Violations of Security Council Sanctions Against UNITA.* S/2000/203, New York, 10 March 2000.

————. *Report of the Secretary-General in Pursuance of Paragraph 13(a) of Resolution 1343 (2001) Concerning Liberia.* S/2001/939, New York, 5 October 2001.

————. *Report of the Secretary-General on the Humanitarian Implications of the Measures Imposed by the Security Council Resolutions 1267 (1999) and 1333 (2000).* S/2001/241, New York, 20 March 2001.

————. *Report of the Secretary-General on the Humanitarian Implications of the Measures Imposed by Security Council Resolutions 1267 (1999) and 1333 (2000) on Afghanistan.* S/2001/695, New York, 13 July 2001.

————. *Report of the Secretary-General on the United Nations Office in Angola.* S/2000/304, New York, 11 April 2000.

————. *Report of the Secretary-General Pursuant to Paragraph 5 of Resolution 1330 (2000).* S/2001/505, New York, 18 May 2001.

————. *Report of the Secretary-General Pursuant to Paragraph 5 of Resolution 1360 (2001).* S/2001/919, New York, 28 September 2001.

————. *Review and Assessment of the Implementation of the Humanitarian Programme Established Pursuant to Security Council Resolution 986 (1995), December 1996–November 1998.* S/1999/481, New York, 28 April 1999.

————. *Security Council Committee Established Pursuant to Resolution 864 (1993) Concerning the Situation in Angola Report on the Chairman's Visit to Central and Southern Africa, May 1999.* S/1999/644, New York, 4 June 1999.

————. *Security Council Committee Established Pursuant to Resolution 864 (1993) Concerning the Situation in Angola Report on the Chairman's Visit to Europe and Participation in the Seventieth Ordinary Session of the Council of Ministers of the Organization of African Unity, July 1999.* S/1999/829, New York, 28 July 1999.

————. *Security Council Committee Issues List of Persons Affected by Resolution 1343 (2001) on Liberia.* Press release SC/7068, New York, 4 June 2001.

————. *Security Council Committee on Sierra Leone Issues List of Junta Members Affected by Sanctions.* Press release SC/6464, New York, 8 January 1998.

————. *Security Council Ponders Establishment of Sanctions-Monitoring Mechanism for Afghanistan.* SC/7069, New York, 5 June 2001.

————. *Security Council Resolution 661 (1990)*. S/RES/661, New York, 6 August 1990.

————. *Security Council Resolution 670 (1990)*. S/RES/670, New York, 25 September 1990.

————. *Security Council Resolution 678 (1990)*. S/RES/678, New York, 29 November 1990.

————. *Security Council Resolution 687 (1991)*. S/RES/687, New York, 3 April 1991.

————. *Security Council Resolution 706 (1991)*. S/RES/706, New York, 15 August 1991.

————. *Security Council Resolution 713 (1991)*. S/RES/713, New York, 25 September 1991.

————. *Security Council Resolution 748 (1992)*. S/RES/748, New York, 31 March 1992.

————. *Security Council Resolution 757 (1992)*. S/RES/757, New York, 30 May 1992.

————. *Security Council Resolution 787 (1992)*. S/RES/787, New York, 16 November 1992.

————. *Security Council Resolution 820 (1993)*. S/RES/820, New York, 17 April 1993.

————. *Security Council Resolution 841 (1993)*. S/RES/841, New York, 16 June 1993.

————. *Security Council Resolution 864 (1993)*. S/RES/864, New York, 15 September 1993.

————. *Security Council Resolution 883 (1993)*. S/RES/883, New York, 11 November 1993.

————. *Security Council Resolution 917 (1994)*. S/RES/917, New York, 6 May 1994.

————. *Security Council Resolution 986 (1995)*. S/RES/986, New York, 14 April 1995.

————. *Security Council Resolution 997 (1995)*. S/RES/997, New York, 9 June 1995.

————. *Security Council Resolution 1013 (1995)*. S/RES/1013, New York, 7 September 1995.

————. *Security Council Resolution 1044 (1996)*. S/RES/1044, New York, 31 January 1996.

————. *Security Council Resolution 1051 (1996)*. S/RES/1051, New York, 27 March 1996.

————. *Security Council Resolution 1054 (1996)*. S/RES/1054, New York, 25 April 1996.

————. *Security Council Resolution 1070 (1996)*. S/RES/1070, New York, 16 August 1996.

————. *Security Council Resolution 1127 (1997)*. S/RES/1127, New York, 28 August 1997.

————. *Security Council Resolution 1132 (1997)*. S/RES/1132, New York, 8 October 1997.

————. *Security Council Resolution 1134 (1997)*. S/RES/1134, New York, 23 October 1997.

————. *Security Council Resolution 1137 (1997)*. S/RES/1137, New York, 12 November 1997.

————. *Security Council Resolution 1153 (1998)*. S/RES/1153, New York, 20 February 1998.

————. *Security Council Resolution 1171 (1998)*. S/RES/1171, New York, 5 June 1998.

————. *Security Council Resolution 1173 (1998)*. S/RES/1173, New York, 12 June 1998.

————. *Security Council Resolution 1237 (1999)*. S/RES/1237, New York, 7 May 1999.

————. *Security Council Resolution 1267 (1999)*. S/RES/1267, New York, 15 October 1999.

————. *Security Council Resolution 1284 (1999)*. S/RES/1284, New York, 17 December 1999.

————. *Security Council Resolution 1295 (2000)*. S/RES/1295, New York, 18 April 2000.

————. *Security Council Resolution 1298 (2000)*. S/RES/1298, New York, 17 May 2000.

————. *Security Council Resolution 1302 (2000)*. S/RES/1302, New York, 8 June 2000.

————. *Security Council Resolution 1306 (2000)*. S/RES/1306, New York, 5 July 2000.

————. *Security Council Resolution 1333 (2000)*. S/RES/1333, New York, 19 December 2000.

————. *Security Council Resolution 1336 (2001)*. S/RES/1336, New York, 23 January 2001.

————. *Security Council Resolution 1343 (2001)*. S/RES/1343, New York, 7 March 2001.

————. *Security Council Resolution 1348 (2001)*. S/RES/1348, New York, 19 April 2001.

————. *Security Council Resolution 1352 (2001)*. S/RES/1352, New York, 1 June 2001.

————. *Security Council Resolution 1360 (2001)*. S/RES/1360, New York, 3 July 2001.

————. *Security Council Resolution 1363 (2001)*. S/RES/1363, New York, 30 July 2001.

————. *Security Council Resolution 1372 (2001)*. S/RES/1372, New York, 28 September 2001.

————. *Security Council Resolution 1373 (2001)*. S/RES/1373, New York, 28 September 2001.

————. *Security Council Resolution 1374 (2001)*. S/RES/1374, New York, 19 October 2001.

————. *Security Council Resolution 1382 (2001)*. S/RES/1382, New York, 29 November 2001.

————. *Security Council Resolution 1390 (2002)*. S/RES/1390, New York, 16 January 2002.

————. *The Situation in Afghanistan and Its Implications for International Peace and Security: Report of the Secretary-General*. S/2001/384-A/55/907, New York, 19 April 2001.

————. *Statement by the President of the Security Council*. S/PRST/2001/14, New York, 15 May 2001.

————. *Supplementary Report of the Monitoring Mechanism on Sanctions Against UNITA*. S/2001/966, New York, 12 October 2001.

————. *Towards a Comprehensive Approach to Durable and Sustainable Solutions to Priority Needs and Challenges in West Africa: Report of the Inter-Agency Mission to West Africa.* S/2001/434, New York, 2 May 2001.

U.S. Agency for International Development, Office of Transition Initiatives. *Sierra Leone: "Conflict" Diamonds: Progress Report on Diamond Policy and Development Program.* New York: USAID, 30 March 2001.

"U.S. Commission on National Security in the 21st Century: After the Attack—A New Urgency." Transcript of the 14 September 2001 General Meeting, Council on Foreign Relations, Washington, D.C., 25 September 2001, 12–13.

U.S. Department of State. "Liberia Country Report on Human Rights Practices for 1997." Washington, D.C.: Government Printing Office, 30 January 1998.

————. *Patterns of Global Terrorism—1996.* Publication 10535. Washington, D.C.: Government Printing Office, 1996.

————. *Patterns of Global Terrorism—2000.* Washington, D.C.: Government Printing Office, April 2001.

————. "Taliban Fact Sheet." Washington, D.C.: Government Printing Office, 20 December 2000.

————. *World Military Expenditure and Arms Transfer 1998.* Washington, D.C.: Government Printing Office, April 2000.

U.S. Department of State. Bureau for International Narcotics and Law Enforcement Affairs. *International Narcotics Control Strategy Report, 1996.* Washington, D.C.: Government Printing Office, March 1997.

————. Bureau for International Narcotics and Law Enforcement Affairs. *International Narcotics Control Strategy Report, 1997.* Washington, D.C.: Government Printing Office, March 1998.

U.S. General Accounting Office. *Money-laundering: FinCEN's Law Enforcement, Support, Regulatory and International Roles*, T-GGD-98-83. Washington, D.C.: Government Printing Office, 1 April 1998.

U.S. House of Representatives. Committee on the Armed Services. "Statement of General Anthony C. Zinni." 106th Cong., 2d sess. *Congressional Record,* 15 March 2000.

————. International Relations Committee, Africa Subcommittee. "Testimony of Susan E. Rice." 106th Cong., 1st sess. *Congressional Record,* 25 May 1999.

U.S. News and World Report. *Triumph Without Victory: The History of the Persian Gulf War.* New York: Random House, 1992.

U.S. Senate. Committee on Banking, Housing, and Urban Affairs. "Testimony of the Honorable Carl Levin Before the Hearings on the Administration's National Money Laundering Strategy for 2001." 107th Cong., 1st sess. *Congressional Record,* 26 September 2001.

————. Committee on Banking, Housing, and Urban Affairs. "Statement of Stuart Eizenstat before the Hearings on the Administration's National Money Laundering Strategy for 2001." 107th Cong., 1st sess. *Congressional Record,* 26 September 2001.

Wechsler, William F. "Follow the Money." *Foreign Affairs* 80, no. 4 (July–August 2001).

Weiss, Thomas G., David Cortright, George A. Lopez, and Larry Minear, eds. *Political Gain and Civilian Pain: Humanitarian Impacts of Economic Sanctions.* Lanham, Md.: Rowman and Littlefield, 1997.

Wood, Brian, and Johan Peleman. *The Arms Fixers: Controlling the Brokers and Shipping Agents.* Research report 99.3. London: British American Security Information Council, November 1999.

World Food Programme. *Assessment of the Adequacy of SCR 986 Food Basket.* North Coordination Office, Erbil, Iraq, 2001.

Zartman, I. William, ed. *Collapsed States: The Disintegration and Restoration of Legitimate Authority.* Boulder, Colo.: Lynne Rienner Publishers, 1995.

# Index

Abu Sayyaf group (Philippines), 120
Afghanistan/Taliban regime sanctions:
arms embargo in, 49–50, 101, 166,
171–172; and arms flow from
Pakistan, 166, 203; and assets
freezes, 51, 96; counterterrorist provisions in, 49, 51; delayed implementation of, 104; on designated
individuals, 101; and economic
reconstruction incentives, 121;
enforcement and monitoring of,
53–58; and great power concerns,
47; and human rights violations,
50–51; humanitarian/social consequences of, 49, 51–53, 58, 209, 210;
and narcotics trafficking, 56–57;
Pakistan's role in, 12; and panel of
experts, 205; political impacts of,
56–58; and release of seized funds,
120–121; restructuring of, 49; and
Security Council resolutions, 49–50;
as smart and innovative sanctions,
47, 49–50; Taliban's response to, 14,
15, 57; and time limits, 10; travel
and aviation, 135*tab*, 145; and UN
arms embargo monitoring team,
202–203; and UN neutrality policy,
172
African National Congress (ANC),
95–96
Air Cess, 169
Airliner bombings, and Libya
aviation/diplomatic sanctions,
137–140
al-Assad, Bashar, 37
al-Qaida network, 129; and global counterterrorist cooperation, 115–116;

Sudan's support of, 117; targeted
financial sanctions and, 57, 101
Angola: armed conflict and human
rights abuses in, 61; conflict, regional crisis and, 63; illegal arms trafficking in, 167, 168–169; Luanda
government in, 63, 73, 74; obstacles
to peace in, 72–73; UN policy in,
62–63
Angola/UNITA sanctions, 61–74,
106–107, 173; on arms and petroleum products, 61, 153; and arms flow
reduction, 158; and assets freeze,
99–100; delayed implementation of,
104; and diamond embargo, 63,
66–67, 70–71, 73, 183–184; Fowler
mission/panel of experts reports on,
65–67, 143–144, 205; improvement
and effectiveness of, 71–72; inadequate enforcement of, 201; and military use of air transportation,
147–148; monitoring mechanism
employed in, 68–70; name and
shame approach to, 205; and private
arms brokers, 158; and regional insecurity, 12, 143; and Security Council
resolutions, 61–63, 64; and targeted
officials, 136; and tracing of assets,
100; on travel, 70, 99, 134*tab*,
135–136, 143–145, 147–148; violation of, 157–158
Annan, Kofi, 29, 30, 31, 51–52, 53, 57,
84, 119, 139, 142, 205–206
Arab League, 139
Ariana Afghan Airlines, 120–121, 145
Aristide, Jean-Bertrand, 99
Arms embargoes, 153–175; and Bonn-

Berlin process, 4–5, 174; effectiveness of, 155; and illegal air transport operations, 167–169; and innovative Security Council resolutions, 202–203; investigative panels' recommendations on, 172, 174–175, 217; and language of Security Council resolutions, 173–174; limitations of, 166–167; monitoring and enforcement of, 156, 162–163, 165, 167–169, 172–175, 202–203; and moral/political dilemmas, 171–172; and private/unregulated arms brokers, 158, 168; and regional institutions, 153–154; against Rwandan Hutu rebels, 204; and small arms trafficking, 155; as stand-alone measures, 155, 156; unilateral, 154; and weapons of mass destruction, 154–155

Arms exports: and domestic laws, 170–171; and end-user certification, 168, 173; illegal, air transportation's role in, 167–168; legislative controls and restrictions on, 172–173; and multilateral export control regimes, 173; of major powers, 170–171; and regulation of arms brokers, 168–169, 173, 174–175

Arms spending, global increase in, 170
Australia Group, 173
Axworthy, Lloyd, 8, 65
Aziz, Tariq, 41–42

Balkans crisis, and sanctions assistance missions, 5
Banking industry: and offshore financial havens, 109–111; and screening of illegal financial transactions, 106; secrecy, and new U.S. laws, 124–125; and UN-mandated financial sanctions, 105, 207
Belgium: and Angola sanctions, 67; and conflict diamonds, 185; diamond certification system in, 194
bin Laden, Osama, 14, 47, 49; and targeted financial sanctions , 101, 111, 115–116, 118, 129
Blix, Hans, 26
Bockarie, Sam, 84
Bolton, John, 171

Bonn International Center for Conversion (BICC), 4
Bonn-Berlin process, 4–5, 174
Bosnian war, and Yugoslavia sanctions, 98
Bout, Victor, 168–169
Brahimi Report, 88
Brooking Institution, and Iraq sanctions, 35–36
Brown, Gordon, 122
Bulgaria: and Angola sanctions, 67, 69; arms exports and sanctions violations of, 172–173
Burkina Faso: Angolan conflict and, 67, 68, 69; sanctions violations of, 143, 158, 159
Burundi, and Congo conflict, 188, 189
Bush administration: and multilateral financial regulations, 111; and unilateral arms embargoes, 154
Butler, Richard, 23–25

Cambodia, and log exports embargo, 203
Camdessus, Michel, 108
Campaign to Eliminate Conflict Diamonds, 190
Canada: and conflict diamond trade, 194; and Ethiopia-Eritrea arms embargo, 162; sanctions monitoring of, 72
Captan, Monie, 146
Central Africa: arms flow to, 156, 157; Fowler mission to, 65; regional crisis in, 63
China: and Iraq sanctions, 32; and Liberian timber imports, 187–188
Chowdhury, Anwarul, 8–9
Chowdhury working group on sanctions reform, 8–11, 16; administrative recommendations of, 213–214; agenda, 9; consensus rule of, 9, 10, 213; design recommendations of, 214; formation of, 7–9; and institutionalization of expert panel recommendations, 215–218; and time limits, 9–10
Clean Diamonds Act (U.S.), 194–195
Clinton administration: and Iraq trade sanctions, 34; Sudan sanctions of, 117

Commodity sanctions, 203; defined, 181; effectiveness of, 195; listing of, 182*tab*. *See also* Diamond embargoes; Oil embargoes

Companies, sanctions against, 174

Compaorè, Blaise, 67

Congo: arms flow into, 156; panel of experts, 205; sanctions against Hutu rebels in, 157. *See also* Democratic Republic of the Congo (DRC)

Congo-Brazzaville: sanctions violations of, 158; UNITA support of, 63

Consumer Access to a Responsible Accounting of Trade (CARAT), 194

Convention on the Prohibition of the Use, Stockpiling, Production, and Transfer of Anti-Personnel Mines and on Their Destruction, 175

Côte d'Ivoire, sanctions violations of, 70, 143, 185

Counterterrorism incentives/sanctions, 115–130, 202, 211–212; and aviation/travel sanctions, 137–140; and economic development/debt relief initiatives, 121–122; and financial sanctions, 111–112; and financing curtailment efforts, 122–126, 129–130; and international cooperation, 115, 118, 119–122; Libya and, 118–120; and Security Council resolution 1373, 96, 115, 123–124, 126–129, 127*tab*, 204; and specially designated nationals (SDNs) operation, 129–130; Sudan and, 117–118; against Taliban regime, 49–50, 51, 120–121; and U.S. State Department terrorism list, 116. *See also* 11 September 2001 terrorist attacks

Cuba, as sponsor of terrorism, 116

Cunningham, James, 161

De Beers Corporation, 183, 207; and conflict diamonds, 191–192

Debt relief, as anti-terrorism incentive, 121–122

Defense Trade Security Initiative, 171

Democratic Republic of the Congo (DRC), 188–190; armed conflicts in, 188–189; arms embargo against Hutu rebels in, 156; diamond pro-duction/trade in, 182, 189; and panel of experts' recommendations, 189

DeWine, Mike, 195

Diamond certification system, 81, 83, 86

Diamond embargoes: in Angola, 63, 67, 183–184; and armed conflict funding, 181, 203; private industry's role in, 207; in West Africa, 81, 83, 86, 87, 186

Diamond trade: and certification systems/diamond tracking technologies, 184, 185, 186, 187, 192–193, 194–195, 207; in conflict diamonds, diamond industry's response to, 191–193; in Democratic Republic of the Congo (DRC), 188–190; and funding of rebel movements, 185–186, 187; government regulation of, 193–195; and human rights groups, 190–191; illegal, 181, 182, 185–186, 192; import procedures, 193–194; and Kimberley process, 192, 194; legitimate, 182; Liberia's criminal activities and, 82, 182, 187; in Sierra Leone, 184–186

*Directive on the Prevention of the Use of the Financial System for the Purposes of Money Laundering* (EU), 109

Dos Santos, Jose Eduardo, 63

Durbin, Richard, 195

Eastern Europe, control of arms exports in, 172–173

Economic Community of West African States (ECOWAS), 81, 82–83, 84–85, 88, 158, 188; arms embargoes of, 154; and small arms controls, 173

Economic Community of West African States Military Observer Group (ECOMOG), 158

Economic development aid: as anti-terrorism incentive, 121–122; and compliance with international financial regulations, 110–111

Egmont Group, 109

Environmental degradation, and natural resource exploitation, 189

Ethiopia-Eritrea war: and arms embar-

go/sanctions, 159, 160; and lifting of
sanctions, 162; and military spend-
ing/arms buildup, 159–160, 167;
sanctions violations in, 161; and
time limits on sanctions, 161; and
U.S. policy, 160
European Union (EU): arms embargoes
of, 153; Code of Conduct on Arms
Exports, 173; Common Foreign and
Security Policy, 100; Yugoslavia
sanctions of, 96, 100–101, 133, 136
Executive Order 13067 (Sudan sanctions), 117
Expert panels. *See* Investigative panels
Eyadema, Gnassingbe, 66–67

Failed states: and humanitarian concerns, 11, 13; monitoring and
enforcement of sanctions in, 11–13
Fatal Transactions Campaign, 190
Financial Action Task Force (FATF),
108, 110, 129; list of noncooperative
countries and territories, 124
Financial crime. *See* Money laundering
Financial Crimes Enforcement Network
(FinCEN), 108–109, 129
Financial sanctions: in failed state environment, 12–13; overview of, 202;
and state enforcement aids, 128–129;
and U.S. capability/leadership, 105,
111. *See also* Targeted financial
sanctions
Financial transparency laws, 124–126
Fourth Freedom Forum, study on Iraq
sanctions, 35–36
Fowler, Robert, 65–66; mission and
report of, 63, 143–144, 184, 205
France: and Iraqi disarmament, 25; and
Iraq sanctions, 32; and Liberian timber imports, 187–188; and sanctions
policy reform, 160–161; and time
limits policy, 9, 210–211. *See also*
Chowdbury working group

Gambia, diamond smuggling and, 185
Genoa summit, 122
German government, Bonn-Berlin
process of, 4–5, 174
Gingrich, Newt, 121–122
Global Witness, 86, 175, 183, 186, 187,
188, 190, 193

Great powers: arms exports of,
170–171; and Permanent Five membership, 6–7, 148, 201; sanctions
monitoring and, 167
*Greatest Threat, The*, 23–25
Greenstock, Jeremy, 126
Group of Seven/Group of Eight
(G7/G8) countries, and anti-
money-laundering efforts, 108, 110,
111
Guinea, armed conflict in, 77, 79,
87

Haass, Richard, 36
Haiti: assets freezes in, 96, 99;
Governors Island Agreement in, 14;
oil and arms embargo in, 99, 181;
targeted financial sanctions against,
99; travel sanctions against, 3,
134*tab*, 136–137, 147
Hall, Tony, 194
Halliday, Denis, 32
Hamas (Lebanon), 117
Hezbollah, 117
Hirsch, John, 88
Holbrooke, Richard, 35
Horn of Africa: Ethiopia-Eritrea war in,
159–162; failure of U.S. policy in,
160, 161–162
Human rights abuses: in Afghanistan,
50–51; in Angola, 61; and conflict
diamonds sanctions, 195; of
Revolutionary United Front, 77–
79
Human rights groups, sanctions moni-
toring of, 208. *See also*
Nongovernmental sector
Human Rights Watch, 35, 50, 171, 174,
183, 190
Humanitarian assessment reports,
208–210
Humanitarian concerns, 3, 135; in
Afghanistan, 49, 51–53, 58; and easing of civilian sanctions, 35–36; and
Liberian/Sierra Leone sanctions, 77,
85–86; monitoring of, 208; and timber export ban, 188; and time limits,
210
Hussein, Saddam, 21, 23, 27, 41, 97
Hutu rebels, arms embargoes against,
156, 157, 204

India, U.S. sanctions against, 115
Individuals, sanctions against, 101, 136, 142, 145, 174
Indonesia: armed forces, Bush administration and, 154; money laundering and, 124
Institute for International Economics, Washington, D.C., 16, 17*n*3
Inter-Congolese Dialogue peace process, 190
Interlaken seminars, and UN financial sanctions, 4, 11, 102, 104, 107, 111, 128, 207
Intermon (Spanish international NGO), 190
International Alert, 175
International Atomic Energy Agency (IAEA), 23, 41, 43
International Campaign to Ban Landmines, 175
International Civil Aviation Organization (ICAO), and Liberia aviation sanctions, 146
International Convention for the Suppression of the Financing of Terrorism, 125
International Crisis Group (ICG), 79, 88
International Monetary Fund (IMF), 74, 108, 121, 160
International peacemaking, arms embargoes as tool of, 175
Investigative panel(s), 204–205; on Angola, 65–67, 143–144, 205, 216, 217; and arms embargo enforcement, 172, 174–175, 217; independence of, 206; name and shame approach of, 205–207; recommendations/reports of, 215–218, 219–221; and secondary sanctions, 216; on Sierra Leone, 81, 205, 216
Iran, as sponsor of global terrorism, 116–117
Iraq sanctions, 211; and arms embargo, 155, 163–166; and assets freezes, 96–97; on civilian trade, 34, 35; and disarmament mandate, 21, 42–43; and dual-use imports, 10, 38, 39; effectiveness of, 163; Fourth Freedom Forum/Kroc Institute study on, 35–36; and Goods Review List proposal, 40; impasse and noncom-

pliance in, 21–44; and infant and child mortality, 27, 31; and manipulation of oil contracts, 33–34; military, 35; and military containment, 163–165; and nongovernmental initiatives, 34–36; and oil embargo/revenues, 27–28, 43, 163–164, 165, 181; and oil for food (986) humanitarian program, 27–28, 29–31, 40; Permanent Five disagreements over, 6, 8, 38, 44, 201; opposition of religious and humanitarian groups to, 32–33; and restructuring proposals, 34–42, 163, 174; and Security Council Resolutions, 24–25; targeting designated officials, 141–142; on trade, 3, 21; on travel and aviation, 134*tab*, 39, 140–142; and UK/U.S. smart sanctions plan, 21, 32, 36–41, 141; and UN arms inspection mandate, 23–26, 43, 141, 142
Islamic Jihad (Egypt), Sudan's support of, 117
Israel, money laundering and, 124

Jeker, Rolf, 102
Jordan, Iraq sanctions and, 33, 34

Kabbah, Ahmed Tejan, 77, 81
Kabila, Joseph, 190
Kabila, Laurent, 157, 188, 189
Khmer Rouge, and log exports embargo, 203
Koonjul, Anund Jagdish, 126
Kosovo crisis, and travel bans, 13
Kosovo Liberation Army (KLA), 162
Kroc Institute for International Peace Studies, 35–36; study on Iraq sanctions, 35–36
Kroll Associates, 100
Kuwait, assets freeze on, 96–97

Land mine convention, 175
Latin America, and financial crimes, 109
Lavrov, Sergey, 126, 161
League of Nations, 211
Liberia: armed conflict in, 77; diamond smuggling and criminal activity in, 82, 182, 187; official diamond trade of, 186–187; panel of experts, 205;

and Revolutionary United Front
(RUF), 82, 156, 157; and timber
exports ban proposal, 187; weapons
flow into, 156
Liberia sanctions, 81, 203–204; and
arms embargo, 82–83, 156, 157; on
diamond exports, 83, 86, 186; extension of, 159; and humanitarian
assessment reports, 209; and
log/timber exports, 86, 203; purpose
of, 204; regional crisis and, 12; and
response to threats of, 14, 83–84, 87;
social impacts of, 85–86; and time
limits, 10; on travel and aviation,
135*tab*, 145–146, 148
Liberians United for Reconciliation and
Democracy, 79
Libya, as sponsor of terrorism, 116
Libya sanctions, 15; and assets freeze,
96, 98; economic impact of, 149*n*8;
oil sales exemption in, 98; and
Qaddafi regime's conciliatory offers,
14; and terrorist bombings of airliners, 118–119, 134*tab*, 137–140, 147,
148
Lloyd's Register, 34; dockside inspections of, 165
Lockerbie bombing and trials, 137–140
Log exports embargo, 203
Lomé Convention, 77, 79, 88
Lusaka Protocol, 61, 143, 183

Macedonian National Liberation Army,
162
Mandela, Nelson, 95
Maritime Interception Force, 165
Medico International (Germany), 190
Milosevic Slobodan, 98, 100, 101
Miro, Mohammad Mustapha, 33
Missile Technology Copntrol Regime,
173
Mobutu Sese Seko, 188
Möllander, Anders, 66
Money laundering, 93: and bank secre-
cy, 105, 110, 123, 124–125; and eco-
nomic aid conditioning, 110–111;
Interlaken process and, 4; interna-
tional efforts against, 108–111; and
mutual legal assistance treaties, 125;
and noncooperative countries and
territories (NCCTs) list, 124; and

offshore financial havens, 109–111;
profitability of, 93; and South Asia
*hawala* systems, 125–126
Mubarak, Hosni, 117
Musharaff regime (Pakistan), and
Afghanistan sanctions, 53

Name and shame strategy, 63, 205; dif-
fering perspectives on, 205–207
Namibia, and Angola sanctions, 63, 71
Narcotics trafficking: and
Afghanistan/Taliban regime sanc-
tions 56–57; and money laundering,
108, 110–111
National interests, sanctions and, 2, 6–7
National Patriotic Front of Liberia
(NPFL), 82
National Union for the Total
Independence of Angola. *See* UNITA
Natural resource exploitation, 188–189
Nauru, money laundering and, 124
Netherlands, and Ethiopia-Eritrea arms
embargo, 162
NIZA (Netherlands Institute for
Southern Africa), 190
Nongovernmental sector, 4, 15–16; and
Afghanistan/Taliban sanctions,
50–51; and conflict diamonds,
190–191; independent research of,
16; and Iraq sanctions, 32–33, 34–36
Nonstate actors, as targets of sanctions,
17
North Atlantic Treaty Organization
(NATO), 172; and Yugoslavia arms
embargo, 162
North Korea, as sponsor of terrorism,
116
Novib (Oxfam Netherlands), 190
Nuclear Suppliers Group, 173

Office of Foreign Assets Control
(OFAC), implementation model,
105–106
Offshore banking centers. *See* Money
laundering
Oil embargoes, 99, 203; in Haiti,
humanitarian concerns of, 181; Iraqi,
27–28, 43, 163–164, 165, 181; and
oil for food program (Iraq), 27,
29–31, 32
Omar, Mullah Muhammad, 56, 57

Organization of African Unity (OAU),
139, 145; Council of Ministers of, 65
Organization of American States (OAS),
136
Organization for Economic Cooperation
and Development (OECD) countries,
124; legal/administrative harmonization of, 107–108
O'Sullivan, Meghan, 35–36

Pakistan, 53; arms trade of, 166, 203;
lifting of U.S. sanctions on, 5, 115,
121; *hawala* system in, 125
Partnership Africa Canada, 82, 190
Permanent Five Security Council mem-
bers: and differential costs, 7; and
Iraq sanctions disagreements, 6, 8,
38, 174; power politics among, 6–7,
201; sanctions enforcement commit-
ment of, 148
Physicians for Human Rights, 190
Powell, Colin, 36–38, 118, 121
Prendergast, John, 160
Private sector: sanctions monitoring of,
207–208; and UN-mandated finan-
cial sanctions, 105
Private security firms, Security
Council's hiring of, 207–208

Qaddafi, Muammar, 14, 138, 140

Ragheb, Ali Abu, 33
Rebel movements: and arms sanctions,
153; and aviation sanctions, 148; and
conflict diamonds trade, 181. *See
also* UNITA (National Union for the
Total Independence of Angola);
Revolutionary United Front (RUF)
Regional institutions, arms embargoes
of, 153–154
Regional security crisis: in Angola,
61–65, 72–74; and sanctions focus,
11–12; in western Africa, 77–89, 188
Relief activities, sanctions' impact on,
13
Retrospective reporting proposal, 107
Revolutionary United Front (RUF):
arms embargo against, 158, 159;
asset freeze on, 83; diamond smuggling of, 185–186, 187; gross human
rights violations of, 77–79; Liberia's

military assistance to, 82, 83,
156–157; sanctions against, 81; and
threat of sanctions, 86–87; travel
bans on members of, 142, 145; and
UN's militarily assertive strategy,
88–89; war against Sierra Leone
government, 185
Rice, Condoleezza, 121
Ritter, Scott, 25
Roth, Kenneth, 35
*Rough Trade: The Role of Companies
and Government in the Angolan
Conflict, A*, 183
Russia: and anti-money-laundering
efforts, 124; global arms trade of,
170; and Iraq sanctions, 21, 32,
40–42; and Iraqi disarmament, 25;
power politics of, 6–7; and sanctions
policy reform, 160–161; and Taliban
sanctions, 47, 51; and time limits
policy, 210–211. *See also*
Chowdbury working group
Rwanda: arms embargo, 156; and
Congo conflict, 188, 189; Hutu
rebels in, arms embargo against,
204; sanctions violations in, 158

Saferworld, 175
Saleh, Mehdi, 42
Sanction(s): and cooperation theory, 25;
institutionalization of, 211; scholarly
research on, 16; symbolic/psycho-
logical impacts of, 139; and use of
Chapter VII, 3
*Sanctions Decade, The*, 1
Sanctions monitoring and enforcement,
2; of arms embargoes, 156, 162–163,
165; and Bonn-Berlin process, 4–5,
3, 167; humanitarian concerns in,
208; lack of, 162; monitoring mechanism in, 68–70; and name and
shame process, 63, 205–207; by non-
governmental/private sector organizations, 175, 207–208; and punitive
preventive strategies, 205–207; and
special investigative bodies, 172,
205–207; and threat of sanctions,
13–15, 206
Sanctions policy: great power politics
in, 42; of incentives/ rewards, 5–6,
118, 121, 216; pattern of initial

response to, 13–15; punitive/coercive, 1, 3, 137

Sanctions reform, 2, 3–4; advances and failures in, 201; and broadening of sanctions, 203–204; future of, 211–218; and humanitarian concerns, 208–210; institutionalization of, 3; and Permanent Five political differences, 7–8; and setting of time limits, 10, 160–161, 210–211; and smarter/selective sanctions, 4, 6, 16–17, 49, 153; summary listing of, 212*tab*. *See also* Chowdbury working group

Sanctions targets: changing nature of, 2; and designated targets list, 202; individuals and decisionmaking elites as, 4, 101, 136, 141–142, 145, 174, 202; and pressure from neighboring states, 147

Sanctions violators: governments/private actors identified as, 66–67; imposition of sanctions against, 6, 68, 203–204, 216

Savimbi, Jonas, 61, 63, 65, 66–67, 183

Schengen agreement, travel restrictions and, 144

Shell banks, 124–125

Sierra Leone: Armed Forces Revolutionary Council (AFRC) military government in, 81, 158; cease-fire in, 77, 159; diamond smuggling in, 184–185; humanitarian operations in, 77; investigative panels, 81, 205; official diamond exports from, 185; peaceful transition prospects in, 79; refugee crisis in, 85; Revolutionary United Front (RUF) rebels in, 82, 156, 158–159; UNAMSIL peacekeeping force in, 77; war and atrocities in, 185

Sierra Leone sanctions: arms embargo in, 157, 158; effectiveness of, 158; against military junta, 14, 209; and military use of air transportation, 147–148; and overthrow of Kabbah government, 81; regional crisis and, 12; and Security Council Resolutions, 80; social impacts of, 85–86; targeted and selective, 81;

threats, responses to, 84–85; trade, 81, 85; travel, 134*tab*, 142–145

Smart sanctions, 4, 6; in Afghanistan, 47, 49–50; arms embargoes as, 153

Somalia: arms embargo and arms flow into, 156; sanctions, and cease-fire agreement, 14; U.S. policy failure in, 160

South Africa, sanctions/sanctions violations in, 95–96, 158

Southern Africa: Fowler mission to, 65; regional crisis in, 63

Southern African Development Community (SADC), 71; small arms control protocol, 173

Specially designated nationals (SDNs), tracking of, 105–106, 129–130

Stevens, Siaka, 185

Sudan: aviation sanctions threat against, 117–118, 134*tab*; counterterrorism cooperation of, 118; Ethiopian/Eritrean support for rebels in, 160; and government's conciliatory offers, 14; reward strategy in, 118; and state support for terrorism, 116, 117; and UN/U.S. sanctions, 115, 117–118

Summit of the Americas Ministerial Conference (1995), 109

Switzerland, 48, 103, 128; bank secrecy in, 124. *See also* Interlaken process

Syria: and Iraq sanctions, 33, 37; as sponsor of terrorism, 116

Targeted decisionmaking elites: psychological impacts of sanctions on, 146; and visa/travel bans, 133–137, 141, 142, 143–145, 146

Targeted financial sanctions, 93–112, 97*tab*; advantages of, 93; and asset freezes, 94, 96; and circumvention schemes, 102; effectiveness and strengthening of, 93–94; general lockdown approach to, 104; and harmonization of legal/administrative systems, 107–108; and Interlaken process, 4; and monitoring/implementation capacity, 104–105; and OECD countries' cooperation, 107; regime's vulnerability to, 101–102, 147; and specially designated nationals, 105–106; speed and decisiveness factors in, 103–104; and tracing of assets, 106–107; and visa bans, 135–136

*Targeted Financial Sanctions: A Manual for Design and Implementation*, 128–129

Taylor, Charles, 77, 82–84, 87, 146, 186, 187

Terrorism, international: and bombings of Pan Am flight 103/UTA flight 772, 118–119, 134*tab*, 137–140, 147, 148; and UN Counter-terrorism Committee, 115. *See also* Counterterrorism incentives/sanctions

Terrorist attacks of 11 September 2001: and congressional measures, 116; and economic statecraft, 115; financing of, 122–123; Libya sanctions and, 120; military response to, 47; Pakistan sanctions and, 5, 115; U.S./international response to, 111–112, 115–116, 117, 118

Thomas J. Watson Jr. Institute of International Studies. *See* Watson Institute

Time limits policy, 10, 160–161, 210–211

Togo: and Angola sanctions, 66–67, 68, 69, 72, 143, 158

Trade sanctions, 3, 98

Travel and aviation sanction(s), 133–148; applications of, 133, 134–135*tab*; and Bonn-Berlin process, 4–5; and coercion, 137; enforcement, and political will, 148; and humanitarian needs, 135; and international terrorism, 137–140; monitoring of, 136; and visa bans, 133

Turkey, Iraq sanctions and, 33

Uganda, and Congo conflict, 188, 189

Ukraine, money laundering and, 124

UNITA (National Union for the Total Independence of Angola) rebel movement, 96; human rights abuses of, 61; military capabilities/setbacks of, 65, 72–73; weapons acquisition of, 157–158. *See also* Angola/UNITA sanctions

United Arab Emirates, 169; and conflict diamonds, 185; and terrorist attacks of 11 September 2001, 122

United Kingdom: and Afghani economic reconstruction program, 121; and conflict diamond legislation, 194; global arms transfers of, 170; and Iraqi sanctions/weapons inspection, 21, 26, 34, 141; Liberia intervention of, 87; Maritime Interception Force, 165; power politics of, 6; and smart sanctions policy on Iraq, 38–40; and time limits policy, 210. *See also* Chowdbury working group

United Nations: *Human Development Report*, 206; neutrality policy, 172; peacekeeping mission of, 61, 77, 87, 88–89; West Africa policy of, 87–89

United Nations Conference on the Illicit Trade in Small Arms and Light Weapons in All Its Aspects, 155

United Nations International Commission of Inquiry (UNICOI), 157, 175, 204–205

United Nations Mission in Sierra Leone (UNAMSIL), 77, 86, 87, 88

United Nations Monitoring, Verification, and Inspection Commission (UNMOVIC), 26, 41

United Nations Office for the Coordination of Humanitarian Affairs (OCHA), 49, 209

United Nations Secretariat, monitoring/implementation capacity of, 104–105

United Nations Security Council Counter-Terrorism Committee, 126–128;

United Nations Special Commission (UNSCOM), 23, 25, 26, 34, 141–142

United States: anti-money-laundering laws of, 108–109, 110; arms exports of, 170–171; arms restrictions of, 154; conflict diamond legislation of, 194; and Ethiopia-Eritrea war, 160; financial sanctioning capability of, 105; Haiti sanctions of, 99, 136–137; and Iraq sanctions, 10, 21, 25–26, 34–40, 42, 141; and Maritime Interception Force, 165; power politics of, 6–7; Somalia policy failure

of, 160; and Taliban regime sanctions, 47, 51, 121; and time limits policy, 210; and weapons trafficking restrictions, 171. *See also* Chowdbury working group
United States Agency for International Development (USAID), 186
United States Treasury Department's Office of Foreign Assets Control, 129
USA Patriot Act, 116

Valdivieso, Alfonso, 126
Vienna Convention Against Illicit Traffic in Narcotic Drugs and Psychotropic Substances, 108, 110
Visa bans, 133–135; and targeted financial sanctions, 135–136
Voices in the Wilderness (U.S.), 32
von Sponeck, Hans, 32

Wassenaar Arrangement, 173, 174
Watson Institute for International Studies, 107–108, 208; design and implementation manual of, 107, 111; financial sanctions roundtables/simulations exercise, 36, 102–103, 104, 128
Weapons of mass destruction, arms embargoes and, 154–155
West Africa: commodity/environmental devastation in, 188–189; diamond certification system in, 187; inade-

quate enforcement of sanctions in, 201; moratorium on arms shipments to, 158; security crisis in, 79, 188; UN peacekeeping in, 77; UN shift to coercive policy in, 87–89. *See also specific country;* Diamond sanctions; Diamond trade
Wolf, Frank, 194
Working group on sanctions reform. *See* Chowdhury working group on sanctions reform
World Bank, 116, 160; money laundering and, 111
World Diamond Council, 207
World Food Programme, 53

Yakovenko, Alexander, 41
Yugoslavia sanctions, 3; and arms embargo, 155, 162–163, 171; EU/U.S. targeted financial, 96, 100–101; implementation and enforcement of, 162, 163; and military stockpiles, 162; against Serbian decisionmaking elites, 96, 100–101, 133, 136; on trade and assets, 98; travel, 134*tab*

Zaire: arms embargo against Hutu rebels in, 156; government support for UNITA in, 63; sanctions violations in, 158. *See also* Democratic Republic of the Congo (DRC)
Zambia, and Angola sanctions, 71
Zangger Committee, 173

# About the Book

Following on the publication of *The Sanctions Decade*—lauded as the definitive history and accounting of UN sanctions in the 1990s—David Cortright and George Lopez continue their collaboration to examine the changing context and meaning of sanctions and the security dilemmas that the Security Council now faces.

Cortright and Lopez note that, despite widespread disagreement about the effectiveness of UN sanctions and the need for reform, the Security Council continues to impose sanctions, and it maintains ongoing measures in eight countries. Exploring the dynamics of recent developments, the authors assess a range of new multilateral approaches to sanctions and economic statecraft, review the heated debate over the humanitarian impact of sanctions, and consider the increasingly important role of NGOs in UN policymaking. They conclude with a framework for future policy, as well as specific recommendations for enhancing the viability of "smart sanctions" strategies.

**David Cortright** is president of the Fourth Freedom Forum and research fellow at the Joan B. Kroc Institute for International Peace Studies, University of Notre Dame. **George A. Lopez** is director of policy studies and faculty senior fellow at the Kroc Institute.